MILES MORALES

BRING ON THE BAD GUYS

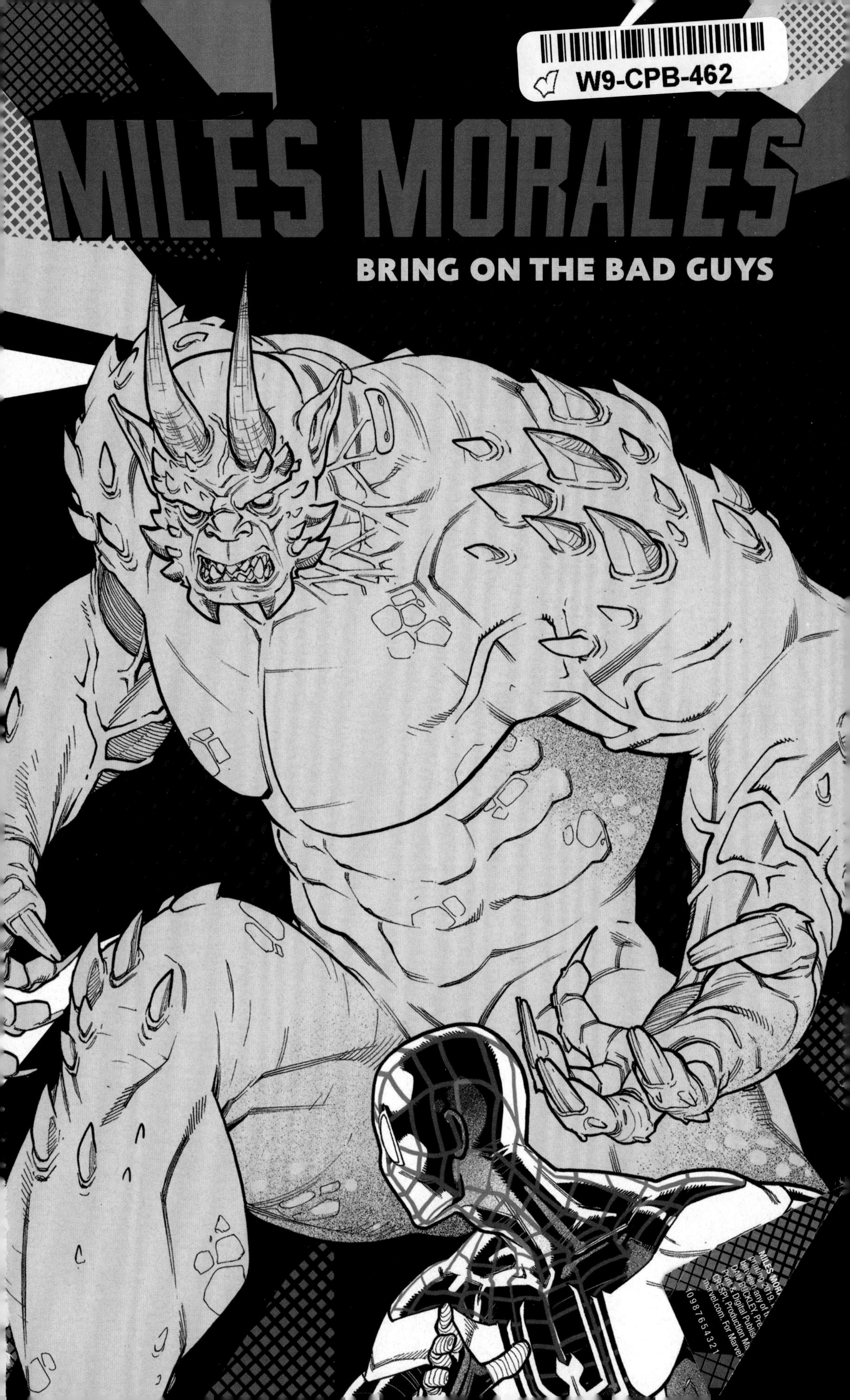

MILES MORALES

BRING ON THE BAD GUYS

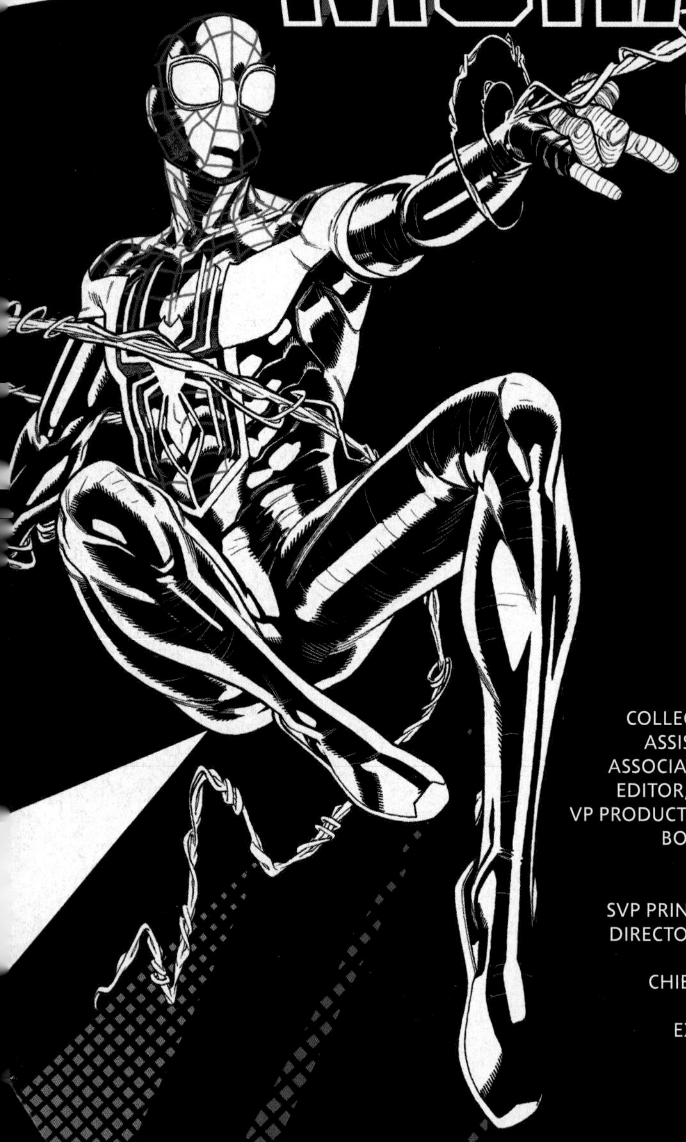

COLLECTION EDITOR **JENNIFER GRÜNWALD**
ASSISTANT EDITOR **CAITLIN O'CONNELL**
ASSOCIATE MANAGING EDITOR **KATERI WOODY**
EDITOR, SPECIAL PROJECTS **MARK D. BEAZLEY**
VP PRODUCTION & SPECIAL PROJECTS **JEFF YOUNGQUIST**
BOOK DESIGNERS **SALENA MAHINA**
WITH **JAY BOWEN**

SVP PRINT, SALES & MARKETING **DAVID GABRIEL**
DIRECTOR, LICENSED PUBLISHING **SVEN LARSEN**
EDITOR IN CHIEF **C.B. CEBULSKI**
CHIEF CREATIVE OFFICER **JOE QUESADA**
PRESIDENT **DAN BUCKLEY**
EXECUTIVE PRODUCER **ALAN FINE**

ALES VOL. 2: BRING ON THE BAD GUYS. Contains material originally published in magazine form as MILES MORALES: SPIDER-MAN (2018) #7-10, and FREE COMIC BOOK DAY 2019 (SPIDER-MAN/VENOM) #1. First SBN 978-1-302-91479-0. Published by MARVEL WORLDWIDE, INC., a subsidiary of MARVEL ENTERTAINMENT, LLC. OFFICE OF PUBLICATION: 135 West 50th Street, New York, NY 10020. © 2019 MARVEL No similarity he names, characters, persons, and/or institutions in this magazine with those of any living or dead person or institution is intended, and any such similarity which may exist is purely coincidental. **Printed in Canada.** sident, Marvel Entertainment; JOHN NEE, Publisher; JOE QUESADA, Chief Creative Officer; TOM BREVOORT, SVP of Publishing; DAVID BOGART, Associate Publisher & SVP of Talent Affairs; DAVID GABRIEL, VP of hing; JEFF YOUNGQUIST, VP of Production & Special Projects; DAN CARR, Executive Director of Publishing Technology; ALEX MORALES, Director of Publishing Operations; DAN EDINGTON, Managing Editor; SUSAN nager; STAN LEE, Chairman Emeritus. For information regarding advertising in Marvel Comics or on Marvel.com, please contact Vit DeBellis, Custom Solutions & Integrated Advertising Manager, at vdebellis@ subscription inquiries, please call 888-511-5480. **Manufactured between 11/8/2019 and 12/10/2019 by SOLISCO PRINTERS, SCOTT, QC, CANADA.**

MILES MORALES: SPIDER-MAN #7

Saladin Ahmed
WRITER

Ron Ackins
PENCILER, PP. 1-5

Dexter Vines
INKER, PP. 1-5

Alitha E. Martinez
ARTIST, PP. 6-10

Vanesa R. Del Rey
ARTIST, PP. 11-16

Javier Garrón
ARTIST: PP. 17-20

David Curiel & Erick Arciniega
COLOR ARTISTS

MILES MORALES: SPIDER-MAN #8-10

Saladin Ahmed & Javier Garrón
STORYTELLERS

David Curiel
COLOR ARTIST

"THE SECRET ORIGIN OF STARLING"

Saladin Ahmed
WRITER

Annie Wu
ARTIST

Rachelle Rosenberg
COLOR ARTIST

VC's Cory Petit (#7, #9-10) & Travis Lanham (#8)
LETTERERS

Patrick O'Keefe (#7-9) AND
Mahmud Asrar & Dave Stewart (#10)
COVER ART

FREE COMIC BOOK DAY 2019

Saladin Ahmed & Tom Taylor
WRITERS

Cory Smith
PENCILER

Jay Leisten
INKER

David Curiel
COLOR ARTIST

VC's Clayton Cowles
LETTERER

Ryan Stegman & Frank Martin
COVER ART

Kathleen Wisneski
ASSISTANT EDITOR

Nick Lowe
EDITOR

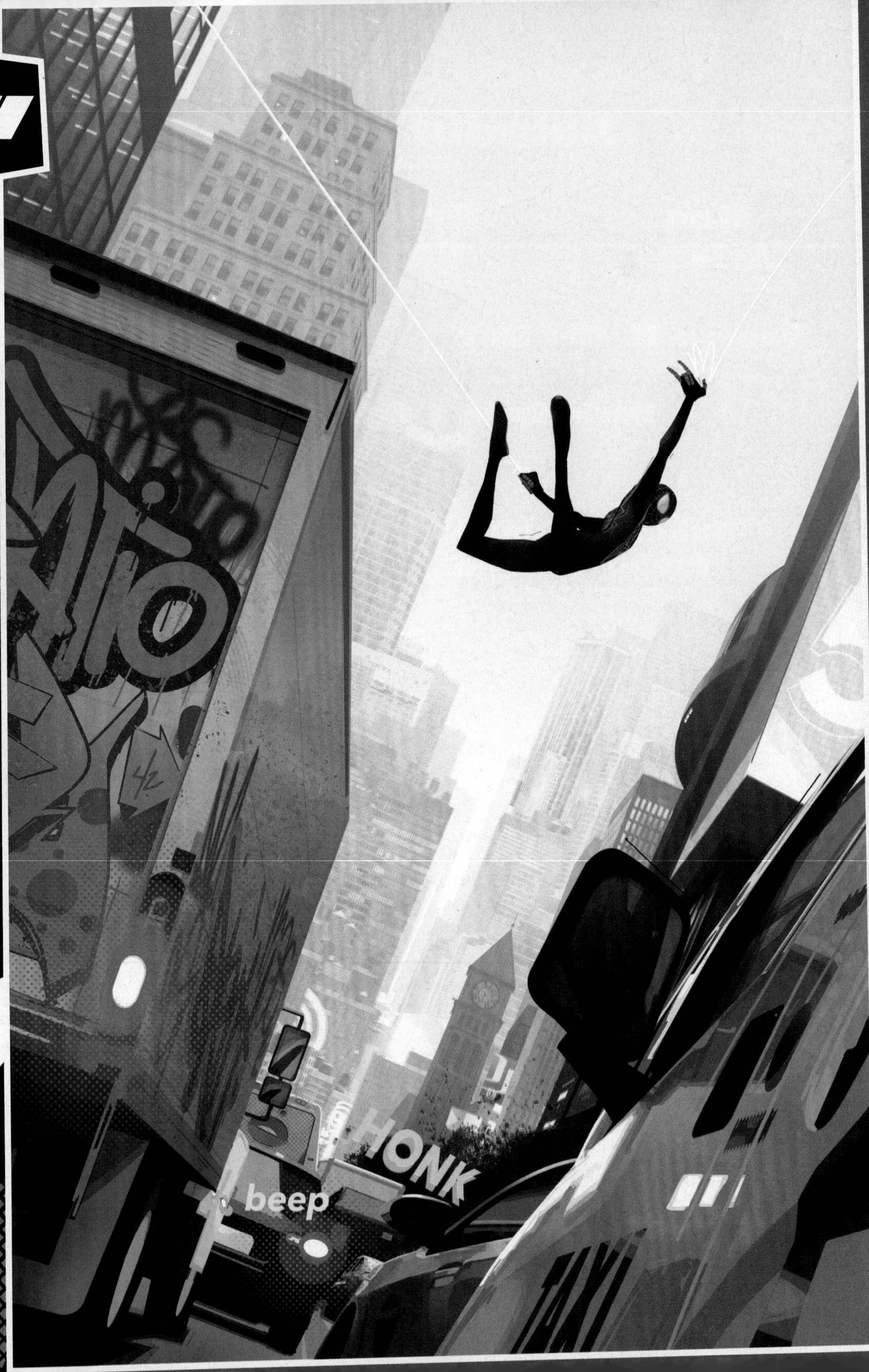
HONK
beep
TAXI

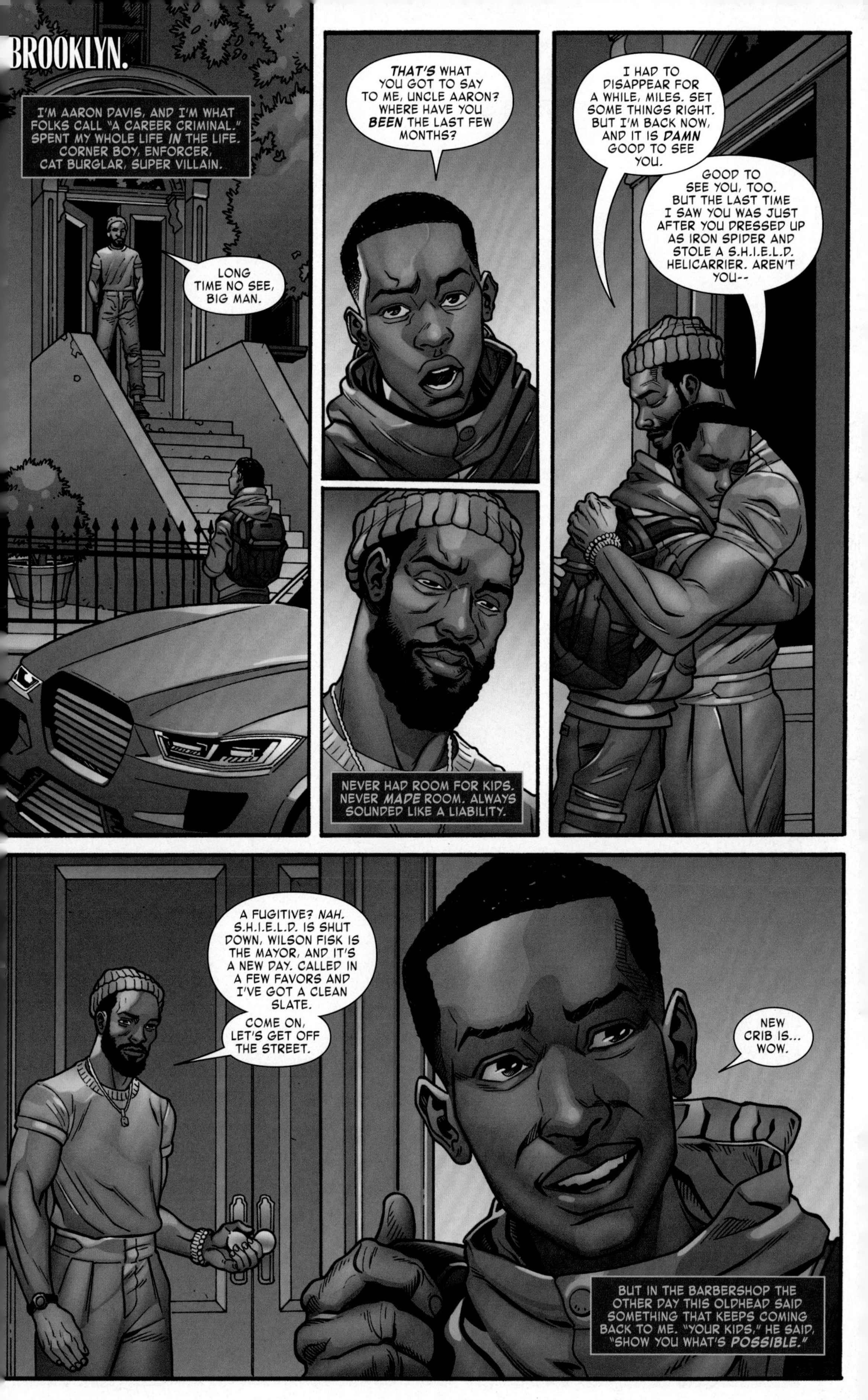
BROOKLYN.
I'M AARON DAVIS, AND I'M WHAT FOLKS CALL "A CAREER CRIMINAL." SPENT MY WHOLE LIFE IN THE LIFE. CORNER BOY, ENFORCER, CAT BURGLAR, SUPER VILLAIN.
LONG TIME NO SEE, BIG MAN.
THAT'S WHAT YOU GOT TO SAY TO ME, UNCLE AARON? WHERE HAVE YOU BEEN THE LAST FEW MONTHS?
NEVER HAD ROOM FOR KIDS. NEVER MADE ROOM. ALWAYS SOUNDED LIKE A LIABILITY.
I HAD TO DISAPPEAR FOR A WHILE, MILES. SET SOME THINGS RIGHT. BUT I'M BACK NOW, AND IT IS DAMN GOOD TO SEE YOU.
GOOD TO SEE YOU, TOO. BUT THE LAST TIME I SAW YOU WAS JUST AFTER YOU DRESSED UP AS IRON SPIDER AND STOLE A S.H.I.E.L.D. HELICARRIER. AREN'T YOU--
A FUGITIVE? NAH. S.H.I.E.L.D. IS SHUT DOWN, WILSON FISK IS THE MAYOR, AND IT'S A NEW DAY. CALLED IN A FEW FAVORS AND I'VE GOT A CLEAN SLATE.
COME ON, LET'S GET OFF THE STREET.
NEW CRIB IS... WOW.
BUT IN THE BARBERSHOP THE OTHER DAY THIS OLDHEAD SAID SOMETHING THAT KEEPS COMING BACK TO ME. "YOUR KIDS," HE SAID, "SHOW YOU WHAT'S POSSIBLE."

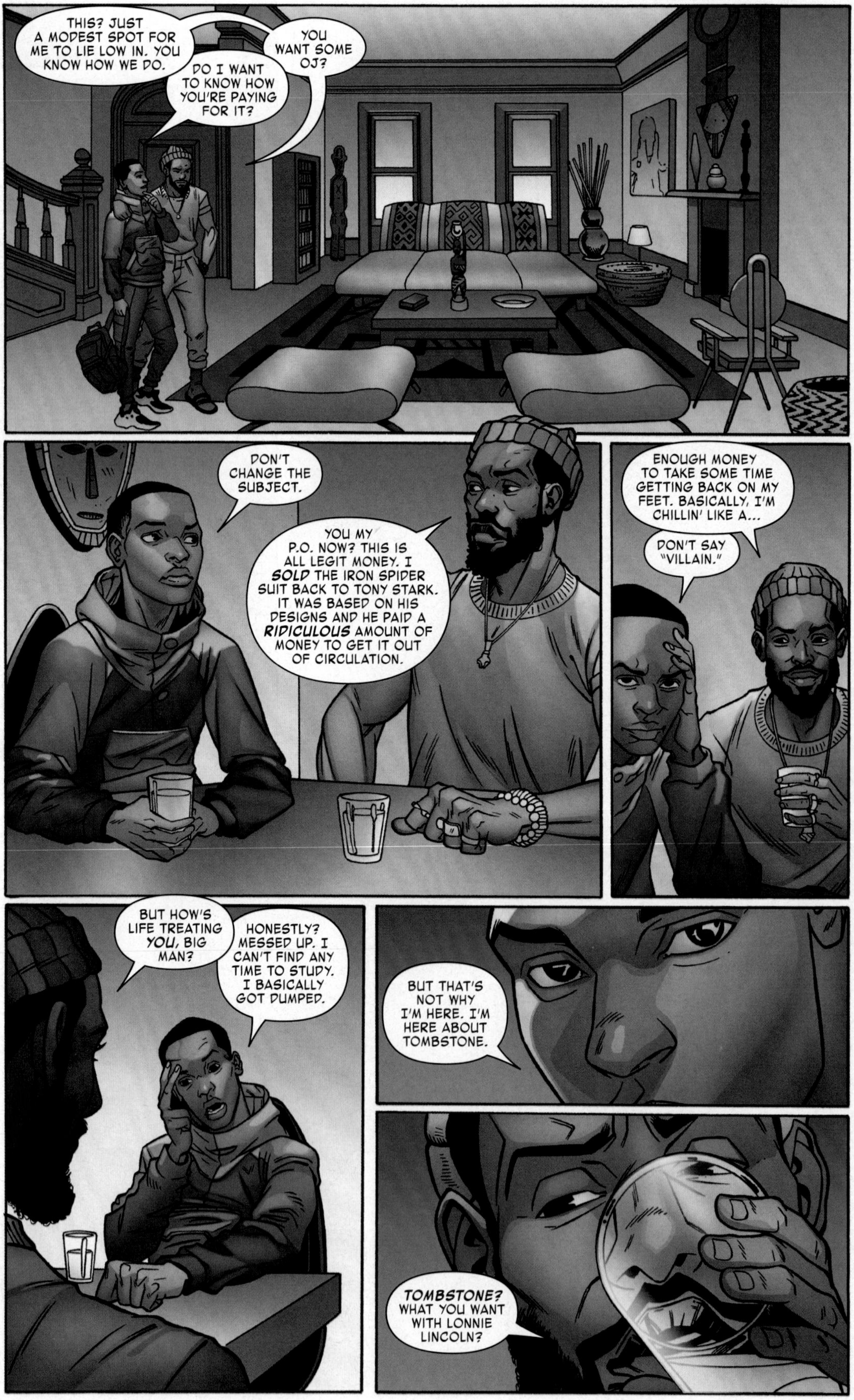

THIS? JUST A MODEST SPOT FOR ME TO LIE LOW IN. YOU KNOW HOW WE DO.
DO I WANT TO KNOW HOW YOU'RE PAYING FOR IT?
YOU WANT SOME OJ?
DON'T CHANGE THE SUBJECT.
YOU MY P.O. NOW? THIS IS ALL LEGIT MONEY. I SOLD THE IRON SPIDER SUIT BACK TO TONY STARK. IT WAS BASED ON HIS DESIGNS AND HE PAID A RIDICULOUS AMOUNT OF MONEY TO GET IT OUT OF CIRCULATION.
ENOUGH MONEY TO TAKE SOME TIME GETTING BACK ON MY FEET. BASICALLY, I'M CHILLIN' LIKE A...
DON'T SAY "VILLAIN."
BUT HOW'S LIFE TREATING YOU, BIG MAN?
HONESTLY? MESSED UP. I CAN'T FIND ANY TIME TO STUDY. I BASICALLY GOT DUMPED.
BUT THAT'S NOT WHY I'M HERE. I'M HERE ABOUT TOMBSTONE.
TOMBSTONE? WHAT YOU WANT WITH LONNIE LINCOLN?

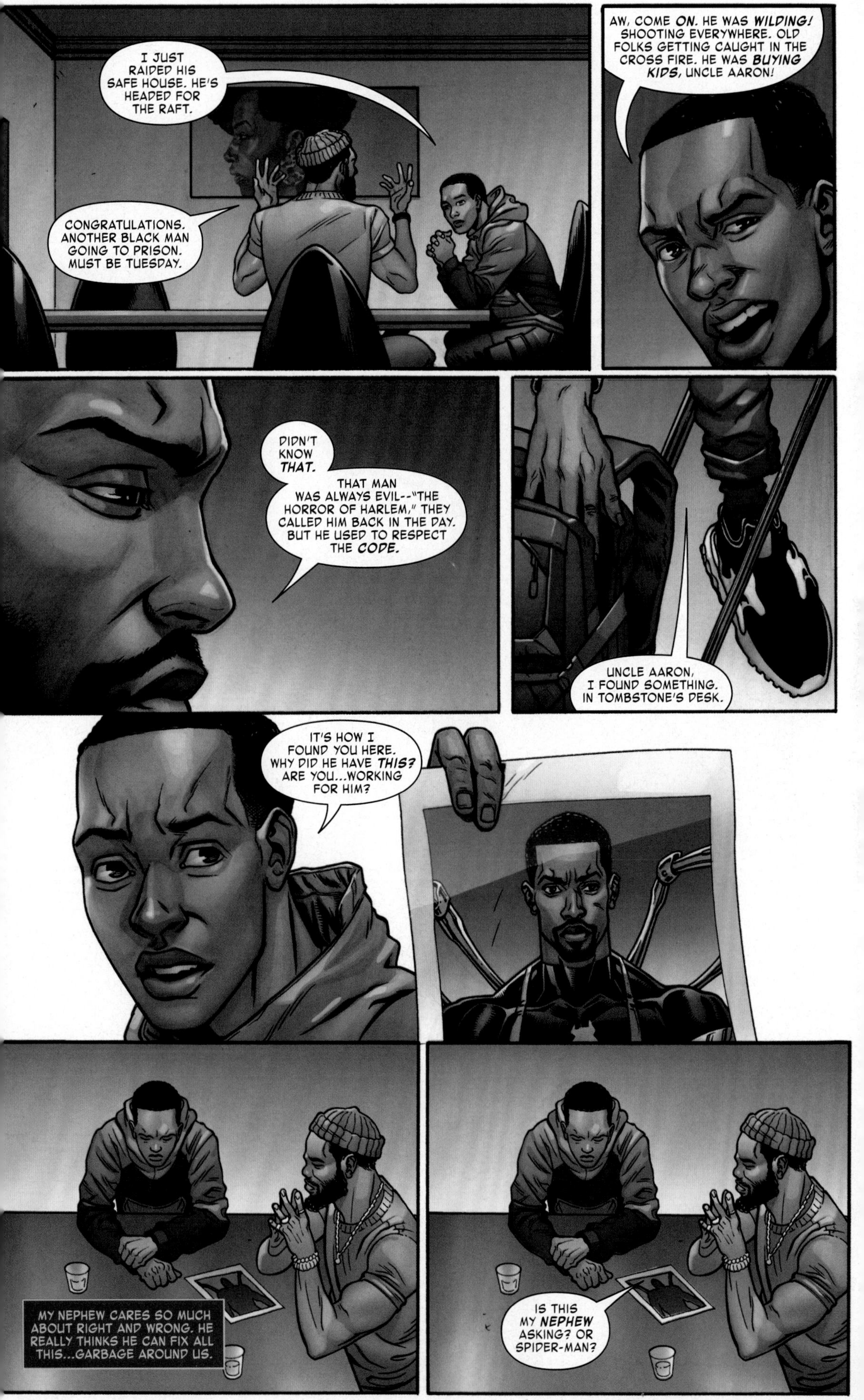
I JUST RAIDED HIS SAFE HOUSE. HE'S HEADED FOR THE RAFT.
CONGRATULATIONS. ANOTHER BLACK MAN GOING TO PRISON. MUST BE TUESDAY.
AW, COME ON. HE WAS WILDING! SHOOTING EVERYWHERE. OLD FOLKS GETTING CAUGHT IN THE CROSS FIRE. HE WAS BUYING KIDS, UNCLE AARON!
DIDN'T KNOW THAT.
THAT MAN WAS ALWAYS EVIL--"THE HORROR OF HARLEM," THEY CALLED HIM BACK IN THE DAY. BUT HE USED TO RESPECT THE CODE.
UNCLE AARON, I FOUND SOMETHING. IN TOMBSTONE'S DESK.
IT'S HOW I FOUND YOU HERE. WHY DID HE HAVE THIS? ARE YOU...WORKING FOR HIM?
MY NEPHEW CARES SO MUCH ABOUT RIGHT AND WRONG. HE REALLY THINKS HE CAN FIX ALL THIS...GARBAGE AROUND US.
IS THIS MY NEPHEW ASKING? OR SPIDER-MAN?

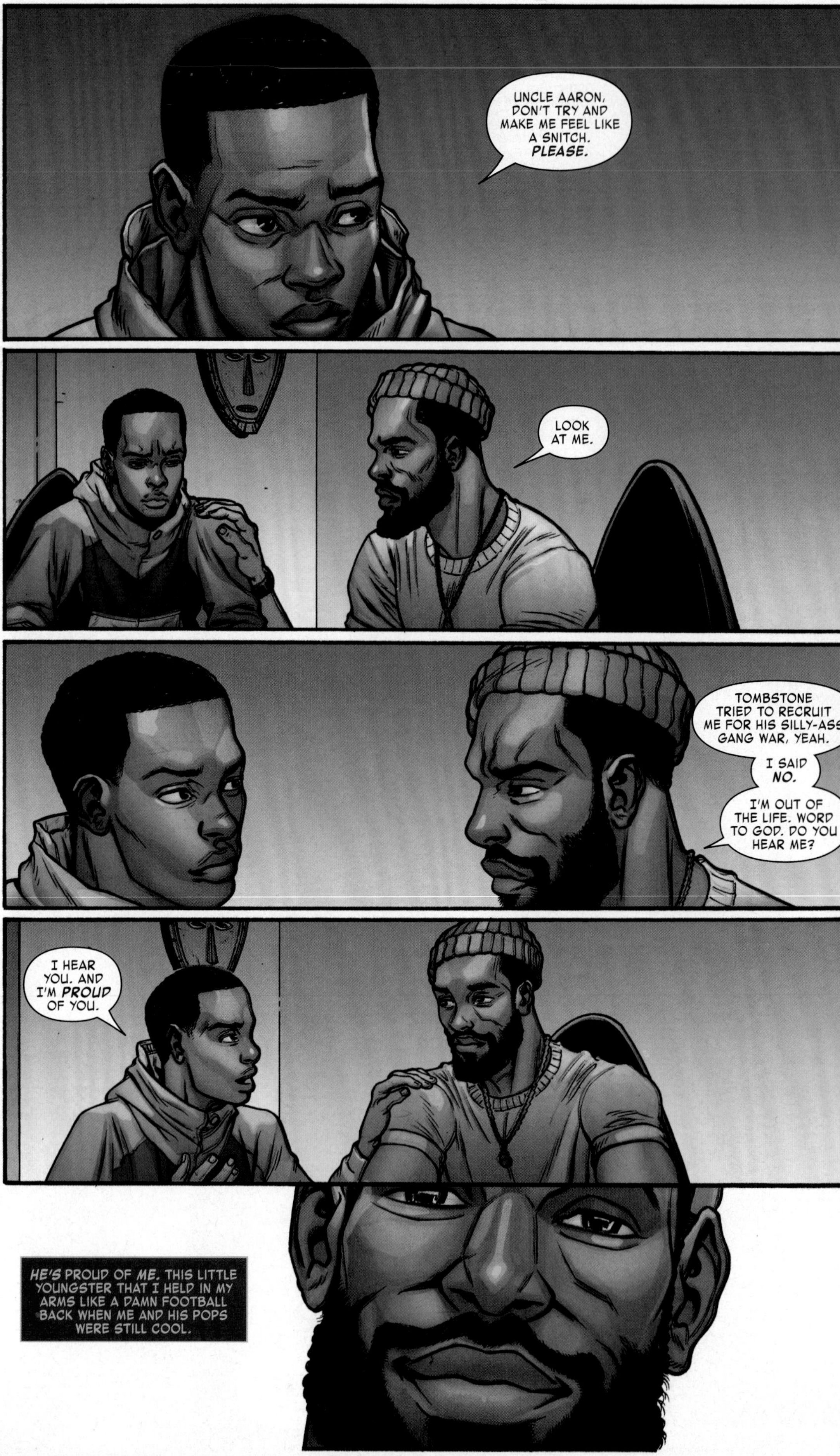
UNCLE AARON, DON'T TRY AND MAKE ME FEEL LIKE A SNITCH. *PLEASE.*
LOOK AT ME.
TOMBSTONE TRIED TO RECRUIT ME FOR HIS SILLY-ASS GANG WAR, YEAH.
I SAID *NO.*
I'M OUT OF THE LIFE. WORD TO GOD. DO YOU HEAR ME?
I HEAR YOU. AND I'M *PROUD* OF YOU.
HE'S PROUD OF *ME.* THIS LITTLE YOUNGSTER THAT I HELD IN MY ARMS LIKE A DAMN FOOTBALL BACK WHEN ME AND HIS POPS WERE STILL COOL.

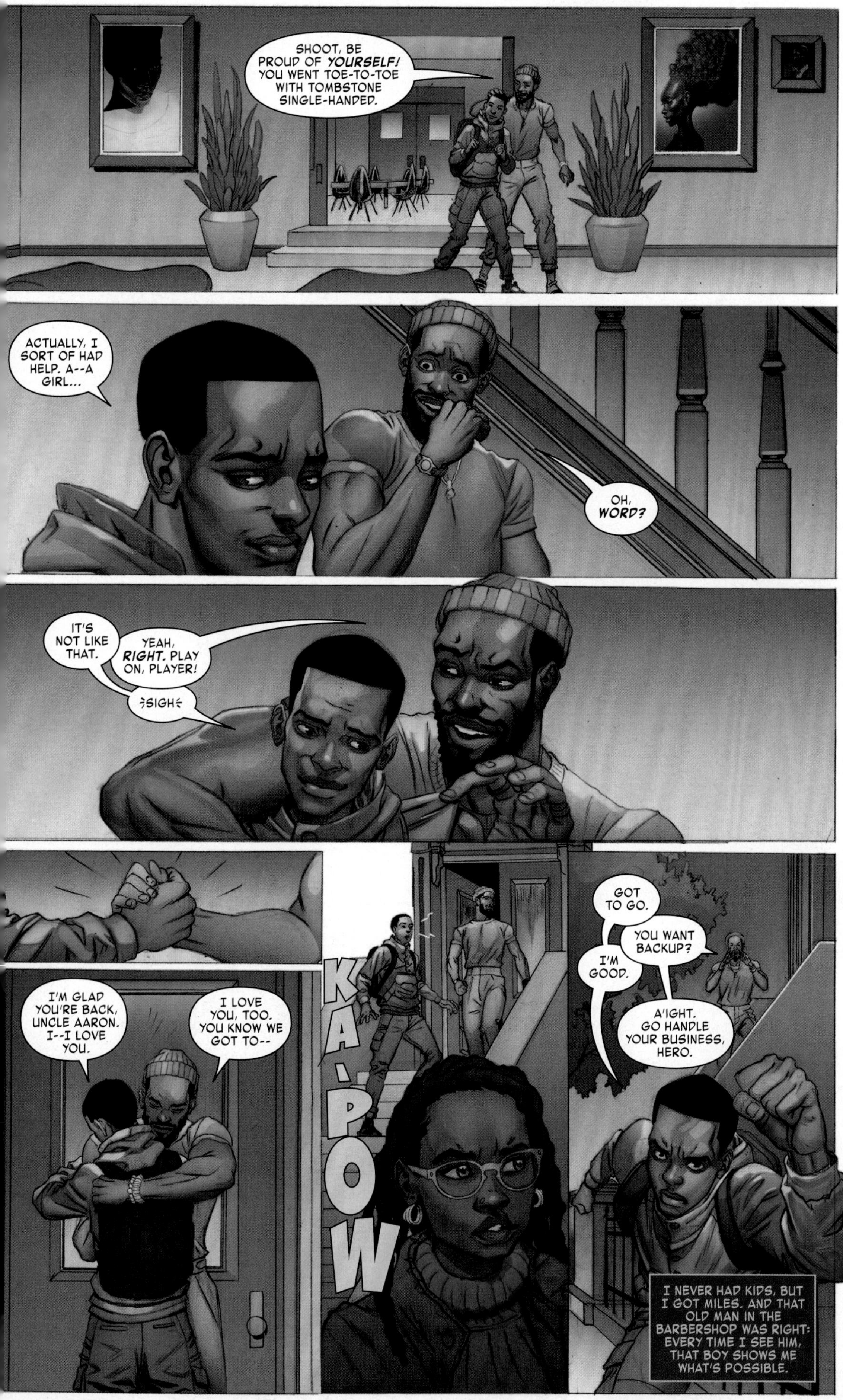
SHOOT, BE PROUD OF YOURSELF! YOU WENT TOE-TO-TOE WITH TOMBSTONE SINGLE-HANDED.
ACTUALLY, I SORT OF HAD HELP. A--A GIRL...
OH, WORD?
IT'S NOT LIKE THAT.
YEAH, RIGHT. PLAY ON, PLAYER!
SIGH
I'M GLAD YOU'RE BACK, UNCLE AARON. I--I LOVE YOU.
I LOVE YOU, TOO. YOU KNOW WE GOT TO--
KA-POW
GOT TO GO.
YOU WANT BACKUP?
I'M GOOD.
A'IGHT. GO HANDLE YOUR BUSINESS, HERO.
I NEVER HAD KIDS, BUT I GOT MILES. AND THAT OLD MAN IN THE BARBERSHOP WAS RIGHT: EVERY TIME I SEE HIM, THAT BOY SHOWS ME WHAT'S POSSIBLE.

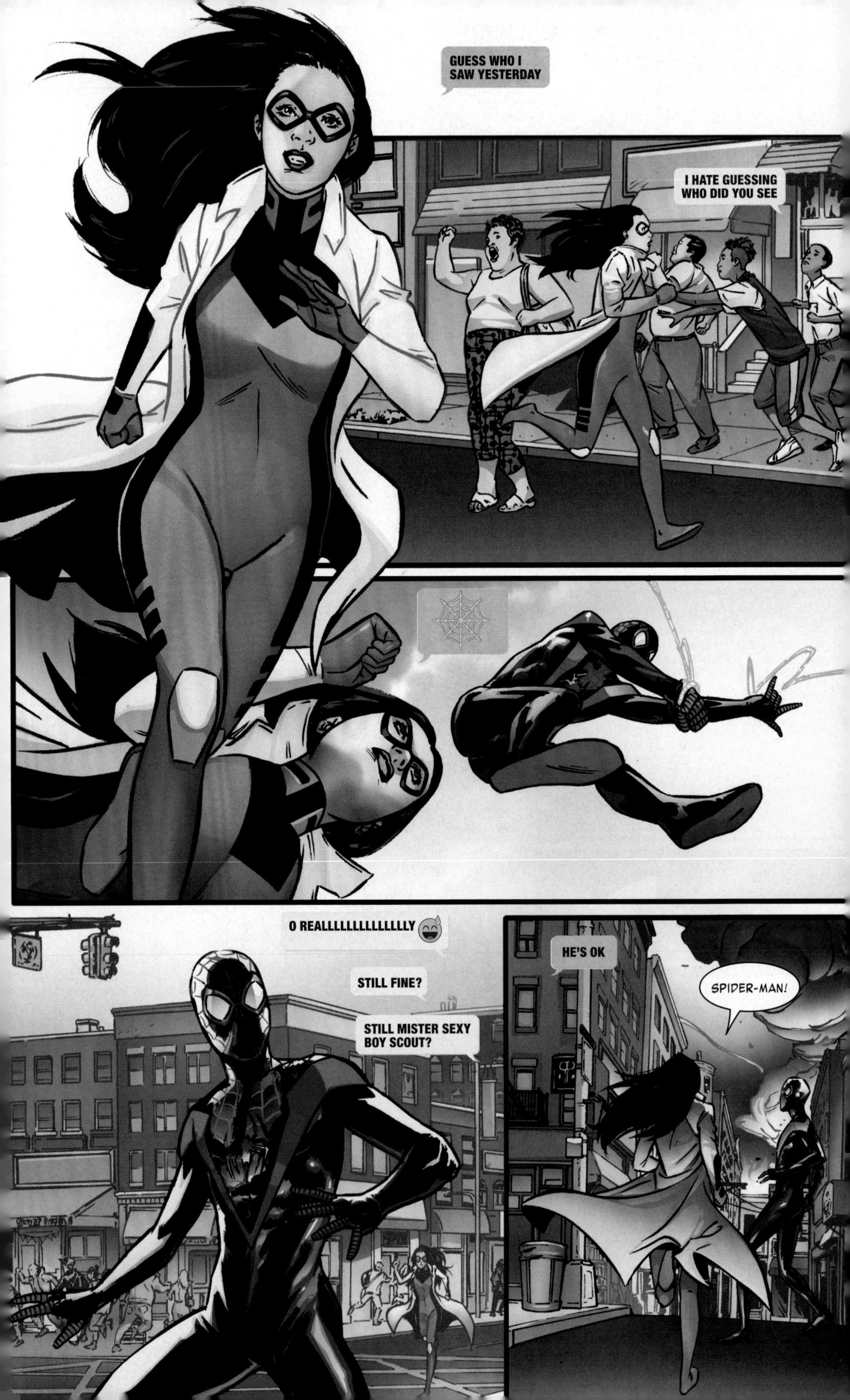
GUESS WHO I SAW YESTERDAY
I HATE GUESSING WHO DID YOU SEE
O REALLLLLLLLLLLLLLY
STILL FINE?
STILL MISTER SEXY BOY SCOUT?
HE'S OK
SPIDER-MAN!

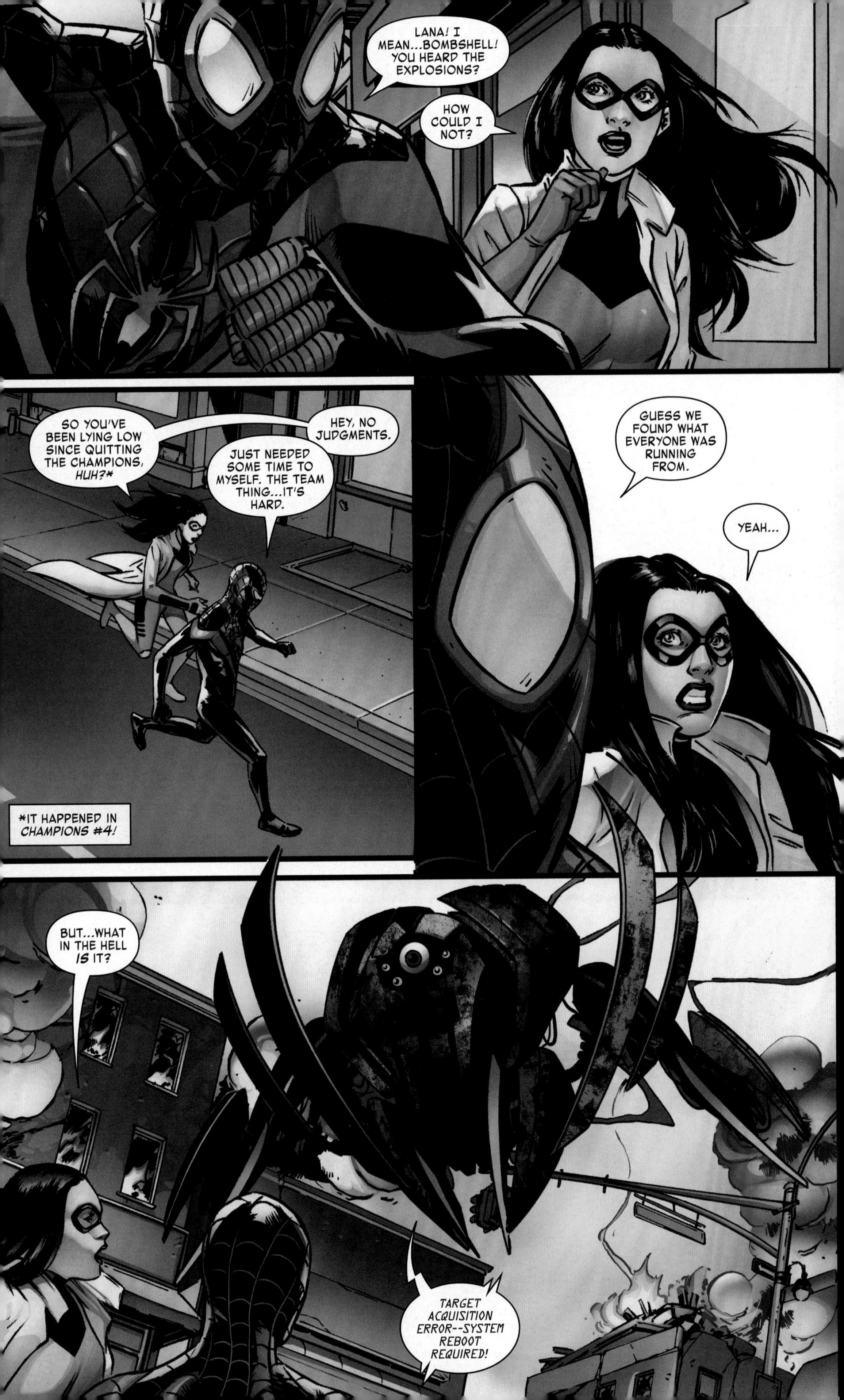
LANA! I MEAN...BOMBSHELL! YOU HEARD THE EXPLOSIONS?
HOW COULD I NOT?
SO YOU'VE BEEN LYING LOW SINCE QUITTING THE CHAMPIONS, *HUH?**
HEY, NO JUDGMENTS.
JUST NEEDED SOME TIME TO MYSELF. THE TEAM THING...IT'S HARD.
*IT HAPPENED IN *CHAMPIONS #4!*
GUESS WE FOUND WHAT EVERYONE WAS RUNNING FROM.
YEAH...
BUT...WHAT IN THE HELL *IS* IT?
TARGET ACQUISITION ERROR--SYSTEM REBOOT REQUIRED!

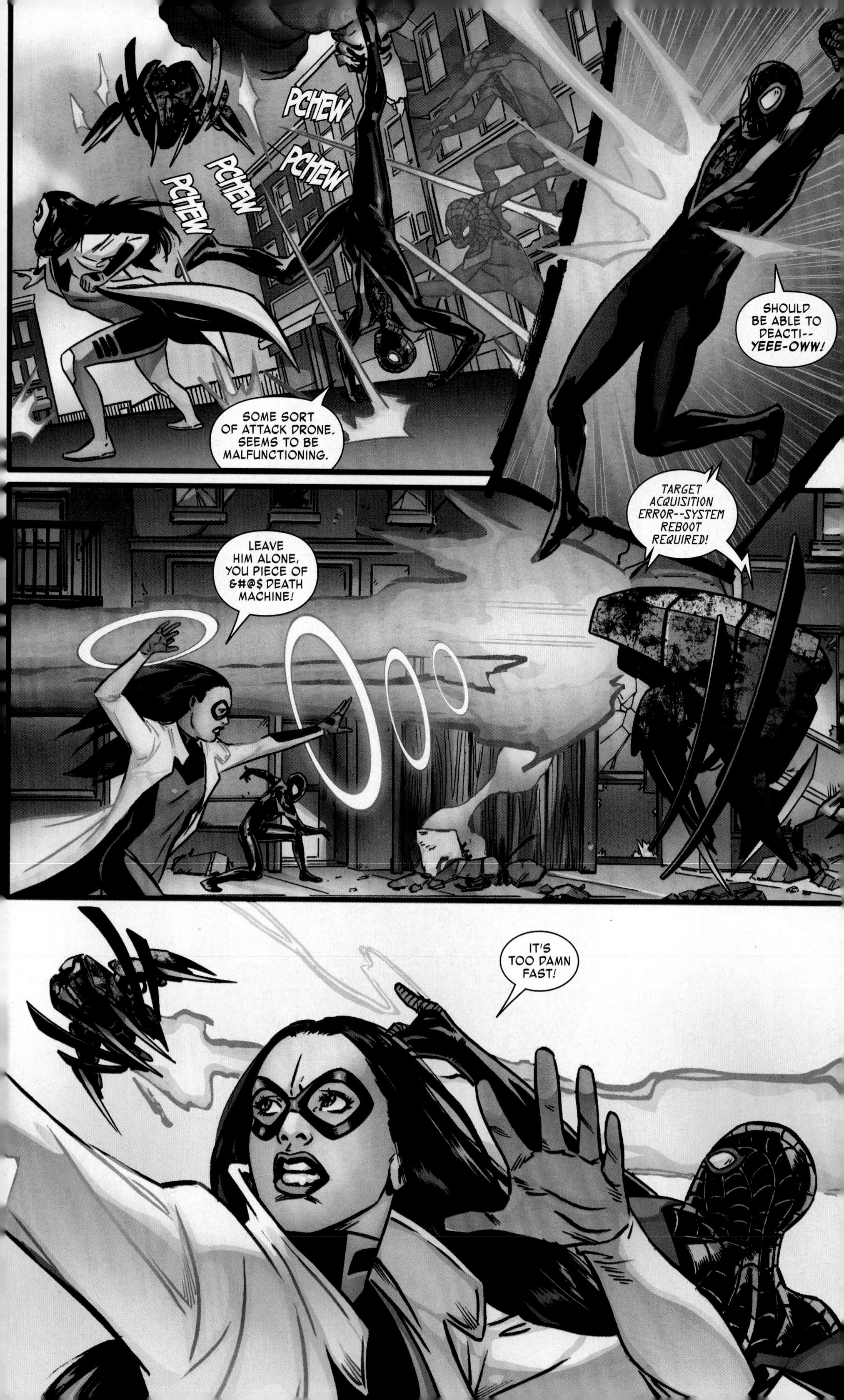
PCHEW
PCHEW
PCHEW
PCHEW
SOME SORT OF ATTACK DRONE. SEEMS TO BE MALFUNCTIONING.
SHOULD BE ABLE TO DEACTI-- YEEE-OWW!
LEAVE HIM ALONE, YOU PIECE OF &#@$ DEATH MACHINE!
TARGET ACQUISITION ERROR--SYSTEM REBOOT REQUIRED!
IT'S TOO DAMN FAST!

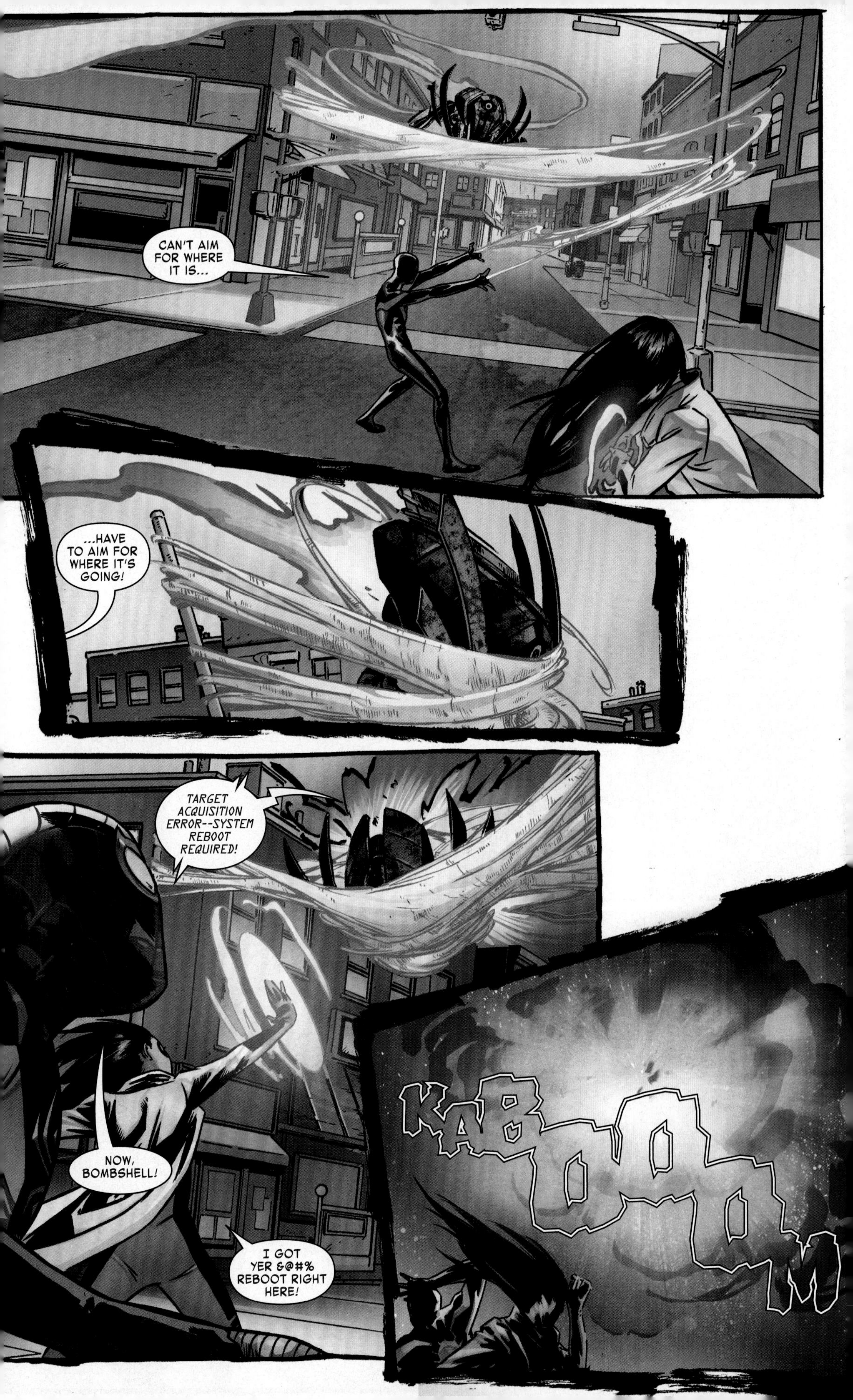
CAN'T AIM FOR WHERE IT IS...
...HAVE TO AIM FOR WHERE IT'S GOING!
TARGET ACQUISITION ERROR--SYSTEM REBOOT REQUIRED!
NOW, BOMBSHELL!
I GOT YER &@#% REBOOT RIGHT HERE!
KABOOOM

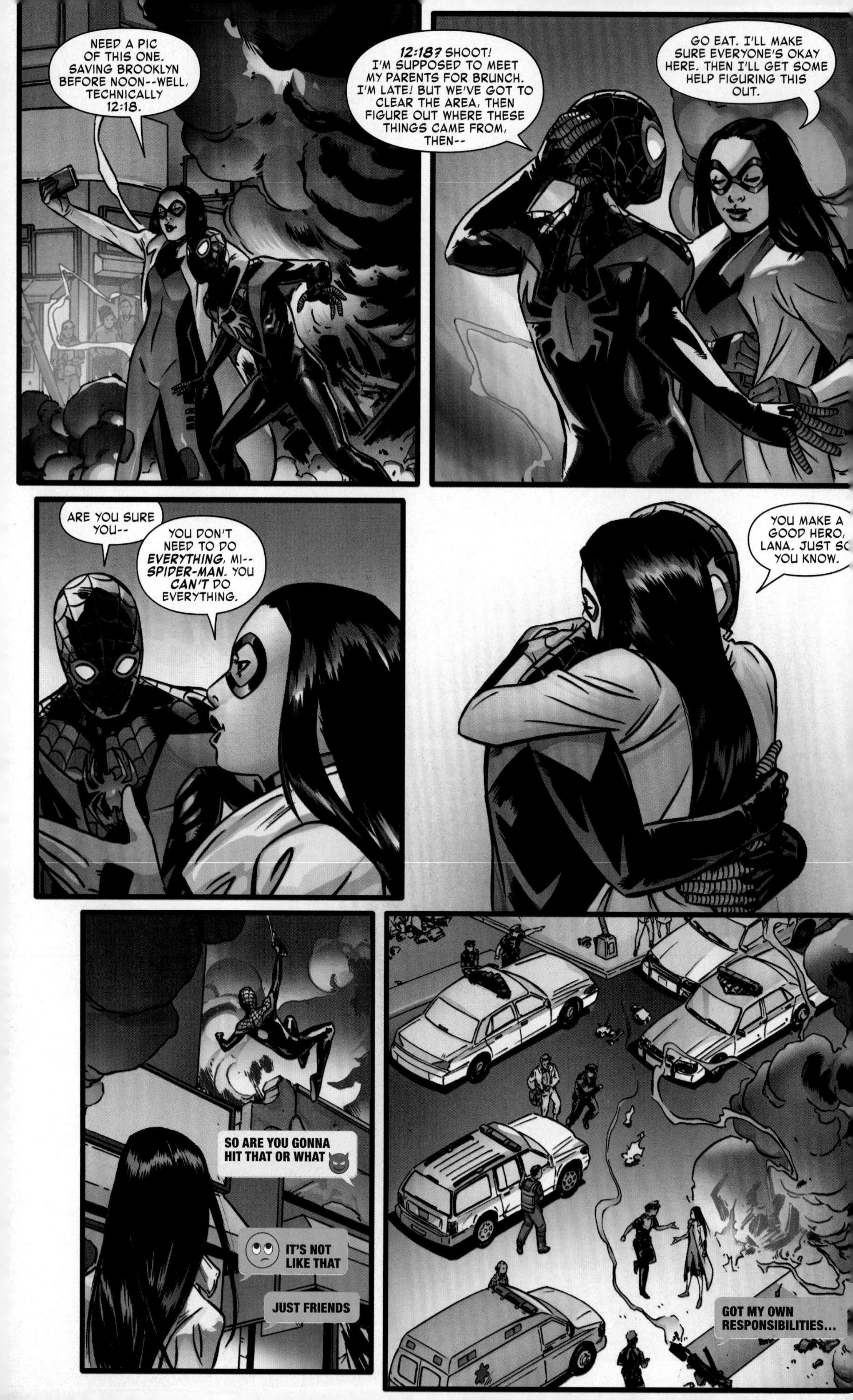

NEED A PIC OF THIS ONE. SAVING BROOKLYN BEFORE NOON--WELL, TECHNICALLY 12:18.
12:18? SHOOT! I'M SUPPOSED TO MEET MY PARENTS FOR BRUNCH. I'M LATE! BUT WE'VE GOT TO CLEAR THE AREA, THEN FIGURE OUT WHERE THESE THINGS CAME FROM, THEN--
GO EAT. I'LL MAKE SURE EVERYONE'S OKAY HERE. THEN I'LL GET SOME HELP FIGURING THIS OUT.
ARE YOU SURE YOU--
YOU DON'T NEED TO DO EVERYTHING, MI-- SPIDER-MAN. YOU CAN'T DO EVERYTHING.
YOU MAKE A GOOD HERO, LANA. JUST SO YOU KNOW.
SO ARE YOU GONNA HIT THAT OR WHAT
IT'S NOT LIKE THAT
JUST FRIENDS
GOT MY OWN RESPONSIBILITIES...

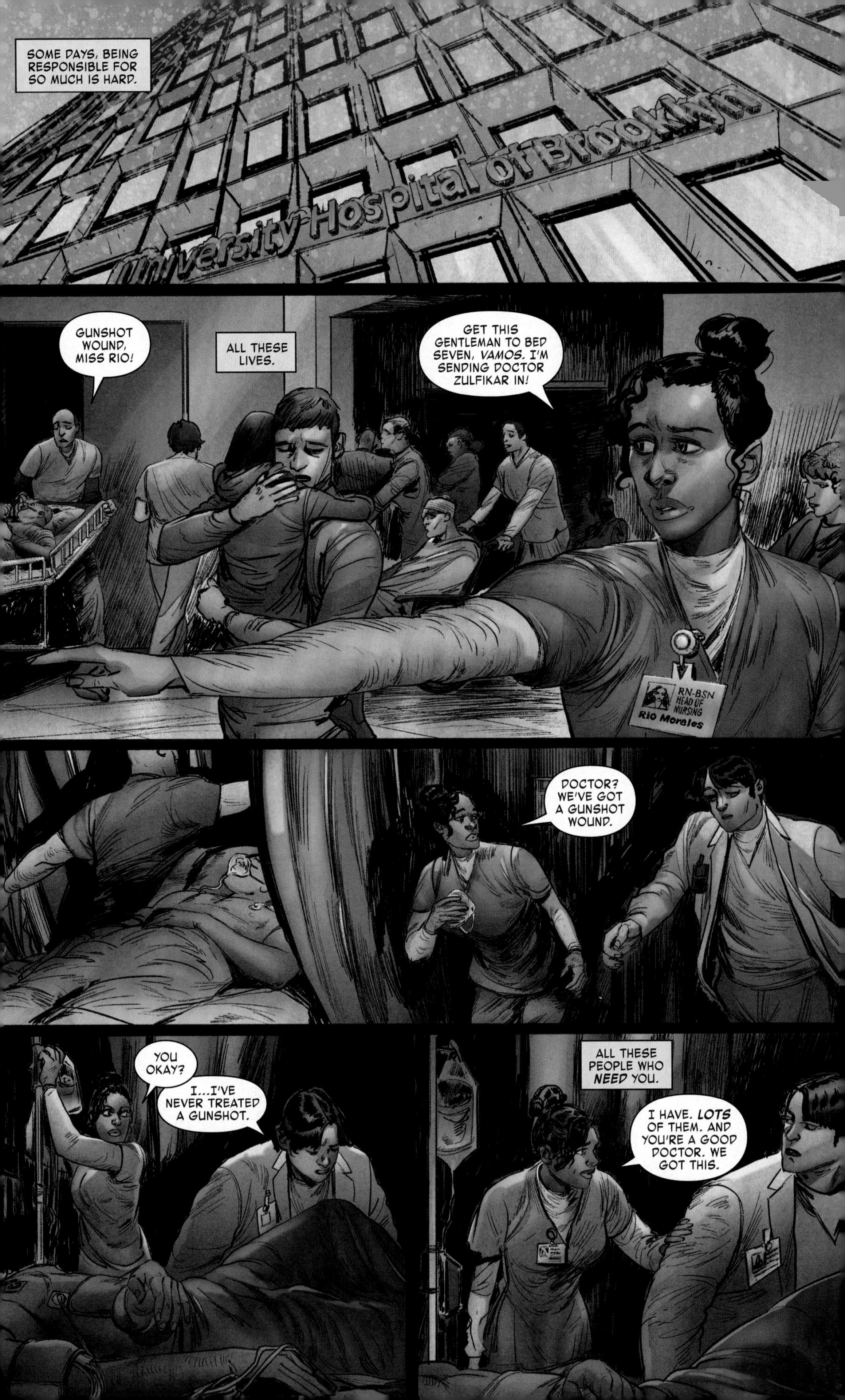
SOME DAYS, BEING RESPONSIBLE FOR SO MUCH IS HARD.
University Hospital of Brooklyn
GUNSHOT WOUND, MISS RIO!
ALL THESE LIVES.
GET THIS GENTLEMAN TO BED SEVEN, *VAMOS.* I'M SENDING DOCTOR ZULFIKAR IN!
RN-BSN
HEAD OF NURSING
Rio Morales
DOCTOR? WE'VE GOT A GUNSHOT WOUND.
YOU OKAY?
I...I'VE NEVER TREATED A GUNSHOT.
ALL THESE PEOPLE WHO ***NEED*** YOU.
I HAVE. ***LOTS*** OF THEM. AND YOU'RE A GOOD DOCTOR. WE GOT THIS.

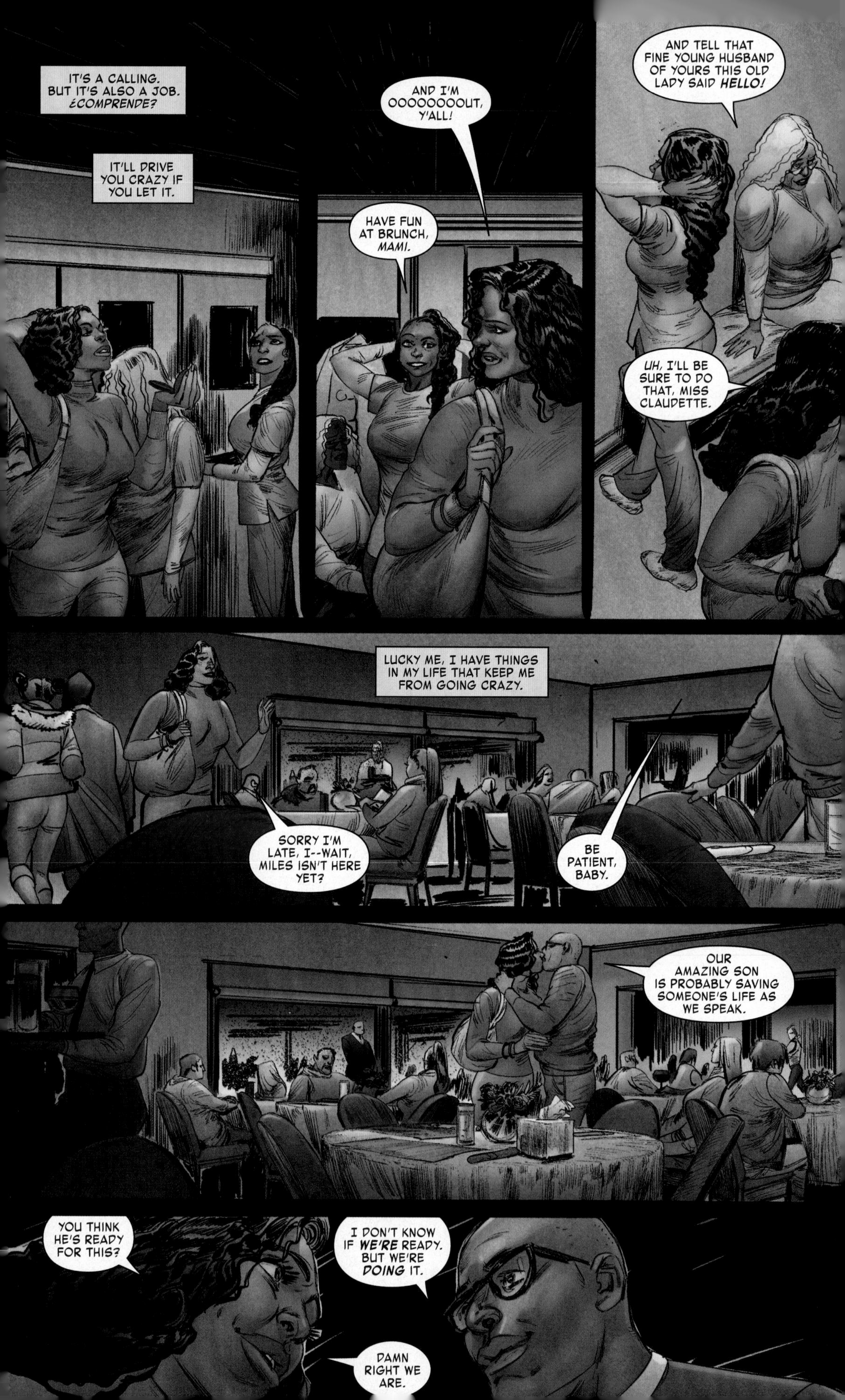
IT'S A CALLING. BUT IT'S ALSO A JOB. ¿COMPRENDE?
IT'LL DRIVE YOU CRAZY IF YOU LET IT.
AND I'M OOOOOOOOUT, Y'ALL!
HAVE FUN AT BRUNCH, MAMI.
AND TELL THAT FINE YOUNG HUSBAND OF YOURS THIS OLD LADY SAID HELLO!
UH, I'LL BE SURE TO DO THAT, MISS CLAUDETTE.
LUCKY ME, I HAVE THINGS IN MY LIFE THAT KEEP ME FROM GOING CRAZY.
SORRY I'M LATE, I--WAIT, MILES ISN'T HERE YET?
BE PATIENT, BABY.
OUR AMAZING SON IS PROBABLY SAVING SOMEONE'S LIFE AS WE SPEAK.
YOU THINK HE'S READY FOR THIS?
I DON'T KNOW IF WE'RE READY. BUT WE'RE DOING IT.
DAMN RIGHT WE ARE.

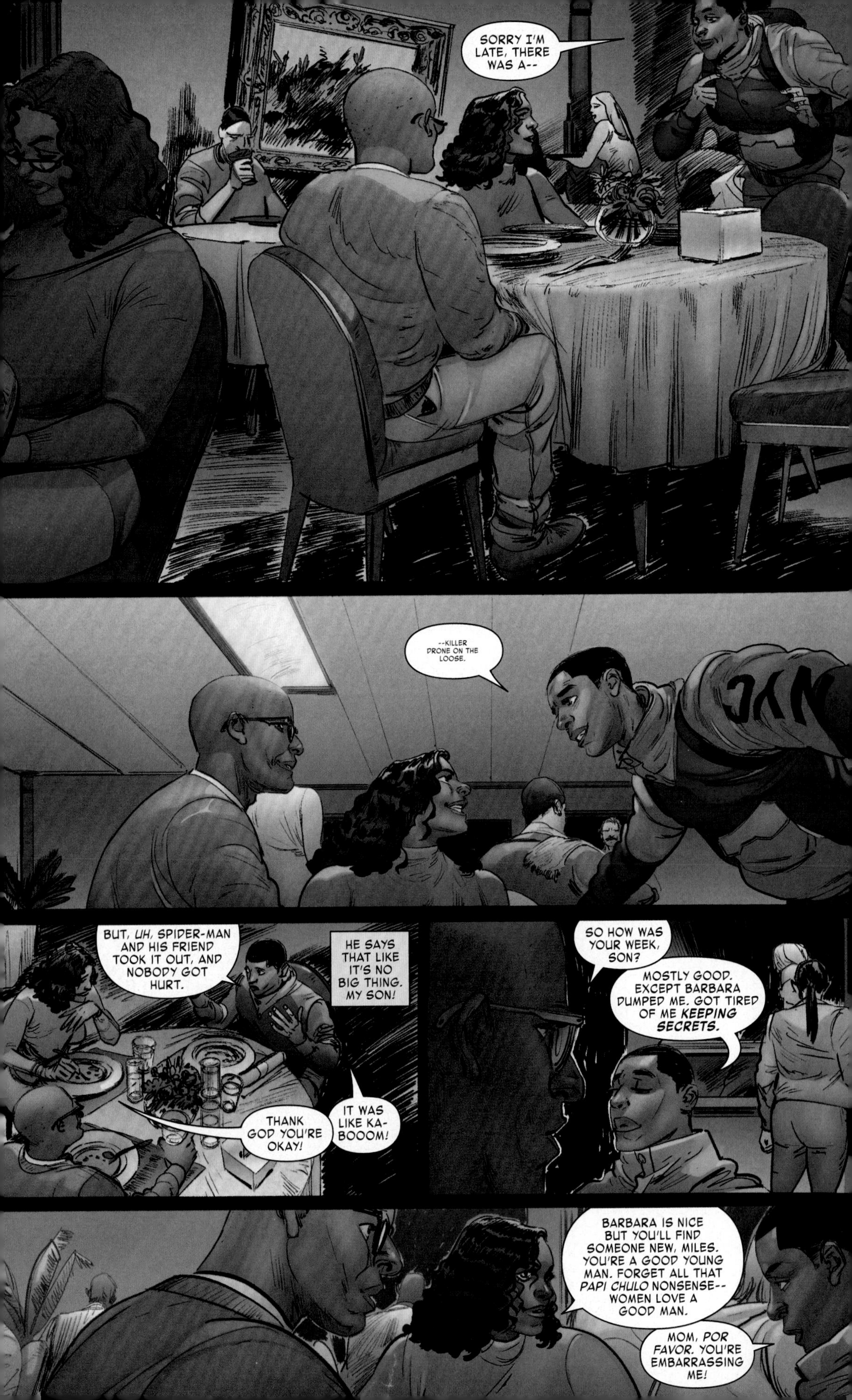
SORRY I'M LATE, THERE WAS A--
--KILLER DRONE ON THE LOOSE.
BUT, UH, SPIDER-MAN AND HIS FRIEND TOOK IT OUT, AND NOBODY GOT HURT.
HE SAYS THAT LIKE IT'S NO BIG THING. MY SON!
THANK GOD YOU'RE OKAY!
IT WAS LIKE KA-BOOOM!
SO HOW WAS YOUR WEEK, SON?
MOSTLY GOOD. EXCEPT BARBARA DUMPED ME. GOT TIRED OF ME KEEPING SECRETS.
BARBARA IS NICE BUT YOU'LL FIND SOMEONE NEW, MILES. YOU'RE A GOOD YOUNG MAN. FORGET ALL THAT PAPI CHULO NONSENSE-- WOMEN LOVE A GOOD MAN.
MOM, POR FAVOR. YOU'RE EMBARRASSING ME!

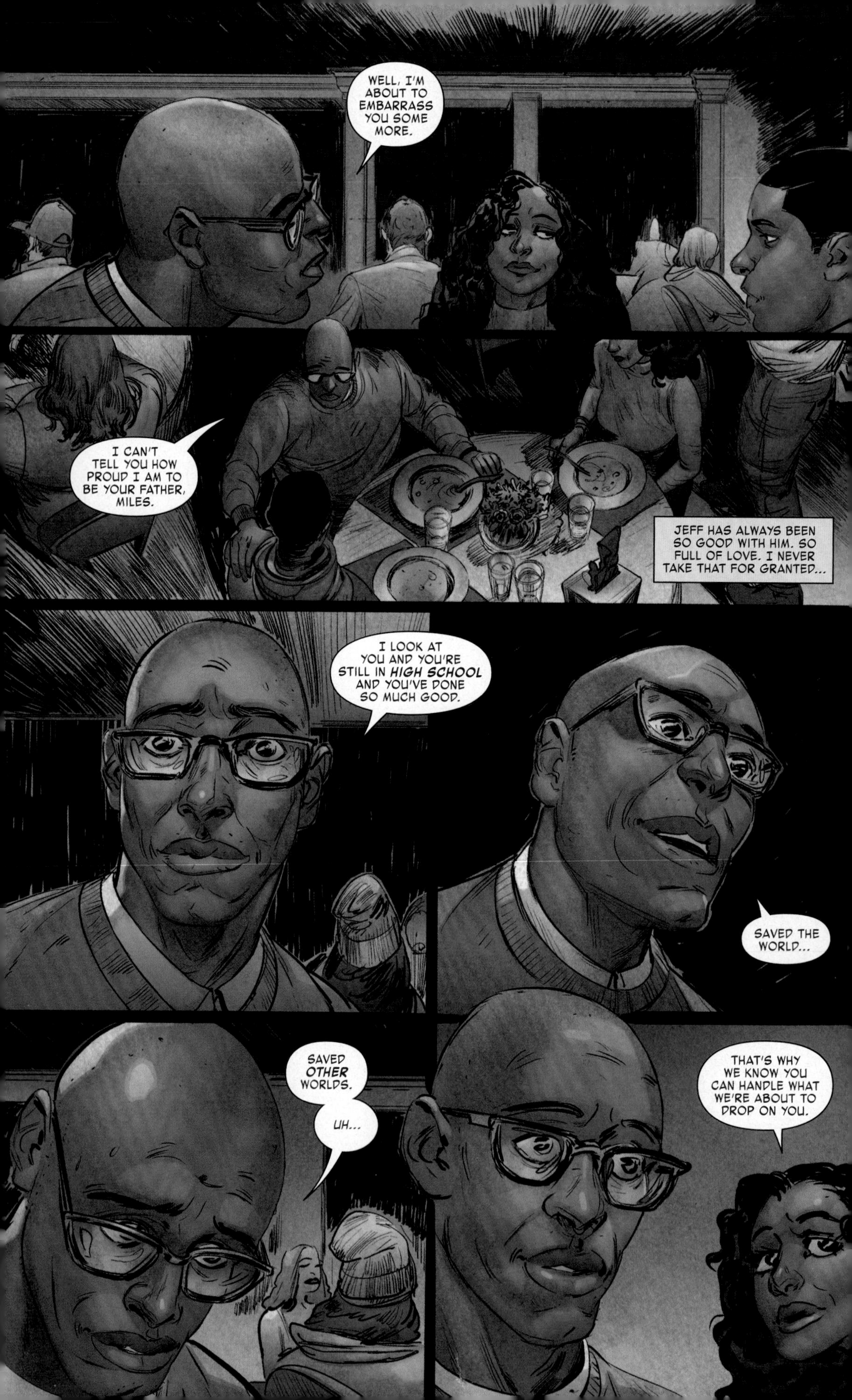
WELL, I'M ABOUT TO EMBARRASS YOU SOME MORE.
I CAN'T TELL YOU HOW PROUD I AM TO BE YOUR FATHER, MILES.
JEFF HAS ALWAYS BEEN SO GOOD WITH HIM. SO FULL OF LOVE. I NEVER TAKE THAT FOR GRANTED...
I LOOK AT YOU AND YOU'RE STILL IN HIGH SCHOOL AND YOU'VE DONE SO MUCH GOOD.
SAVED THE WORLD...
SAVED OTHER WORLDS.
UH...
THAT'S WHY WE KNOW YOU CAN HANDLE WHAT WE'RE ABOUT TO DROP ON YOU.

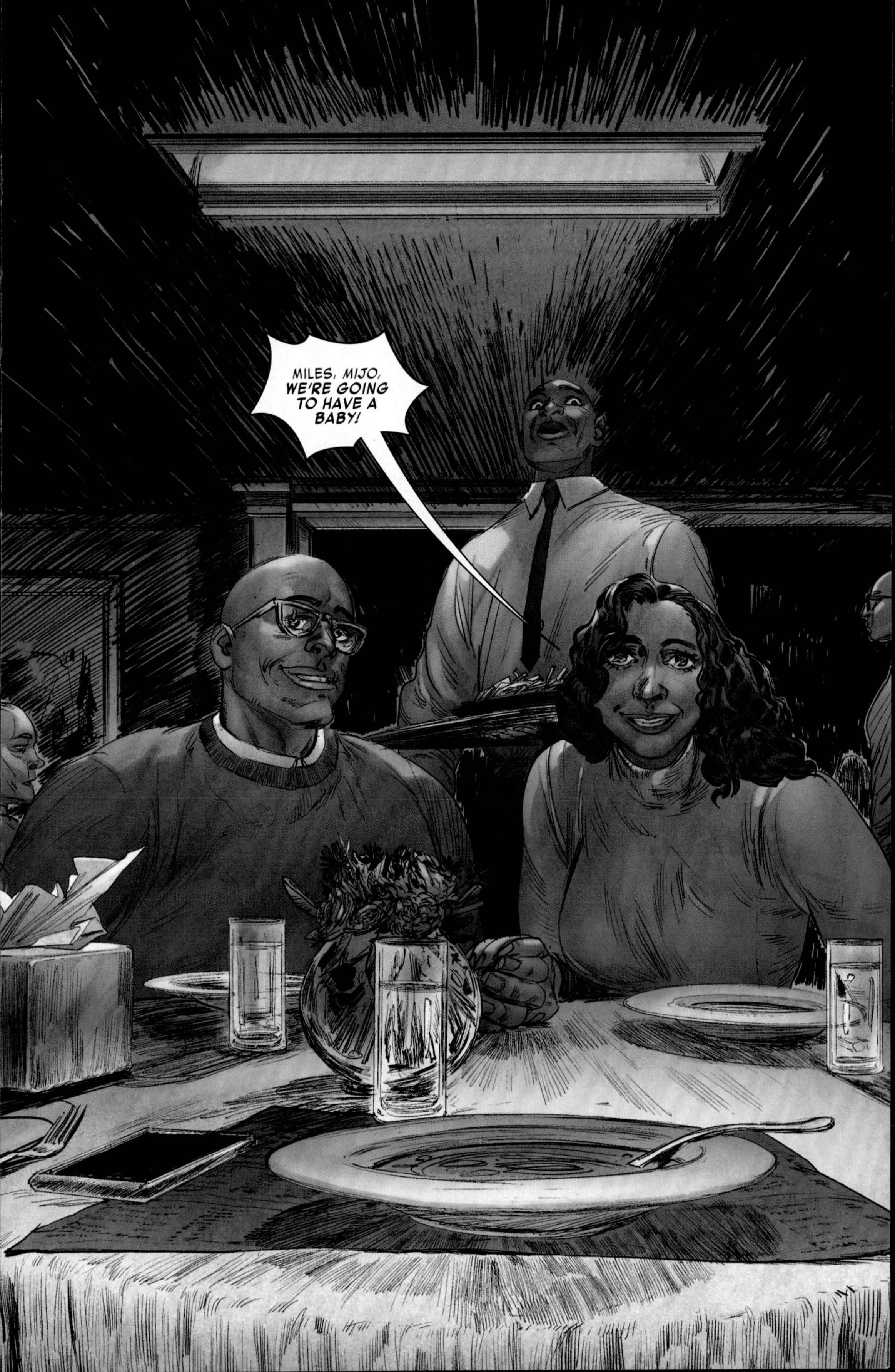
MILES, MIJO, WE'RE GOING TO HAVE A BABY!

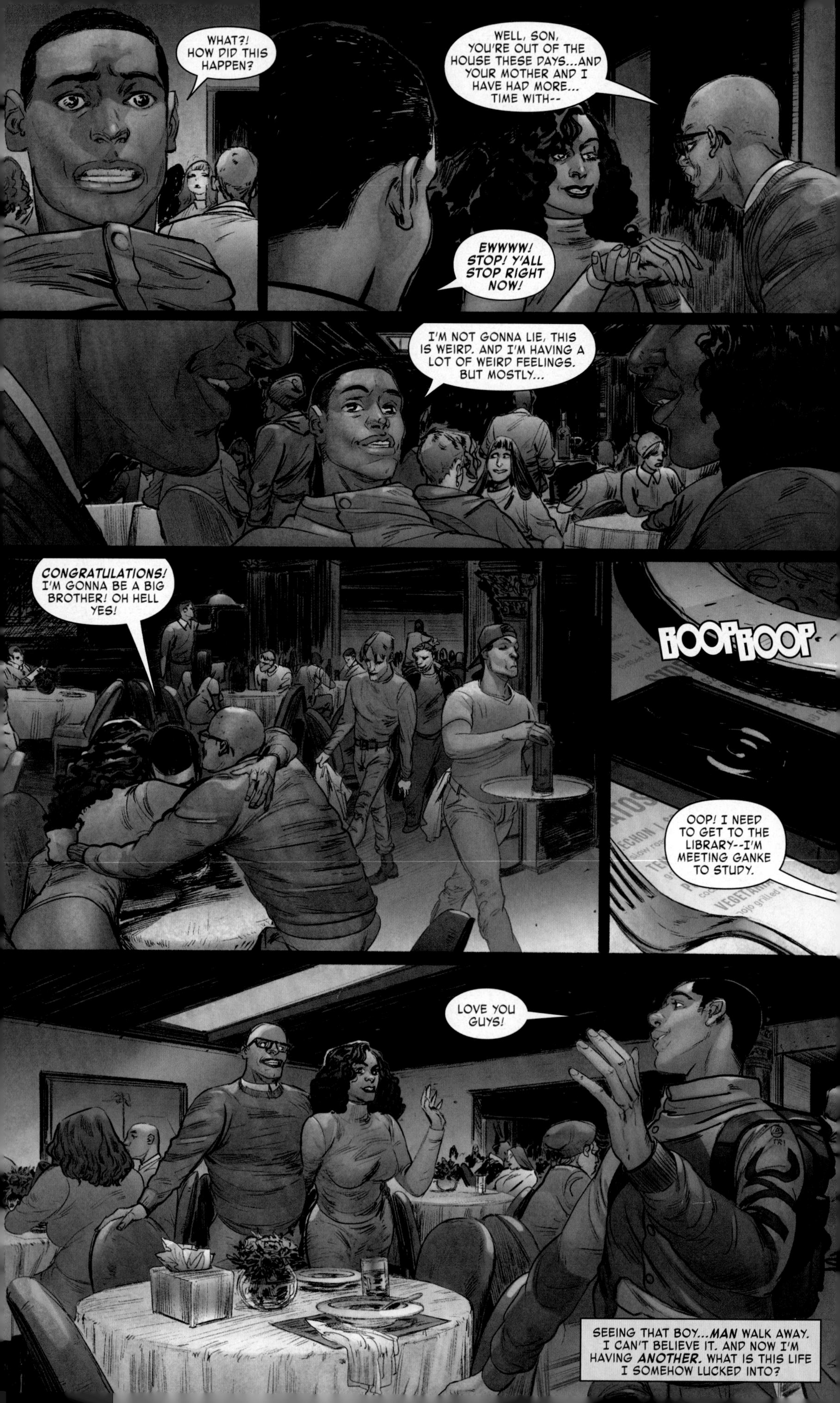
WHAT?! HOW DID THIS HAPPEN?
WELL, SON, YOU'RE OUT OF THE HOUSE THESE DAYS...AND YOUR MOTHER AND I HAVE HAD MORE... TIME WITH--
EWWWW! STOP! Y'ALL STOP RIGHT NOW!
I'M NOT GONNA LIE, THIS IS WEIRD. AND I'M HAVING A LOT OF WEIRD FEELINGS. BUT MOSTLY...
CONGRATULATIONS! I'M GONNA BE A BIG BROTHER! OH HELL YES!
BOOPBOOP
OOP! I NEED TO GET TO THE LIBRARY--I'M MEETING GANKE TO STUDY.
LOVE YOU GUYS!
SEEING THAT BOY...MAN WALK AWAY. I CAN'T BELIEVE IT. AND NOW I'M HAVING ANOTHER. WHAT IS THIS LIFE I SOMEHOW LUCKED INTO?

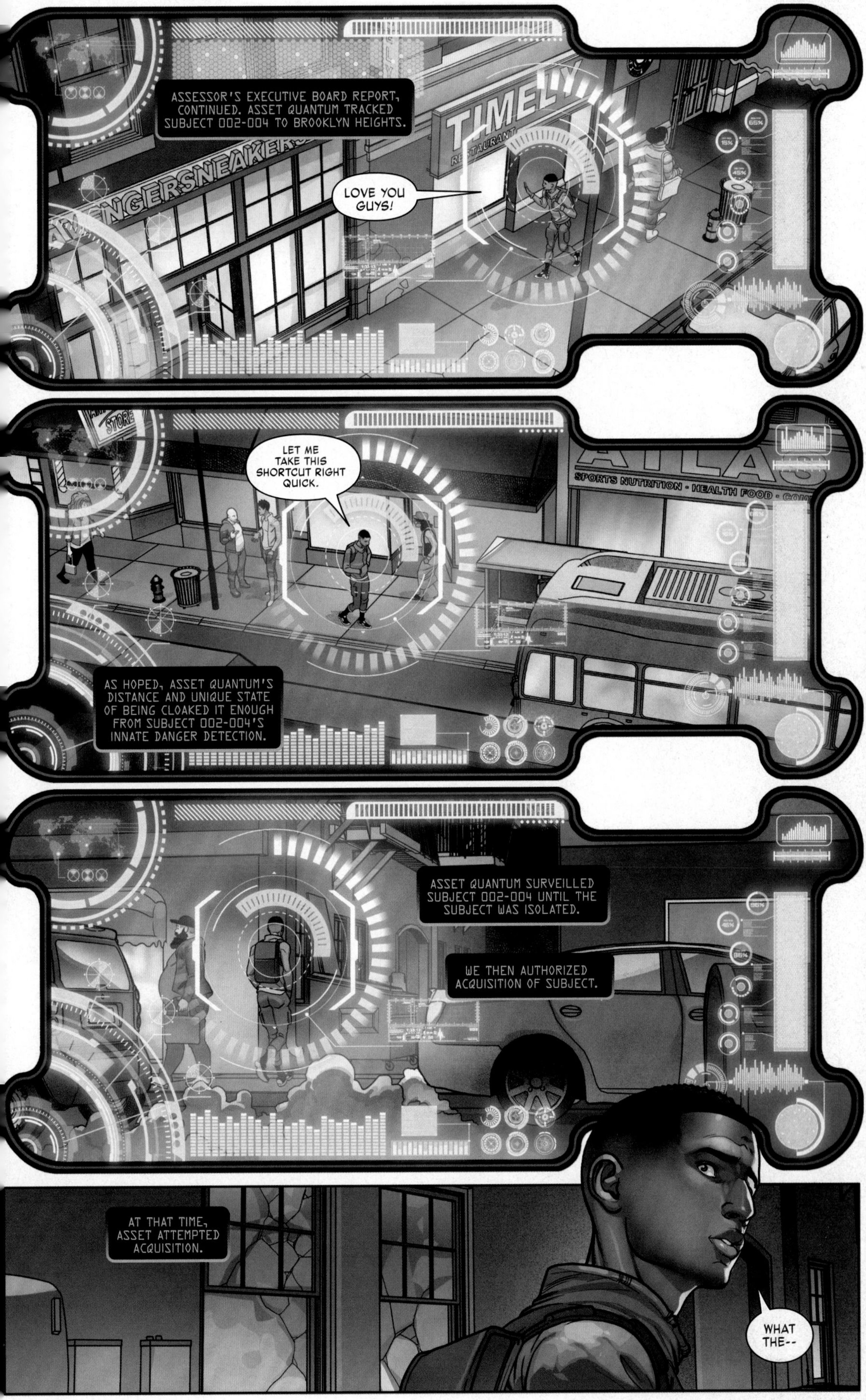
ASSESSOR'S EXECUTIVE BOARD REPORT, CONTINUED. ASSET QUANTUM TRACKED SUBJECT 002-004 TO BROOKLYN HEIGHTS.
TIMELY
RESTAURANT
LOVE YOU GUYS!
LET ME TAKE THIS SHORTCUT RIGHT QUICK.
AS HOPED, ASSET QUANTUM'S DISTANCE AND UNIQUE STATE OF BEING CLOAKED IT ENOUGH FROM SUBJECT 002-004'S INNATE DANGER DETECTION.
ASSET QUANTUM SURVEILLED SUBJECT 002-004 UNTIL THE SUBJECT WAS ISOLATED.
WE THEN AUTHORIZED ACQUISITION OF SUBJECT.
AT THAT TIME, ASSET ATTEMPTED ACQUISITION.
WHAT THE--

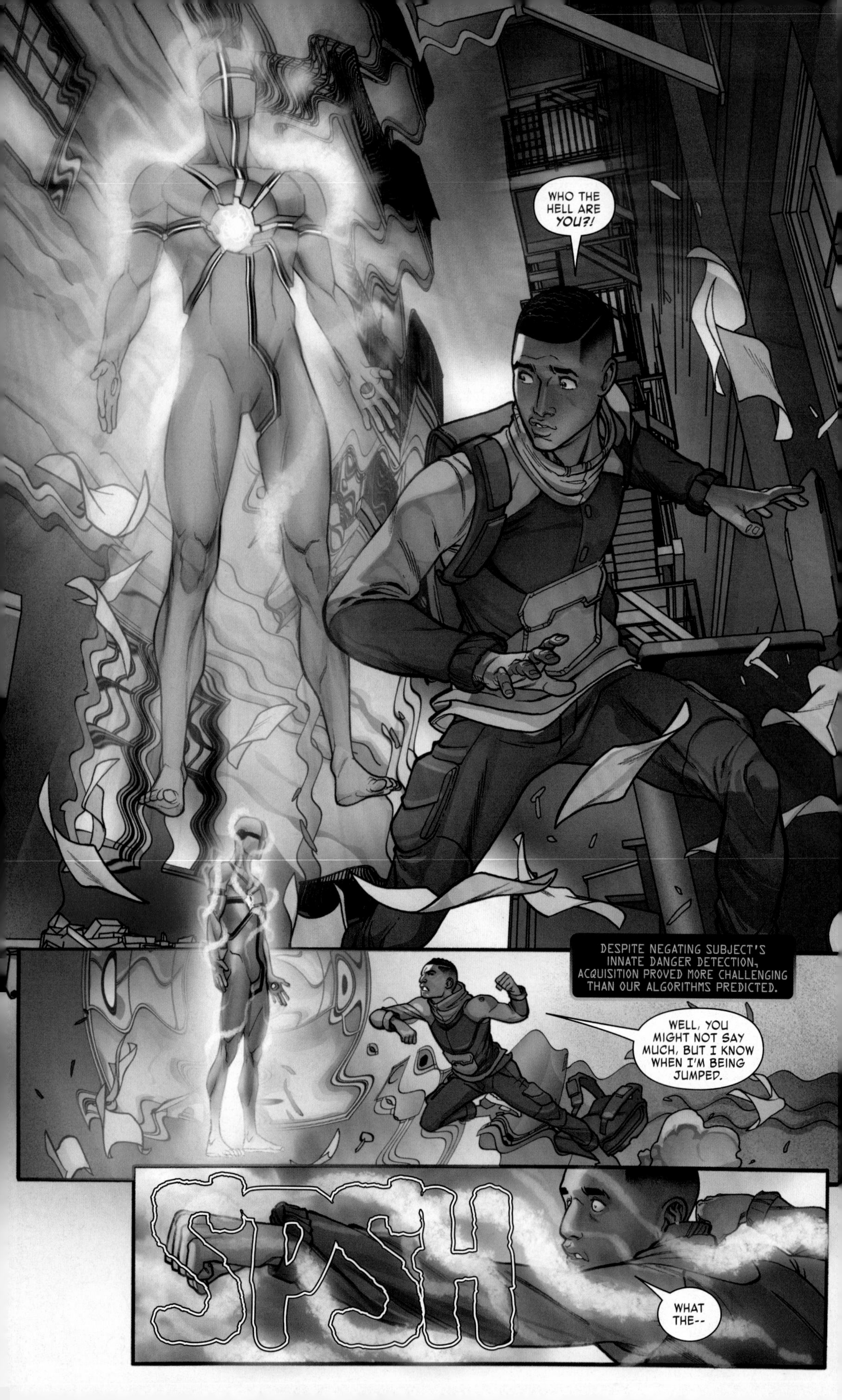
WHO THE HELL ARE YOU?!
DESPITE NEGATING SUBJECT'S INNATE DANGER DETECTION, ACQUISITION PROVED MORE CHALLENGING THAN OUR ALGORITHMS PREDICTED.
WELL, YOU MIGHT NOT SAY MUCH, BUT I KNOW WHEN I'M BEING JUMPED.
SPSH
WHAT THE--

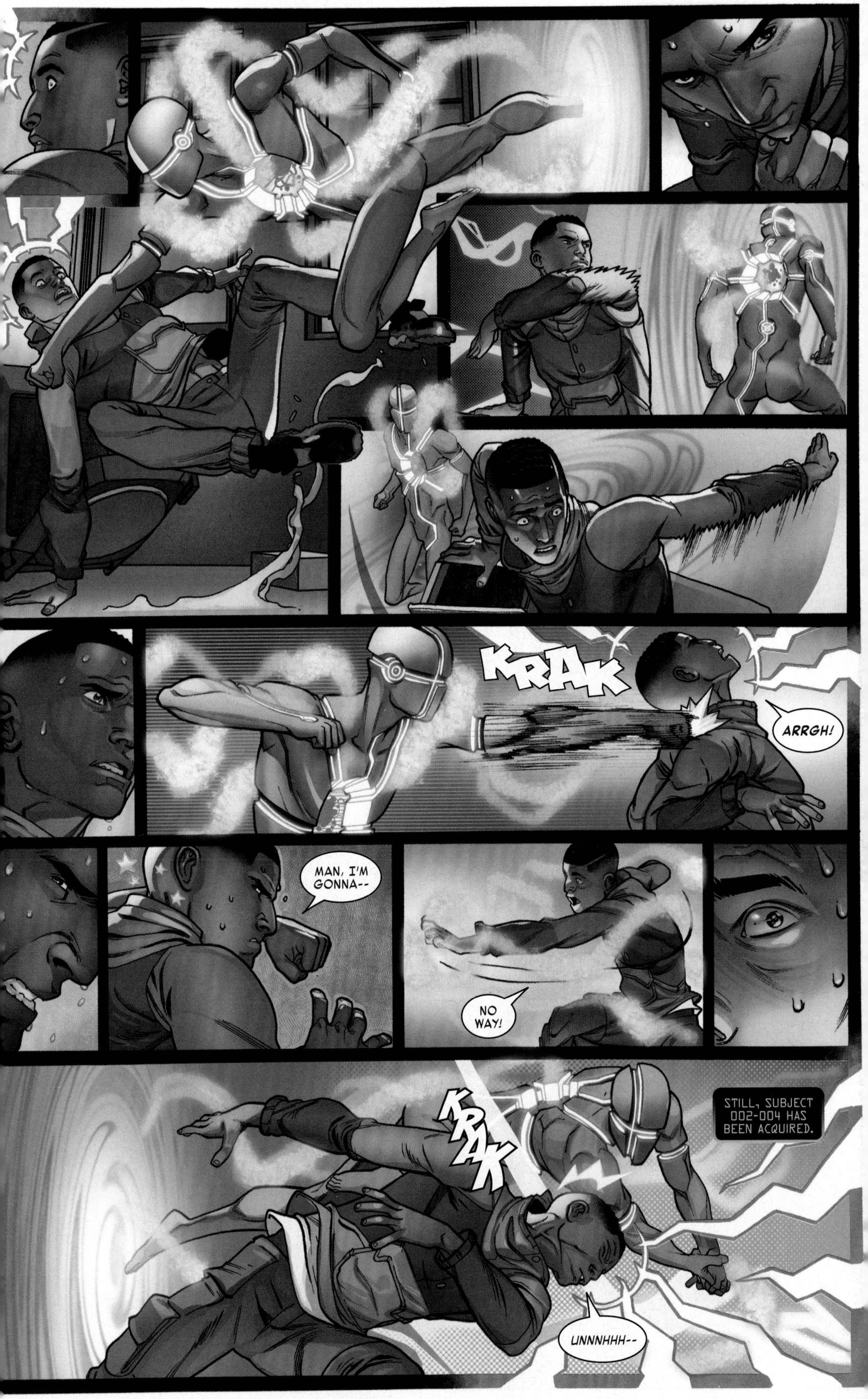
KRAK
ARRGH!
MAN, I'M GONNA--
NO WAY!
KRAK
STILL, SUBJECT 002-004 HAS BEEN ACQUIRED.
UNNNHHH--

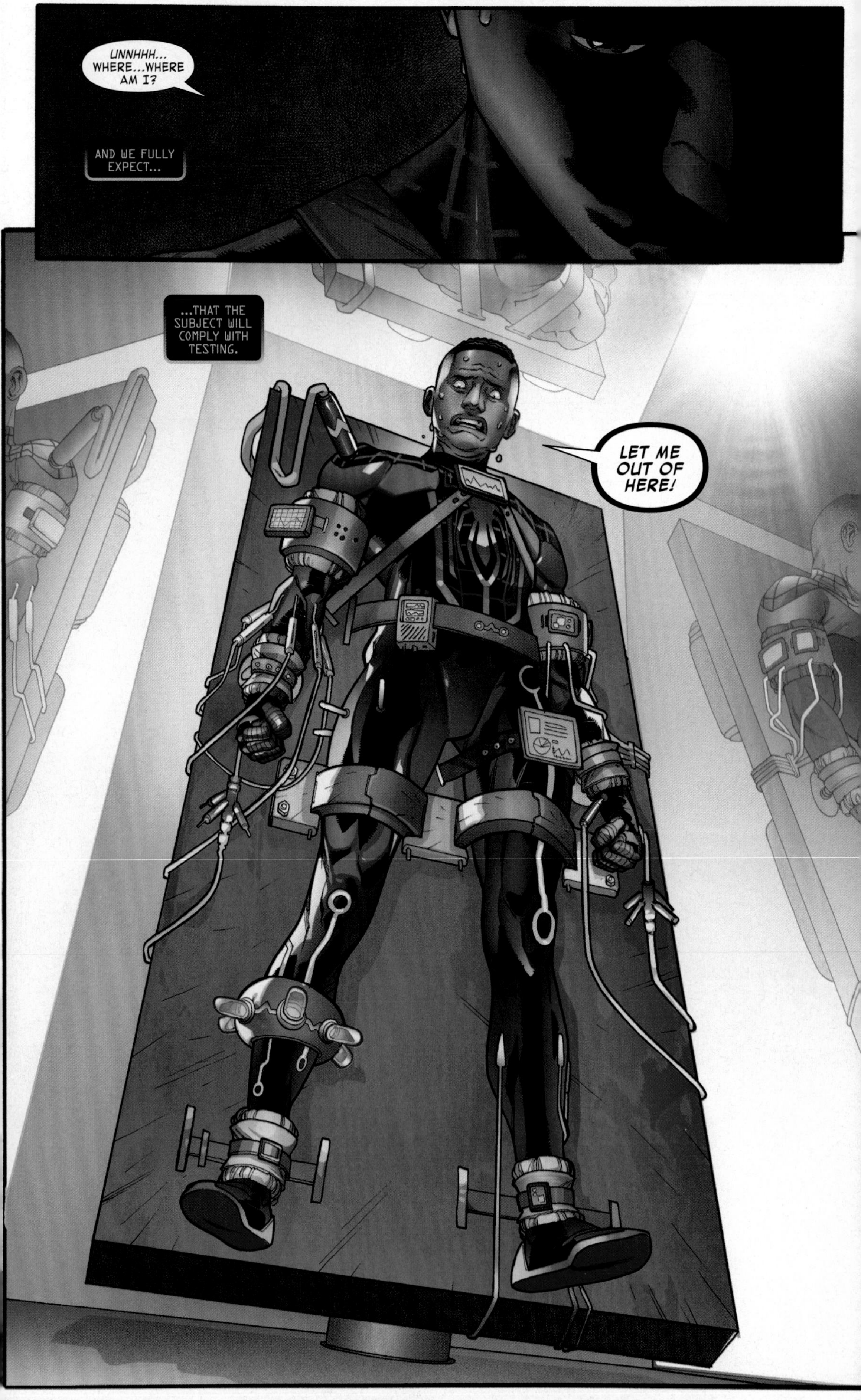
UNNHHH... WHERE...WHERE AM I?
AND WE FULLY EXPECT...
...THAT THE SUBJECT WILL COMPLY WITH TESTING.
LET ME OUT OF HERE!

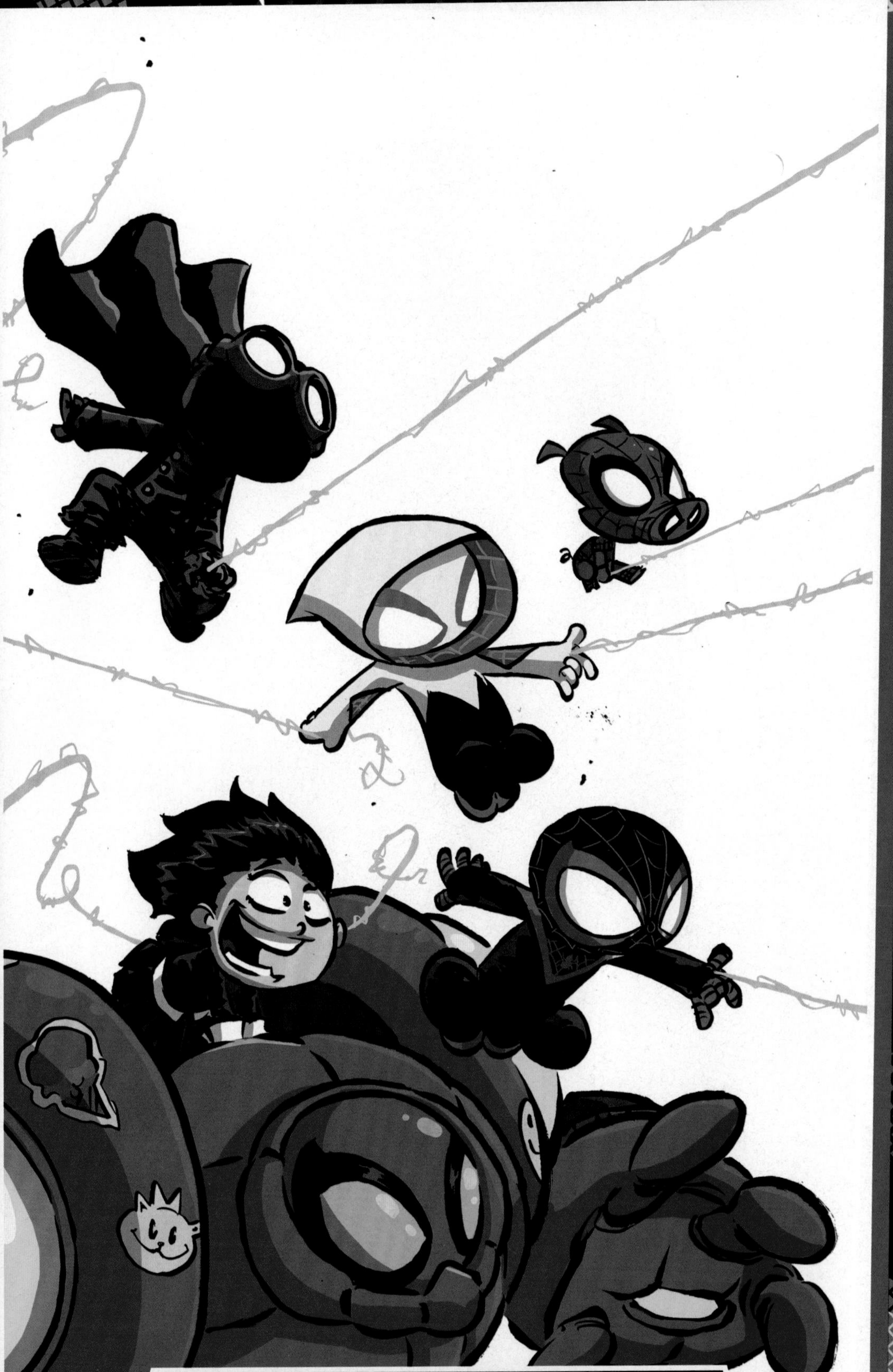

#8 SAN DIEGO COMIC-CON VARIANT BY **SKOTTIE YOUNG**

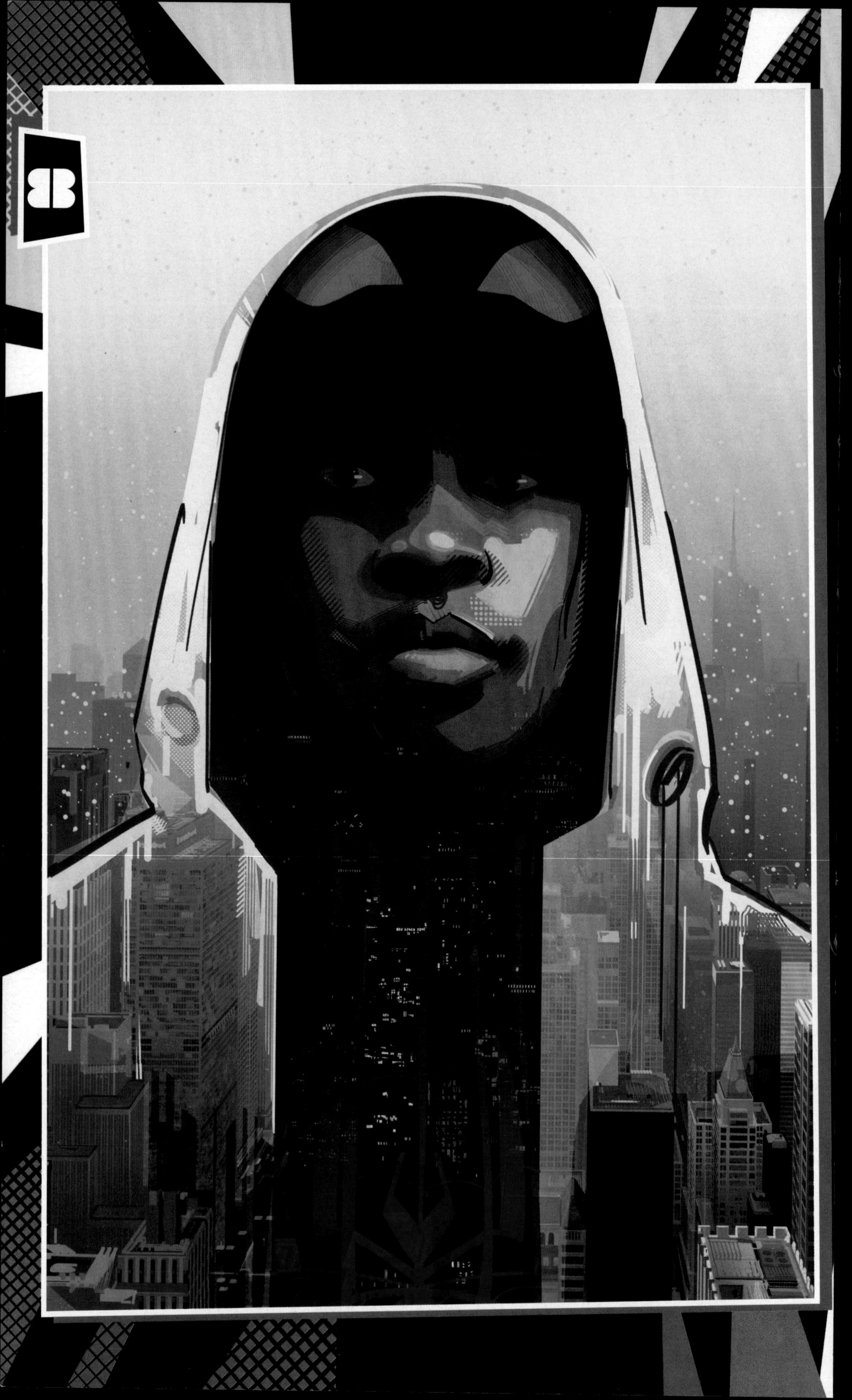

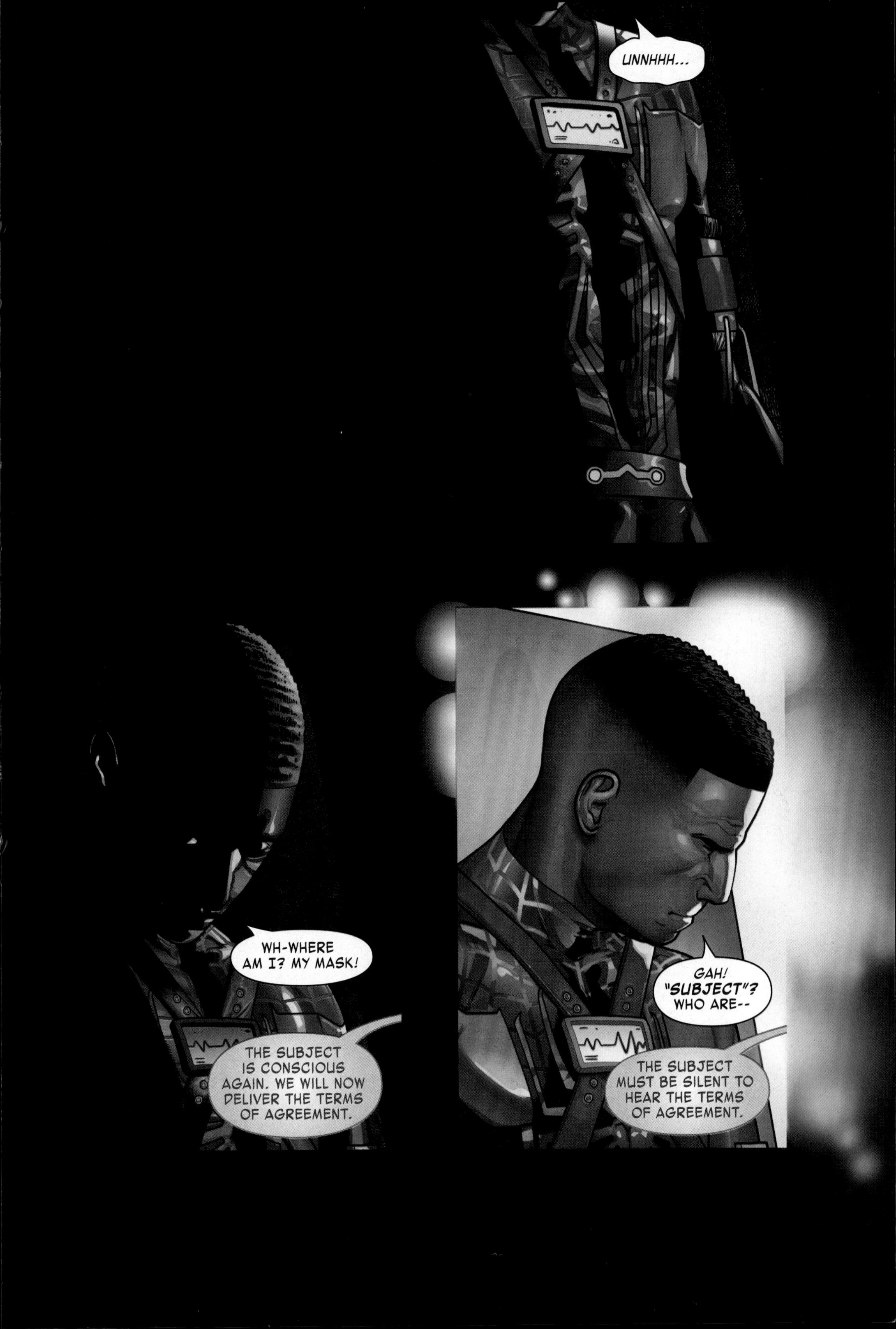
UNNHHH...
WH-WHERE AM I? MY MASK!
THE SUBJECT IS CONSCIOUS AGAIN. WE WILL NOW DELIVER THE TERMS OF AGREEMENT.
GAH! "SUBJECT"? WHO ARE--
THE SUBJECT MUST BE SILENT TO HEAR THE TERMS OF AGREEMENT.

LIKE HELL I WILL! WHO IN THE--

IF THE SUBJECT IS NOT SILENT, THE SUBJECT UNDERSTANDS THAT DISCIPLINARY MEASURES WILL BE INSTITUTED.

WHOEVER YOU ARE, I'M ABOUT TO INSTITUTE SOME DISCIPLINARY MEASURES UPSIDE YOUR HEAD! LEMME OUTTA THIS--

THE SUBJECT HAS ACTIVATED THE DISCIPLINARY MEASURES CLAUSE.

BZZZZZZZ

ARRGHHH!

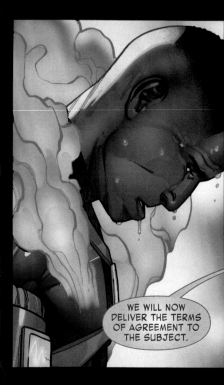

WE WILL NOW DELIVER THE TERMS OF AGREEMENT TO THE SUBJECT.

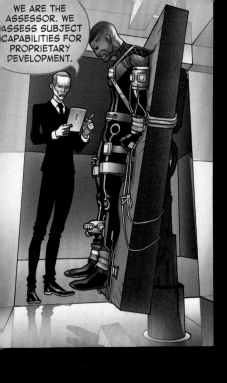

WE ARE THE ASSESSOR. WE ASSESS SUBJECT CAPABILITIES FOR PROPRIETARY DEVELOPMENT.

LOOK, MAN, I DON'T KNOW WHO'S PAYING YOU, BUT THIS AIN'T THE FIRST TIME I'VE BEEN CAPTURED. I *WILL* GET OUT OF HERE, AND WHEN I DO--

THE REDACTED TERMS OF AGREEMENT ARE AS FOLLOWS:

SUBJECT 002-004 WILL PARTICIPATE IN TRIALS ASSIGNED BY THE ASSESOR.

WHO ARE YOU WORKING WITH? TOMBSTONE?

IF THE SUBJECT DOES NOT PARTICIPATE IN TRIALS TO THE ASSESSOR'S SATISFACTION, THE SUBJECT UNDERSTANDS...

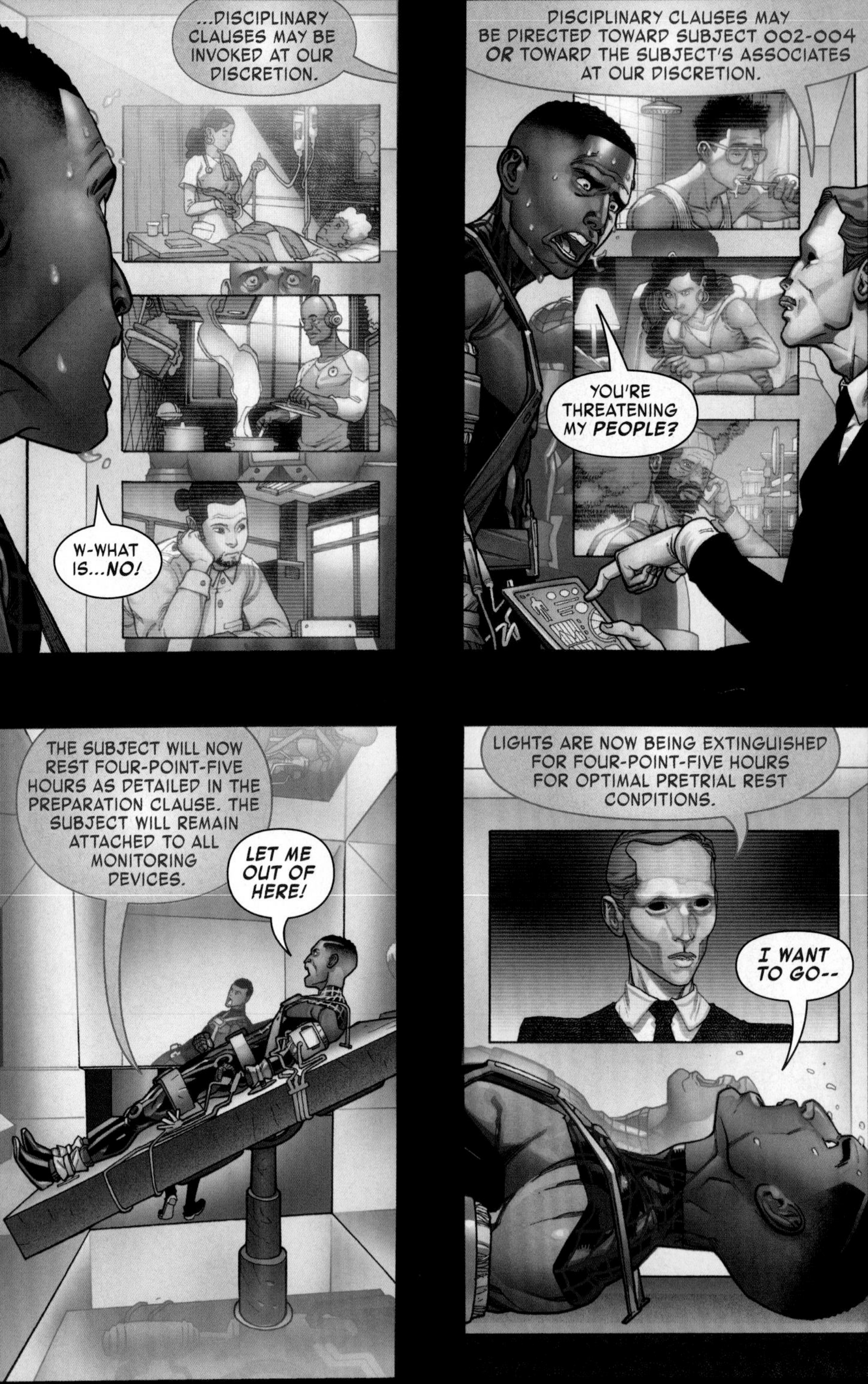
...DISCIPLINARY CLAUSES MAY BE INVOKED AT OUR DISCRETION.
W-WHAT IS...NO!
DISCIPLINARY CLAUSES MAY BE DIRECTED TOWARD SUBJECT 002-004 OR TOWARD THE SUBJECT'S ASSOCIATES AT OUR DISCRETION.
YOU'RE THREATENING MY PEOPLE?
THE SUBJECT WILL NOW REST FOUR-POINT-FIVE HOURS AS DETAILED IN THE PREPARATION CLAUSE. THE SUBJECT WILL REMAIN ATTACHED TO ALL MONITORING DEVICES.
LET ME OUT OF HERE!
LIGHTS ARE NOW BEING EXTINGUISHED FOR FOUR-POINT-FIVE HOURS FOR OPTIMAL PRETRIAL REST CONDITIONS.
I WANT TO GO--

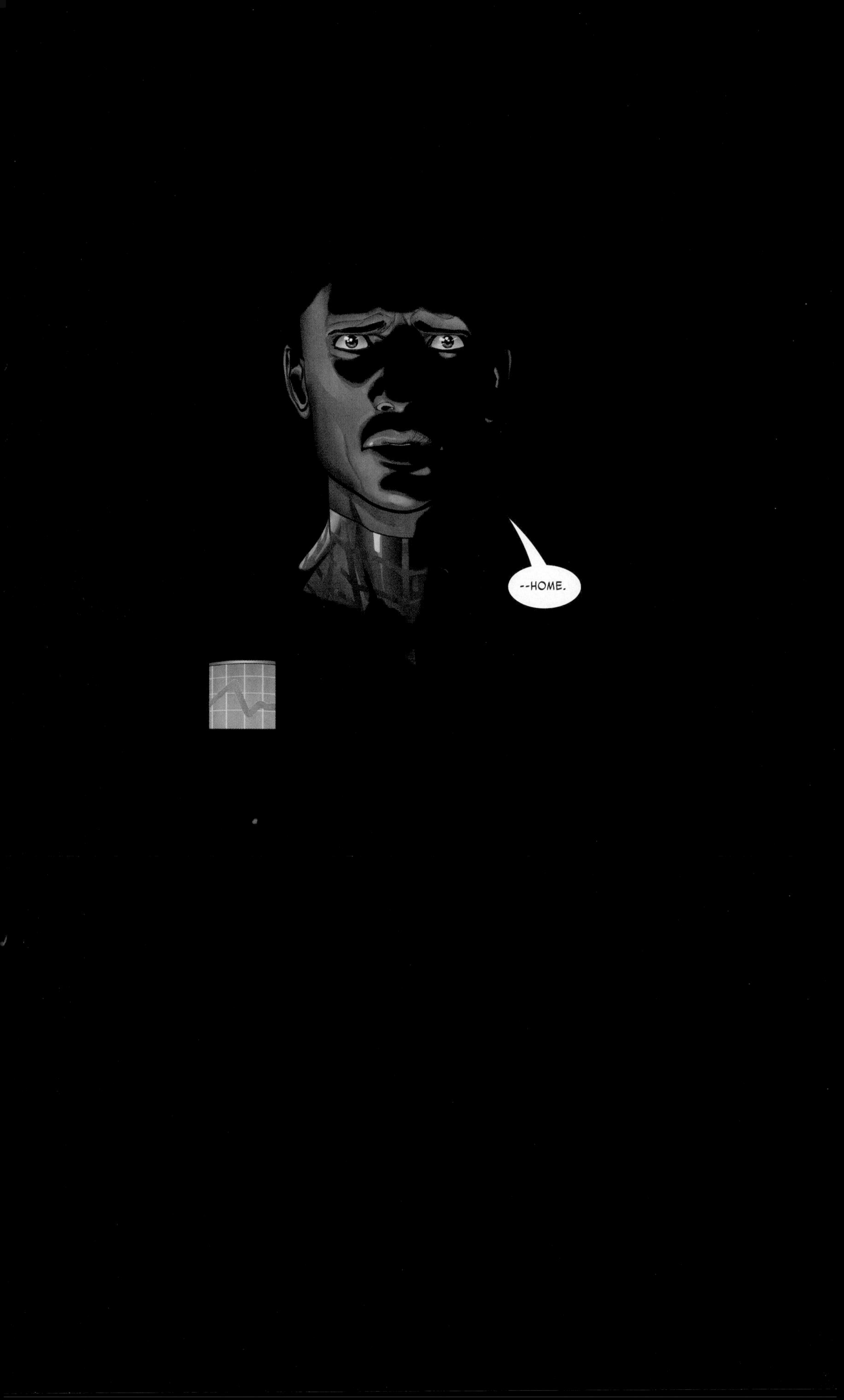
--HOME.

THE SUBJECT WILL NOW WAKE.
HUNH?
CLICK
CLICK
CLICK
CLICK
CLICK
CLICK
NOW COMMENCING ASSESSMENT OF THREAT DETECTION AND ATTENDANT COMBAT SKILL ENHANCEMENT VERSUS MULTIPLE MEDIUM-THREAT TARGETS.
YOU'RE LETTING ME GO?
TRIAL WILL COMMENCE IN THREE...TWO... ONE...
TRIAL? DO I GET A LAWYER OR--
BLAM
BLAM
AAHHHH!
BLAM

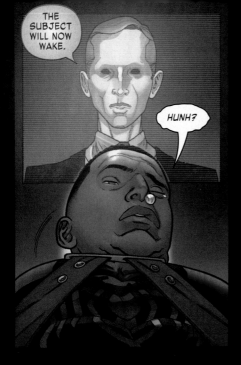

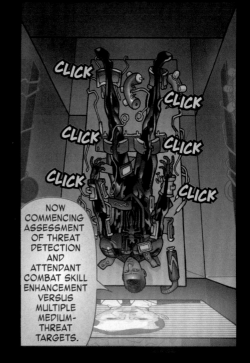

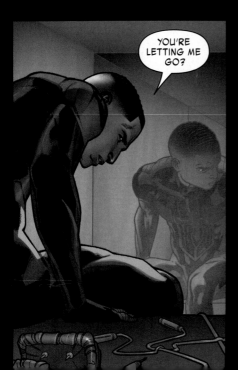

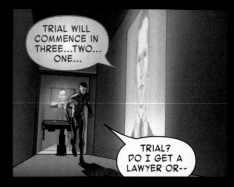

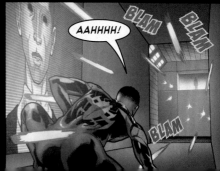

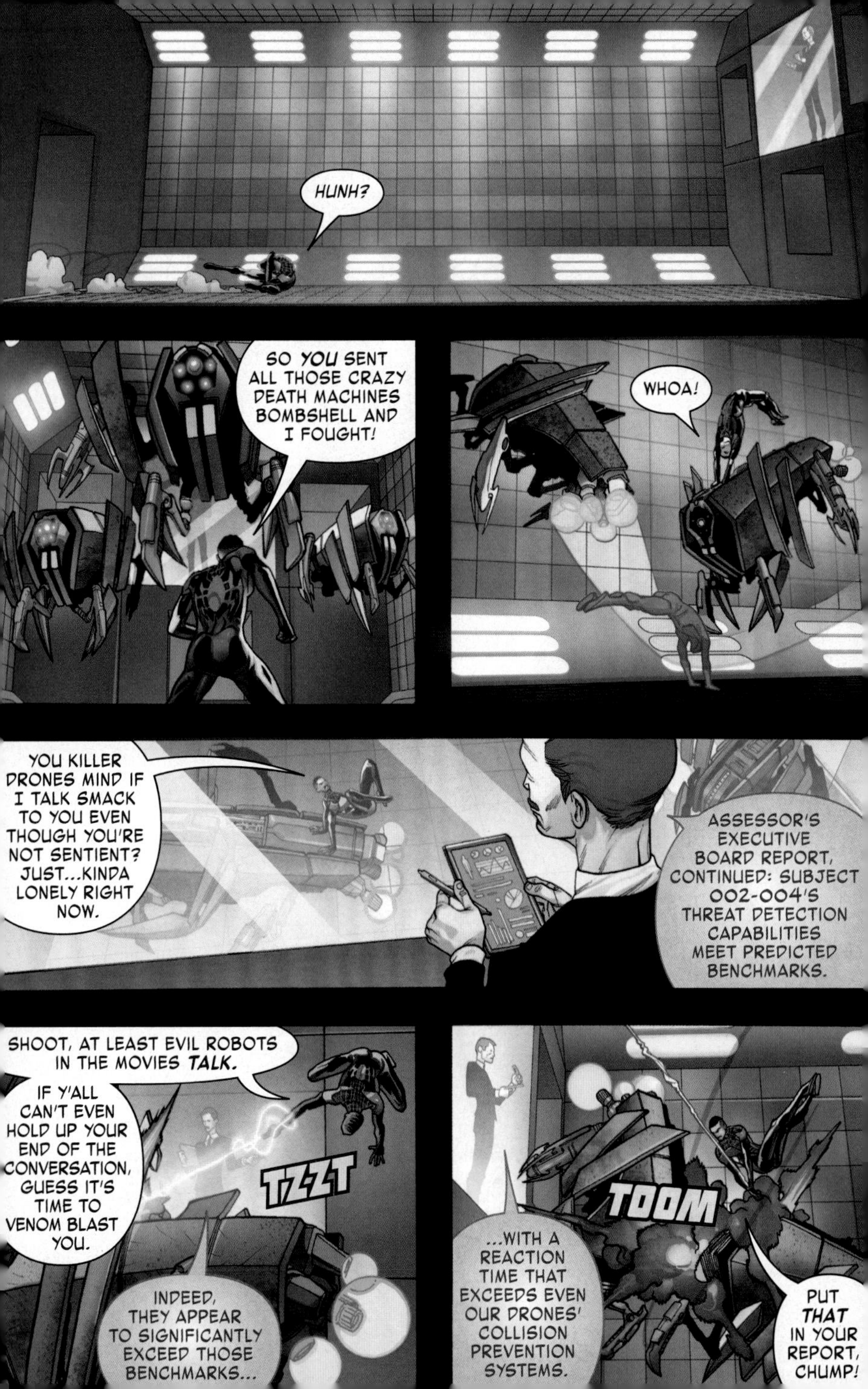
HUNH?
SO YOU SENT ALL THOSE CRAZY DEATH MACHINES BOMBSHELL AND I FOUGHT!
WHOA!
YOU KILLER DRONES MIND IF I TALK SMACK TO YOU EVEN THOUGH YOU'RE NOT SENTIENT? JUST...KINDA LONELY RIGHT NOW.
ASSESSOR'S EXECUTIVE BOARD REPORT, CONTINUED: SUBJECT 002-004'S THREAT DETECTION CAPABILITIES MEET PREDICTED BENCHMARKS.
SHOOT, AT LEAST EVIL ROBOTS IN THE MOVIES TALK.
IF Y'ALL CAN'T EVEN HOLD UP YOUR END OF THE CONVERSATION, GUESS IT'S TIME TO VENOM BLAST YOU.
TZZT
INDEED, THEY APPEAR TO SIGNIFICANTLY EXCEED THOSE BENCHMARKS...
TOOM
...WITH A REACTION TIME THAT EXCEEDS EVEN OUR DRONES' COLLISION PREVENTION SYSTEMS.
PUT THAT IN YOUR REPORT, CHUMP!

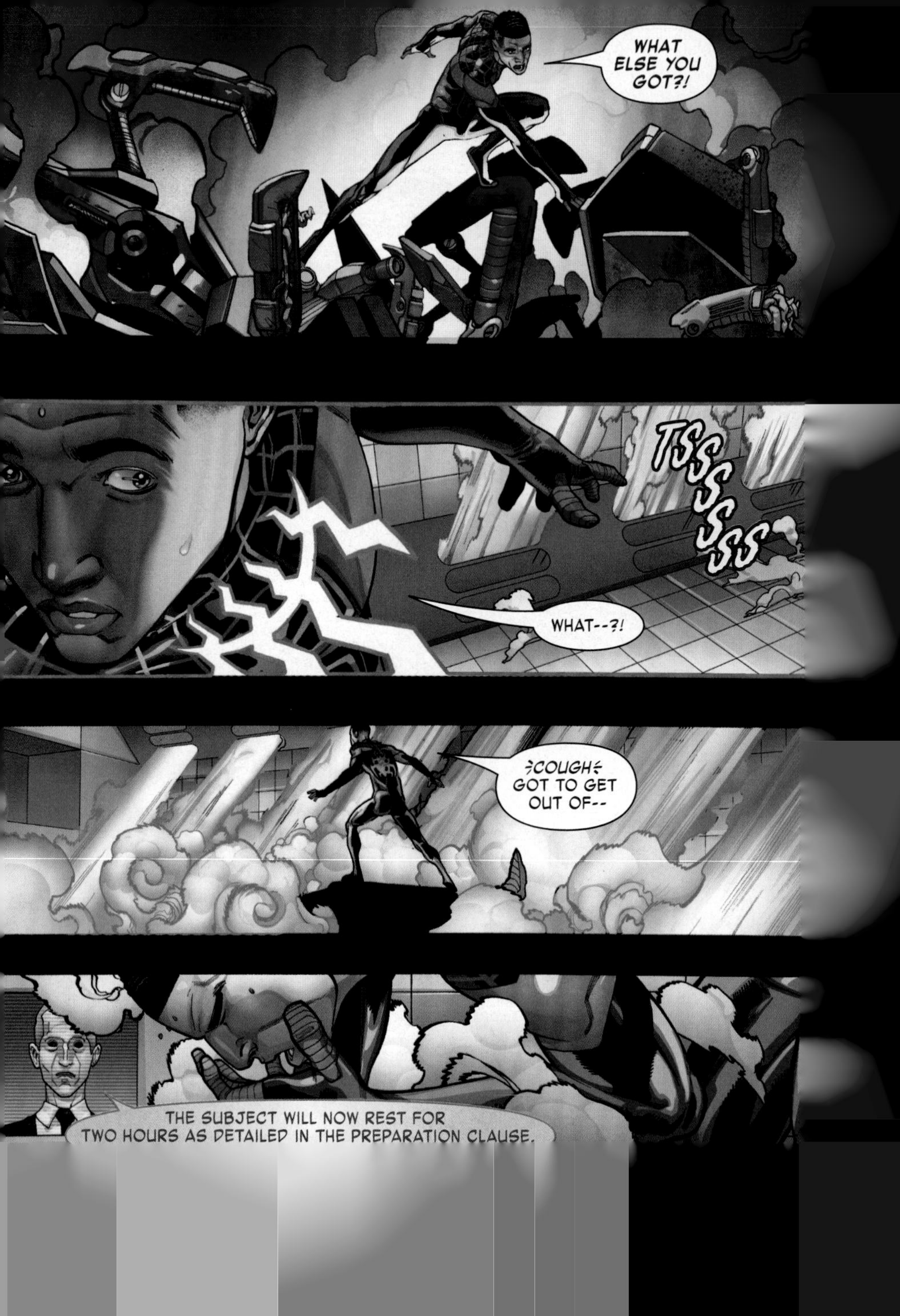
WHAT ELSE YOU GOT?!
TSSSSSS
WHAT--?!
COUGH GOT TO GET OUT OF--
THE SUBJECT WILL NOW REST FOR TWO HOURS AS DETAILED IN THE PREPARATION CLAUSE.

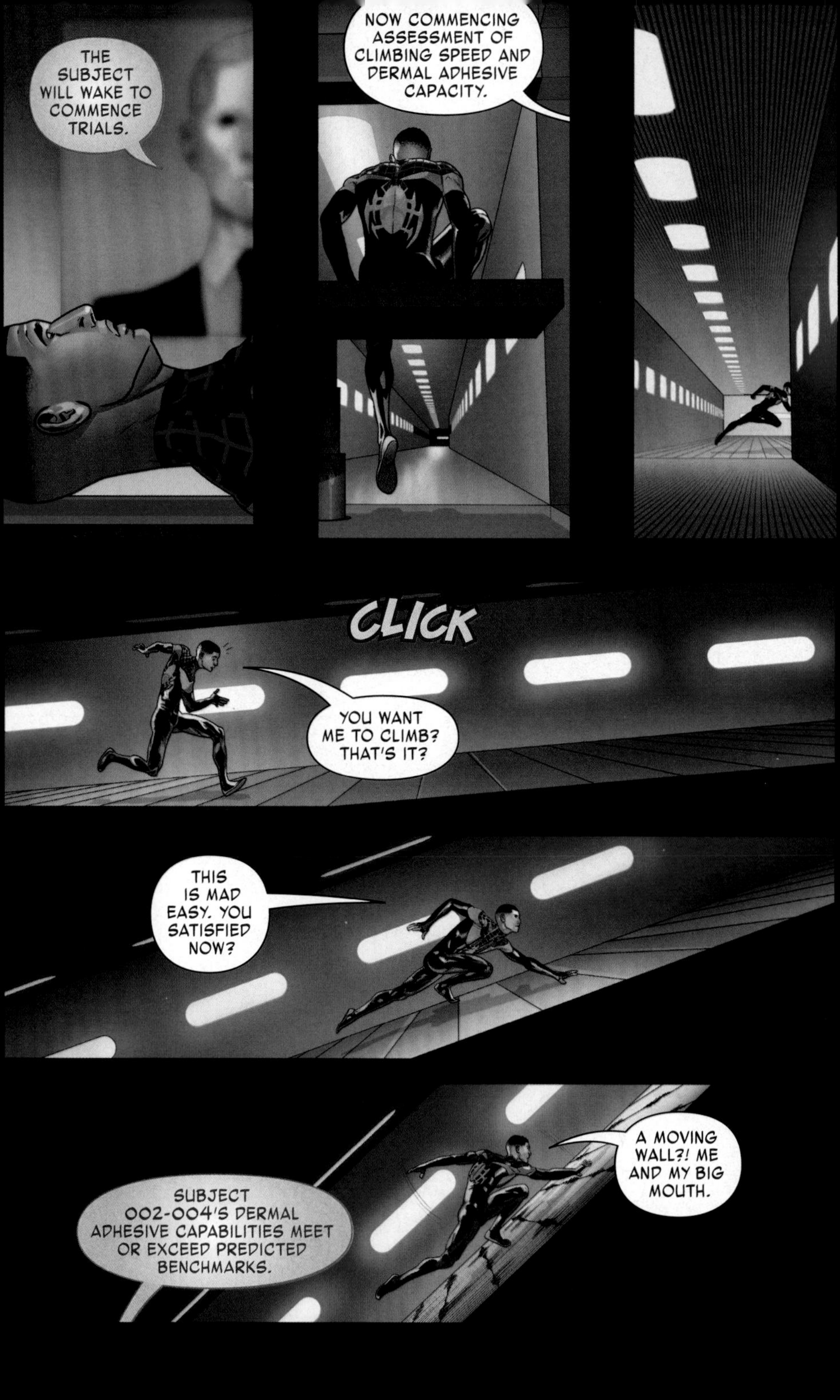
THE SUBJECT WILL WAKE TO COMMENCE TRIALS.
NOW COMMENCING ASSESSMENT OF CLIMBING SPEED AND DERMAL ADHESIVE CAPACITY.
CLICK
YOU WANT ME TO CLIMB? THAT'S IT?
THIS IS MAD EASY. YOU SATISFIED NOW?
A MOVING WALL?! ME AND MY BIG MOUTH.
SUBJECT 002-004'S DERMAL ADHESIVE CAPABILITIES MEET OR EXCEED PREDICTED BENCHMARKS.

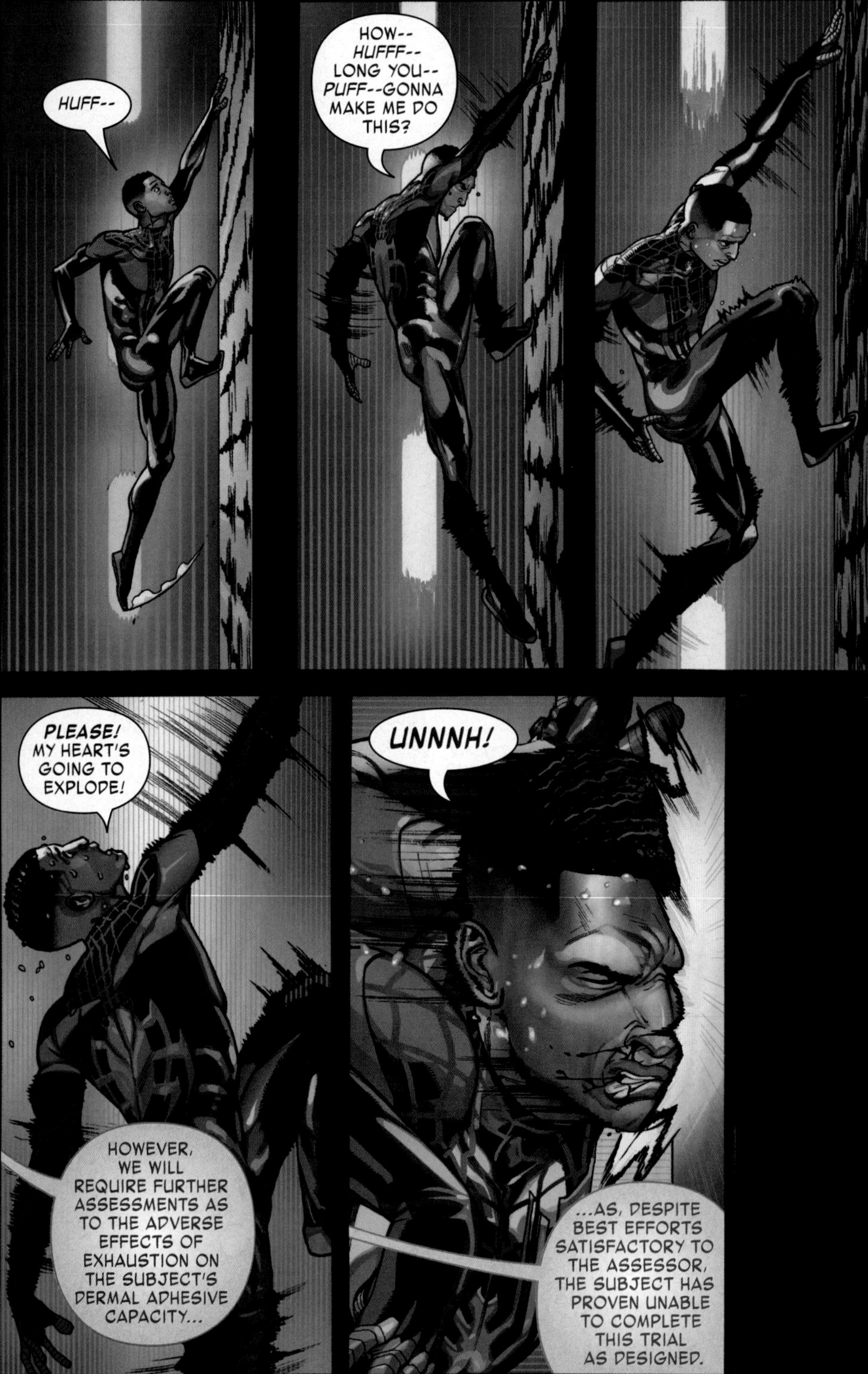
HUFF--
HOW-- HUFFF-- LONG YOU-- PUFF--GONNA MAKE ME DO THIS?
PLEASE! MY HEART'S GOING TO EXPLODE!
UNNNH!
HOWEVER, WE WILL REQUIRE FURTHER ASSESSMENTS AS TO THE ADVERSE EFFECTS OF EXHAUSTION ON THE SUBJECT'S DERMAL ADHESIVE CAPACITY...
...AS, DESPITE BEST EFFORTS SATISFACTORY TO THE ASSESSOR, THE SUBJECT HAS PROVEN UNABLE TO COMPLETE THIS TRIAL AS DESIGNED.

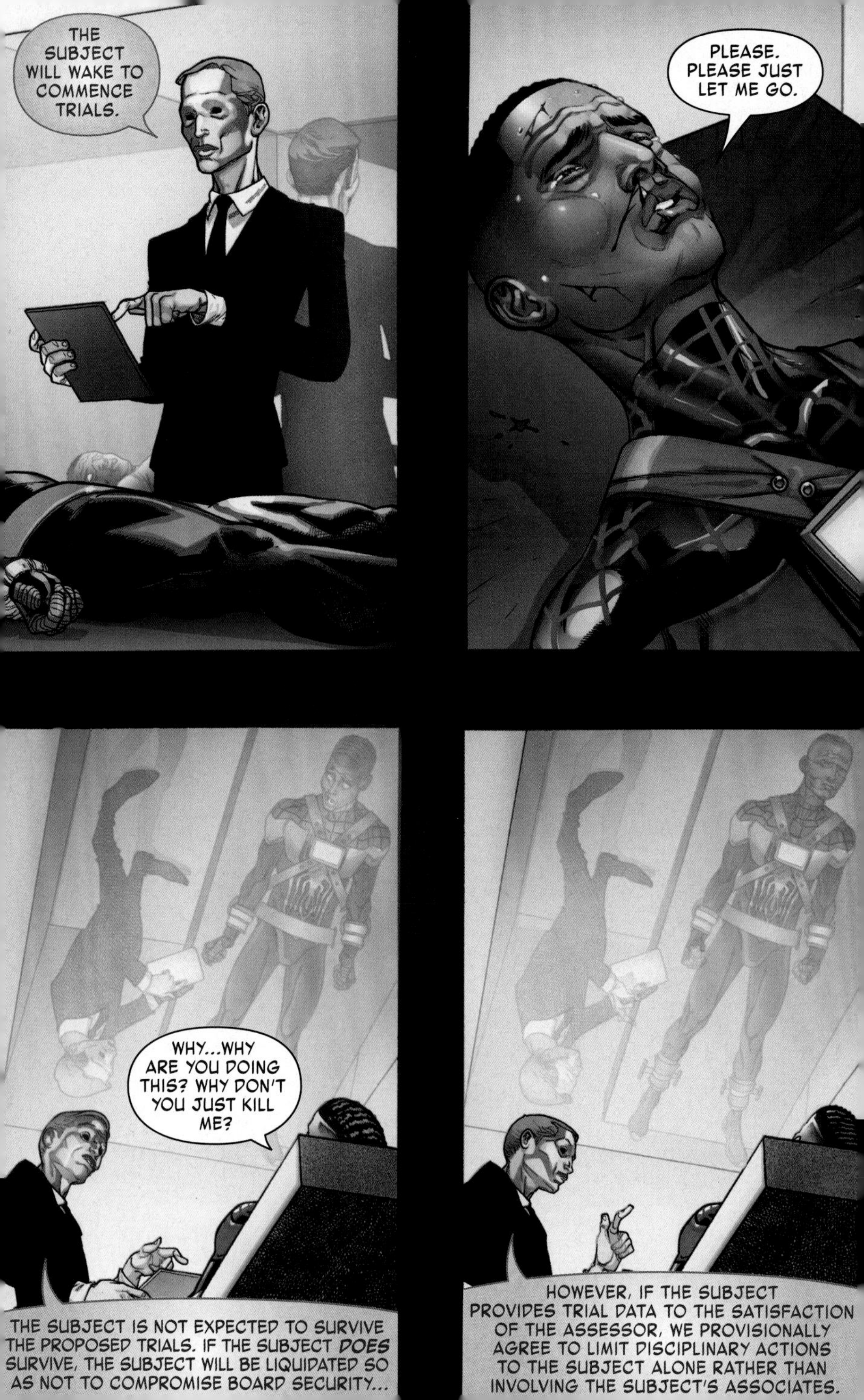
THE SUBJECT WILL WAKE TO COMMENCE TRIALS.
PLEASE. PLEASE JUST LET ME GO.
WHY...WHY ARE YOU DOING THIS? WHY DON'T YOU JUST KILL ME?
THE SUBJECT IS NOT EXPECTED TO SURVIVE THE PROPOSED TRIALS. IF THE SUBJECT *DOES* SURVIVE, THE SUBJECT WILL BE LIQUIDATED SO AS NOT TO COMPROMISE BOARD SECURITY...
HOWEVER, IF THE SUBJECT PROVIDES TRIAL DATA TO THE SATISFACTION OF THE ASSESSOR, WE PROVISIONALLY AGREE TO LIMIT DISCIPLINARY ACTIONS TO THE SUBJECT ALONE RATHER THAN INVOLVING THE SUBJECT'S ASSOCIATES.

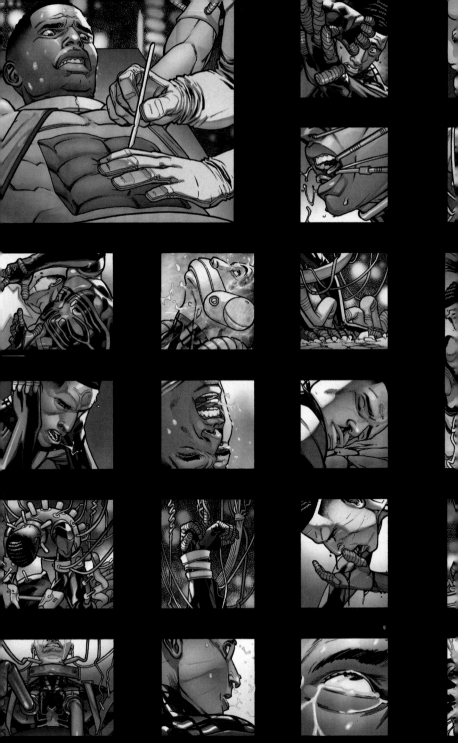

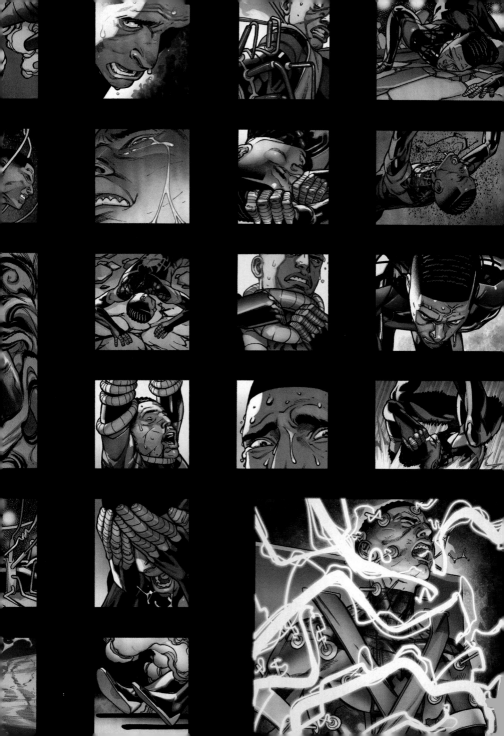

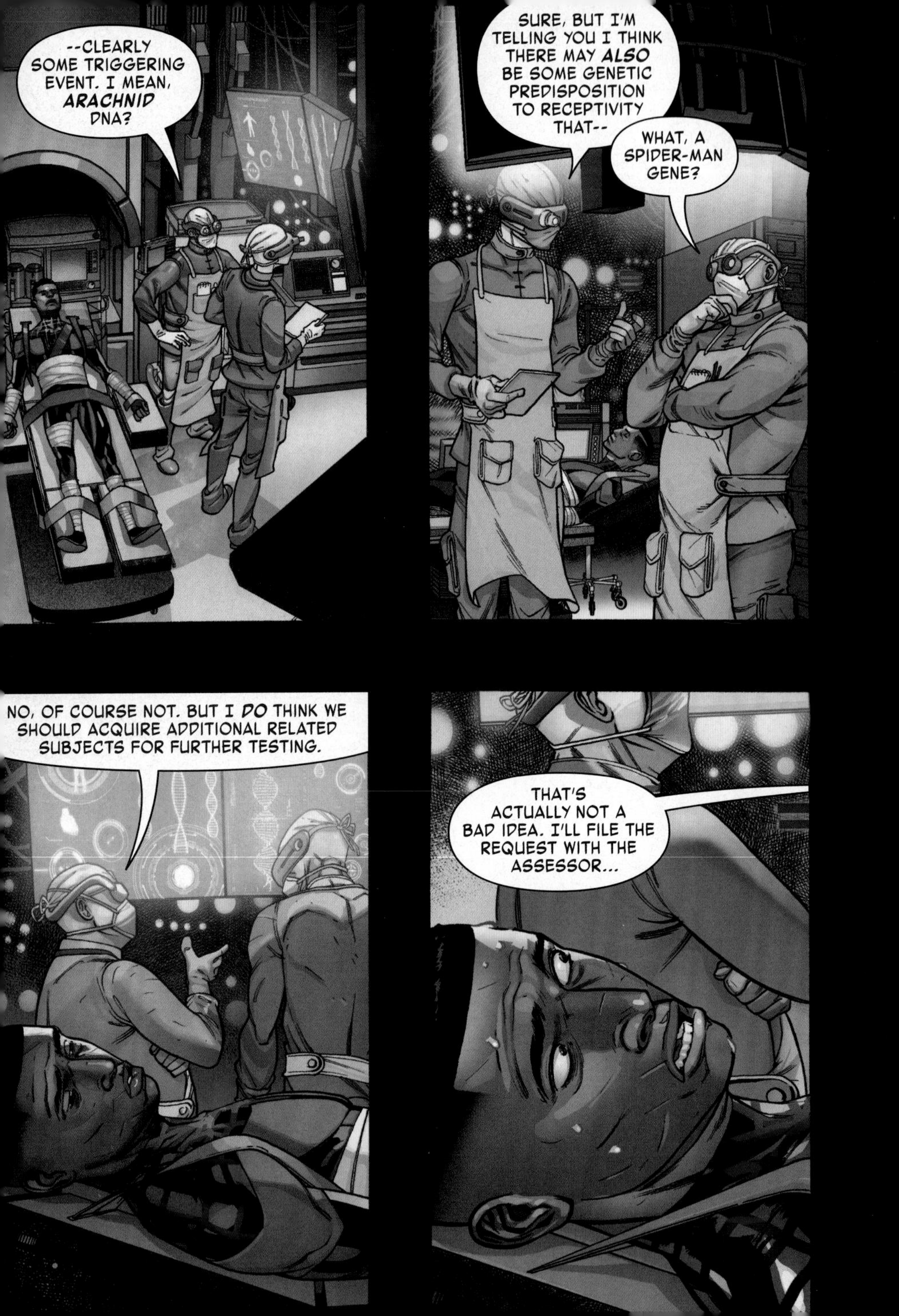
--CLEARLY SOME TRIGGERING EVENT. I MEAN, ARACHNID DNA?
SURE, BUT I'M TELLING YOU I THINK THERE MAY ALSO BE SOME GENETIC PREDISPOSITION TO RECEPTIVITY THAT--
WHAT, A SPIDER-MAN GENE?
NO, OF COURSE NOT. BUT I DO THINK WE SHOULD ACQUIRE ADDITIONAL RELATED SUBJECTS FOR FURTHER TESTING.
THAT'S ACTUALLY NOT A BAD IDEA. I'LL FILE THE REQUEST WITH THE ASSESSOR...

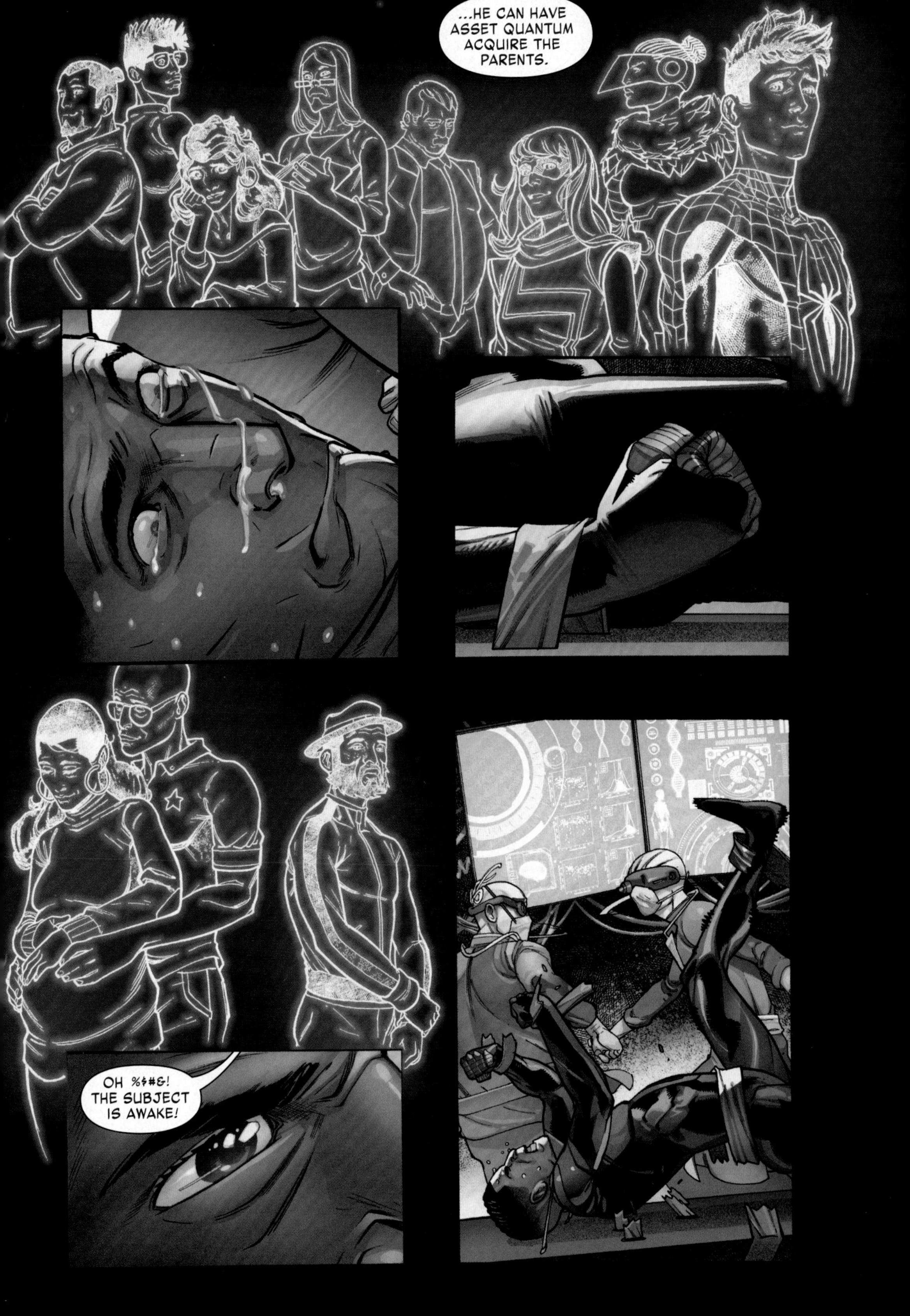
...HE CAN HAVE ASSET QUANTUM ACQUIRE THE PARENTS.
OH %$#&! THE SUBJECT IS AWAKE!

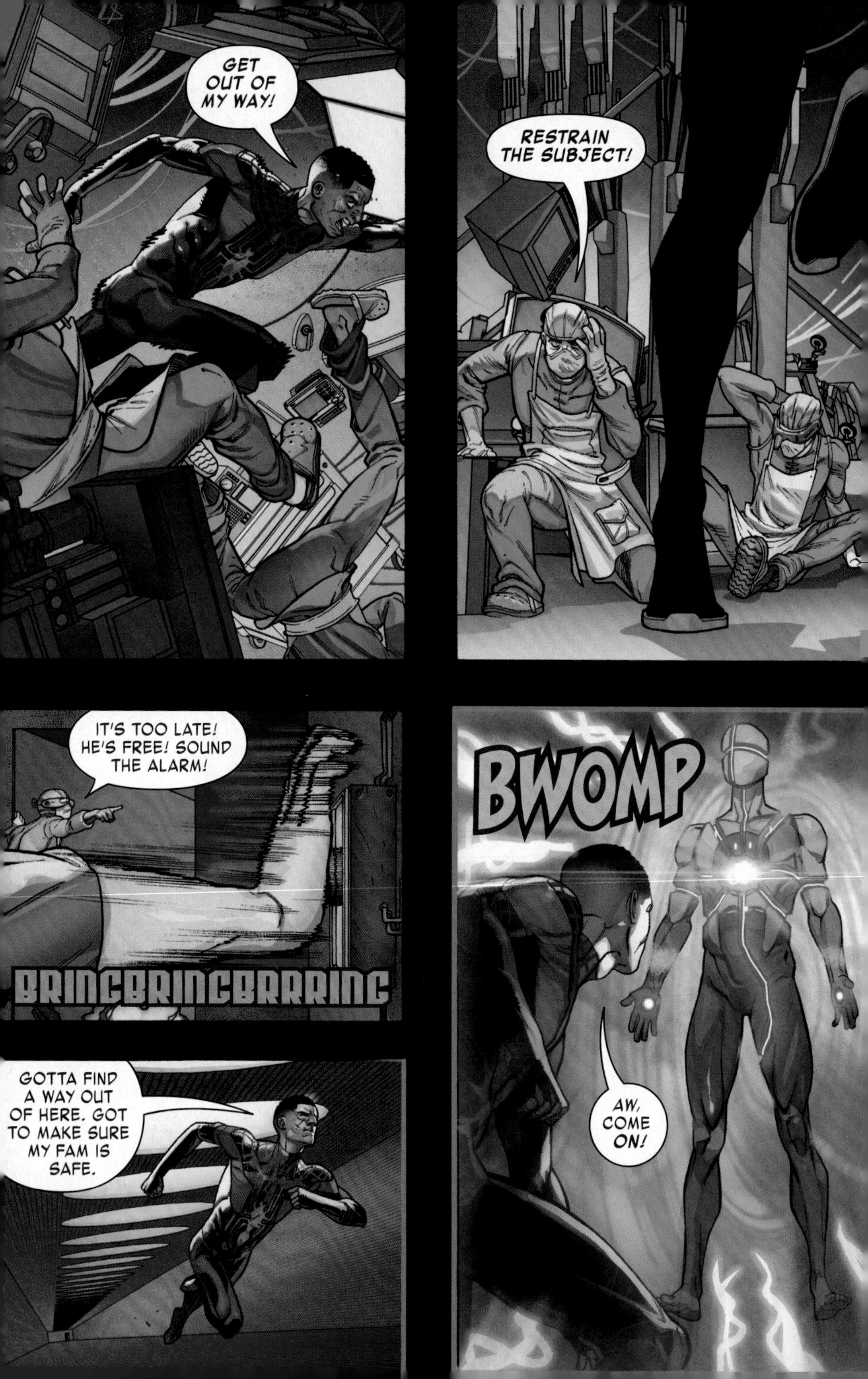
GET OUT OF MY WAY!
RESTRAIN THE SUBJECT!
IT'S TOO LATE! HE'S FREE! SOUND THE ALARM!
BRINGBRINGBRRRING
GOTTA FIND A WAY OUT OF HERE. GOT TO MAKE SURE MY FAM IS SAFE.
BWOMP
AW, COME ON!

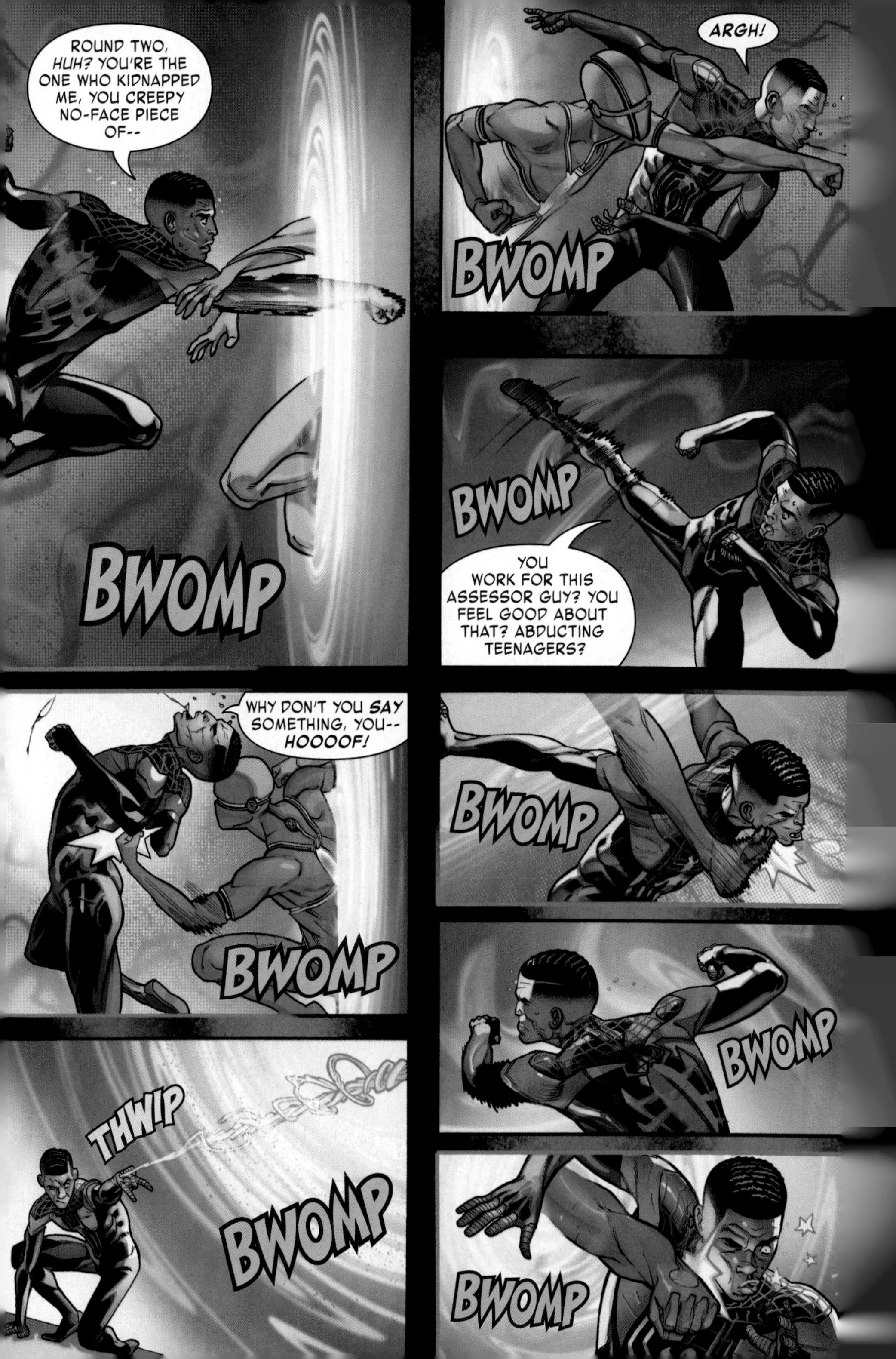
ROUND TWO, HUH? YOU'RE THE ONE WHO KIDNAPPED ME, YOU CREEPY NO-FACE PIECE OF--
BWOMP
ARGH!
BWOMP
BWOMP
YOU WORK FOR THIS ASSESSOR GUY? YOU FEEL GOOD ABOUT THAT? ABDUCTING TEENAGERS?
WHY DON'T YOU SAY SOMETHING, YOU-- HOOOOF!
BWOMP
BWOMP
BWOMP
THWIP
BWOMP
BWOMP

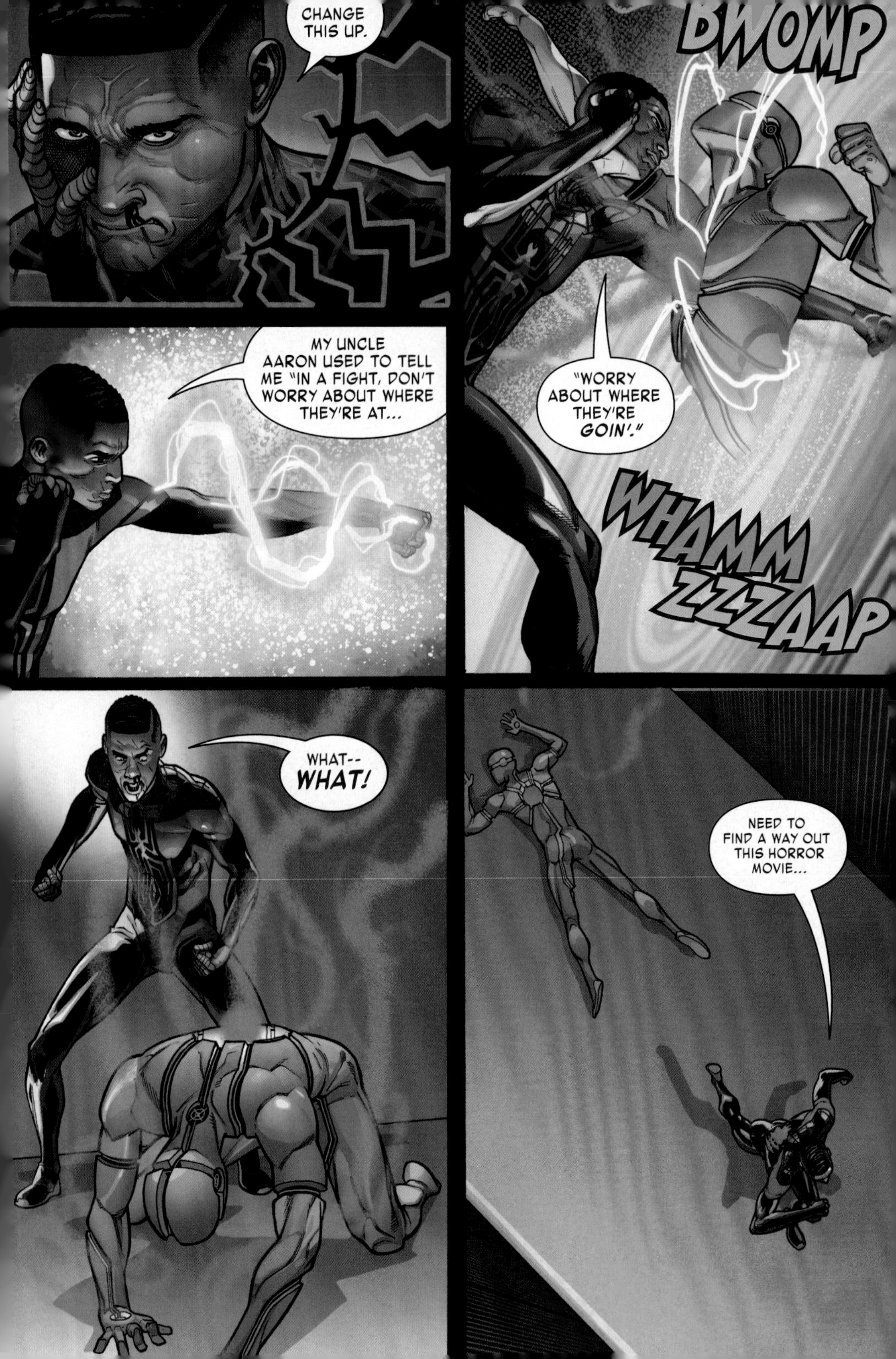
CHANGE THIS UP.
BWOMP
MY UNCLE AARON USED TO TELL ME "IN A FIGHT, DON'T WORRY ABOUT WHERE THEY'RE AT...
"WORRY ABOUT WHERE THEY'RE *GOIN'*."
WHAMM
ZZZAAP
WHAT-- **WHAT!**
NEED TO FIND A WAY OUT THIS HORROR MOVIE...

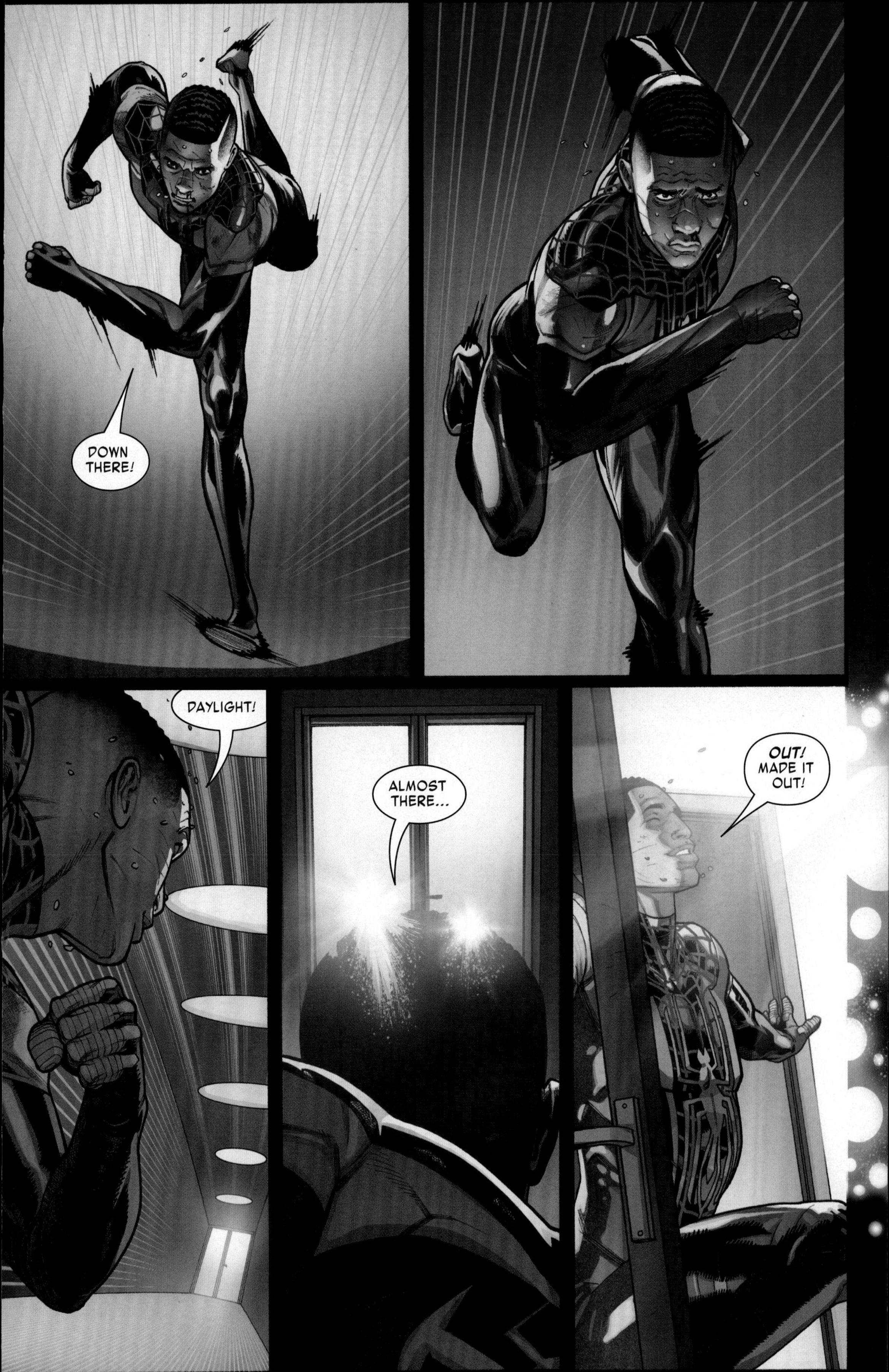
DOWN THERE!
DAYLIGHT!
ALMOST THERE...
OUT! MADE IT OUT!

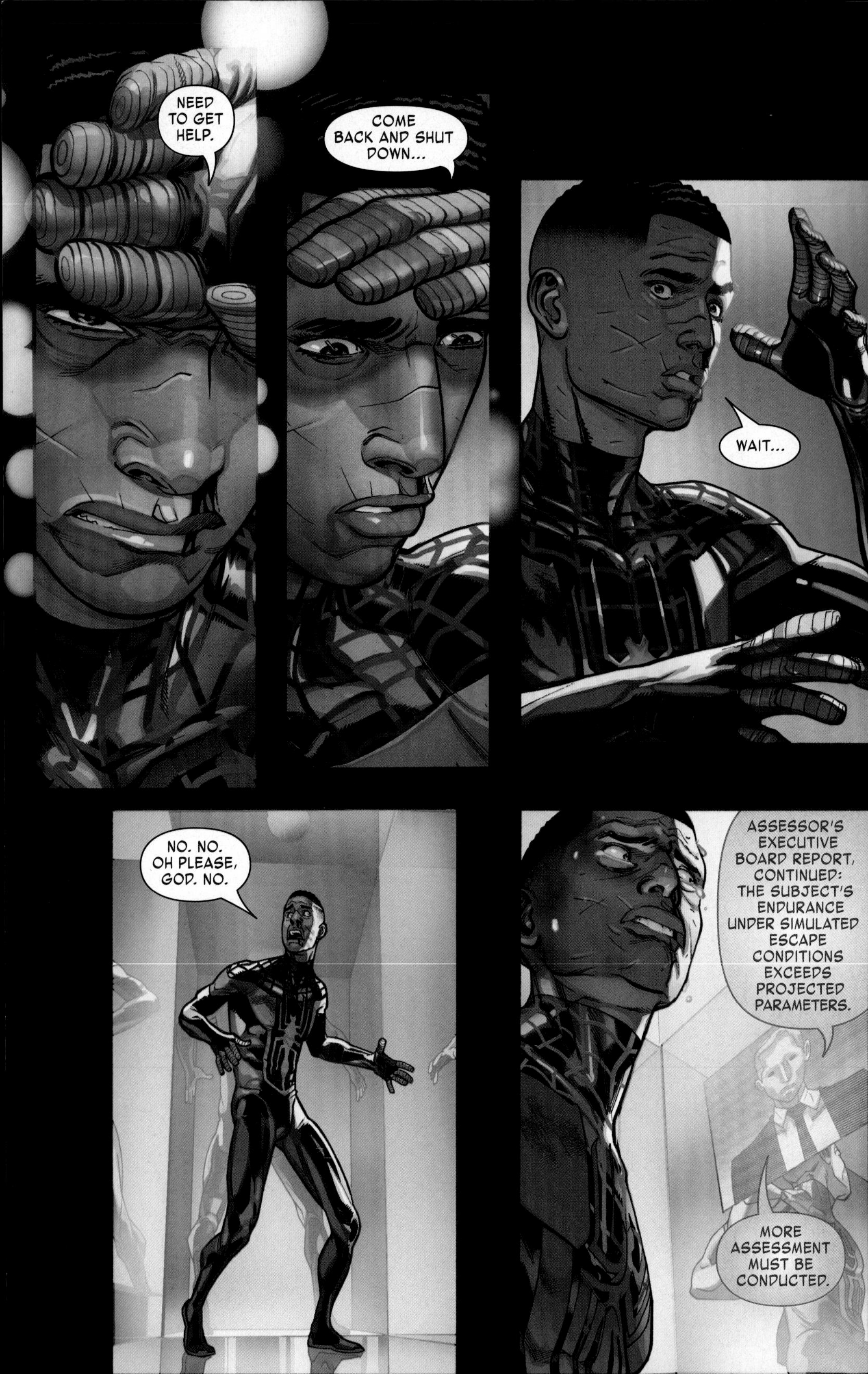
NEED TO GET HELP.
COME BACK AND SHUT DOWN...
WAIT...
NO. NO. OH PLEASE, GOD. NO.
ASSESSOR'S EXECUTIVE BOARD REPORT, CONTINUED: THE SUBJECT'S ENDURANCE UNDER SIMULATED ESCAPE CONDITIONS EXCEEDS PROJECTED PARAMETERS.
MORE ASSESSMENT MUST BE CONDUCTED.

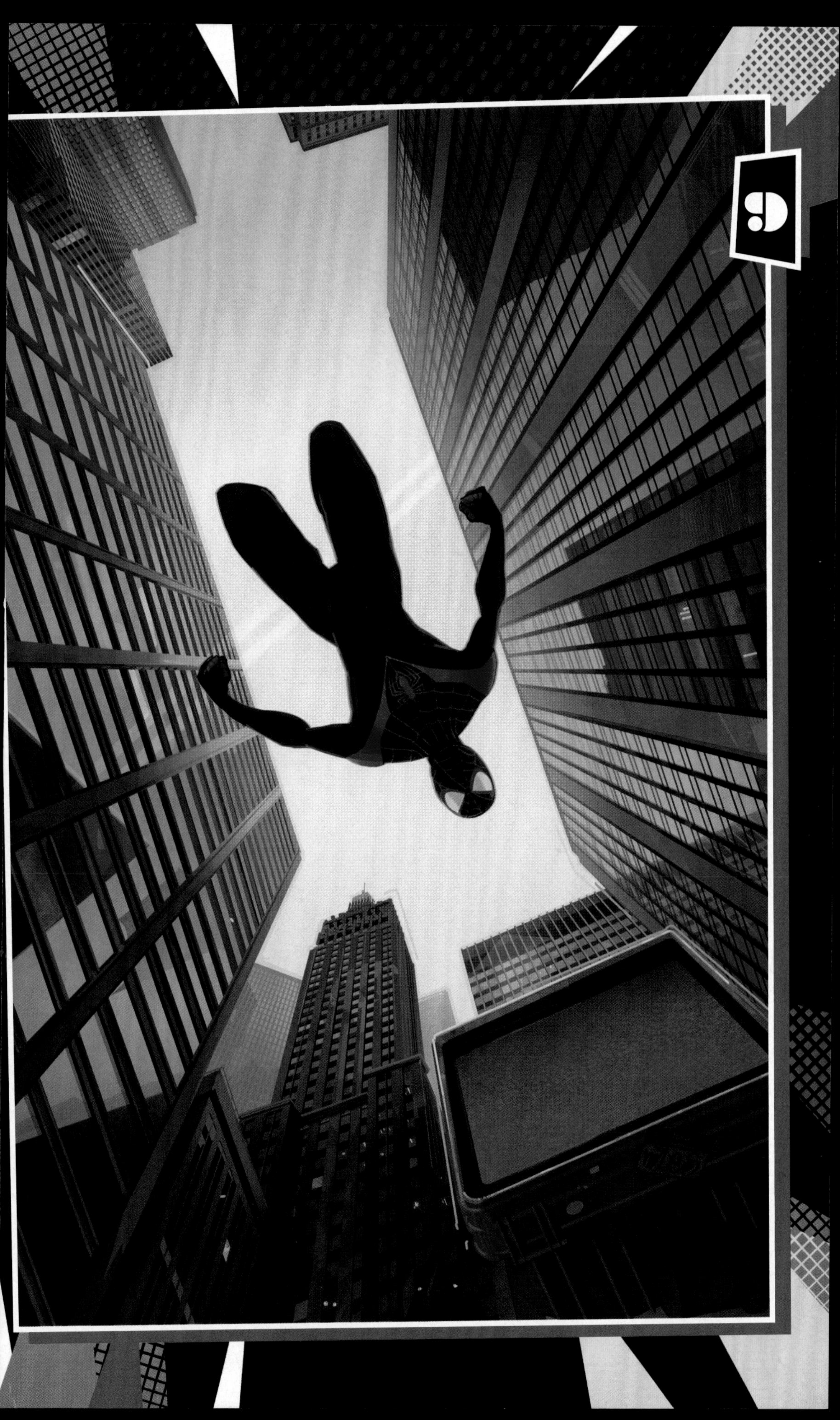
9

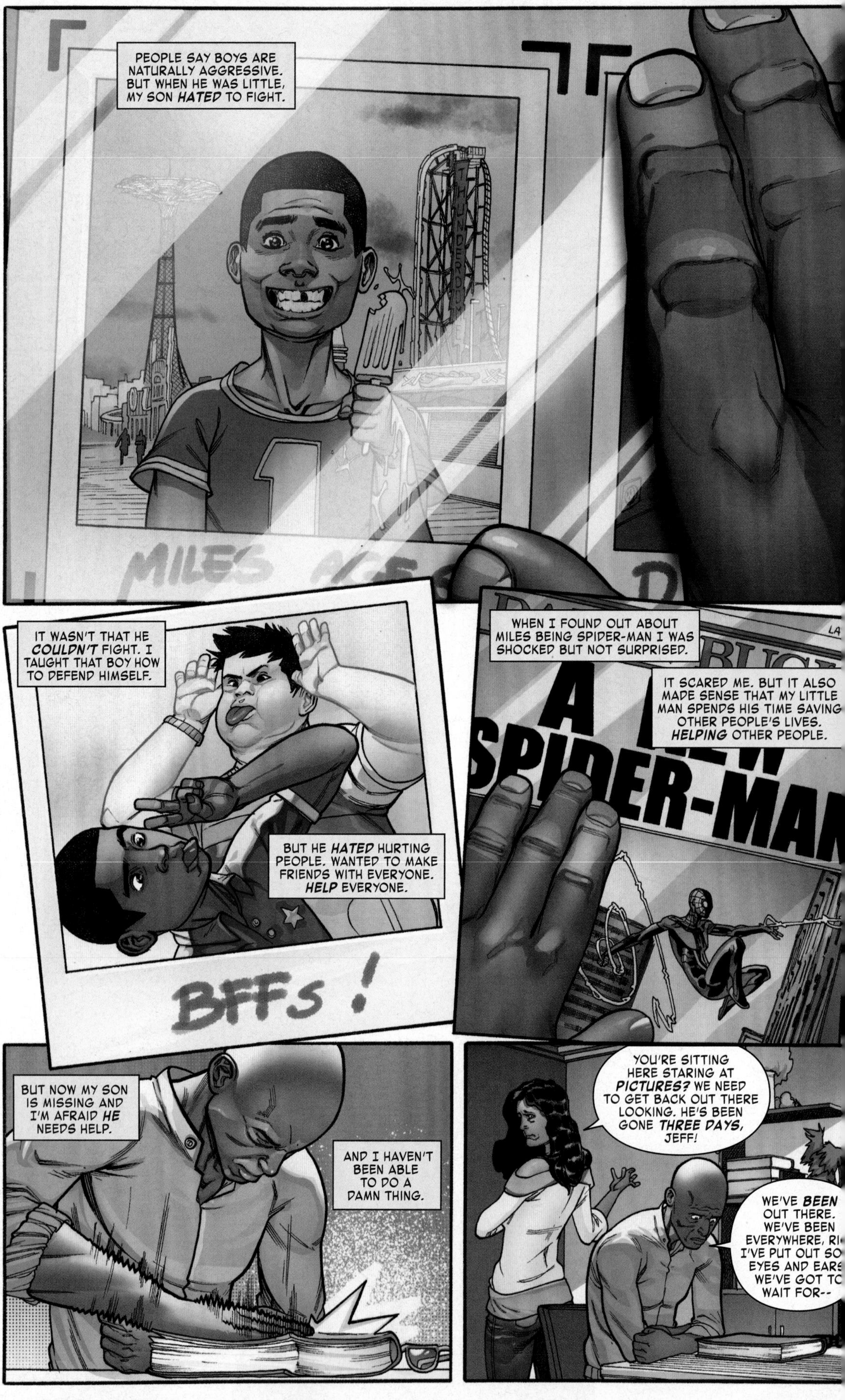

PEOPLE SAY BOYS ARE NATURALLY AGGRESSIVE. BUT WHEN HE WAS LITTLE, MY SON *HATED* TO FIGHT.
MILES
IT WASN'T THAT HE *COULDN'T* FIGHT. I TAUGHT THAT BOY HOW TO DEFEND HIMSELF.
BUT HE *HATED* HURTING PEOPLE. WANTED TO MAKE FRIENDS WITH EVERYONE. *HELP* EVERYONE.
BFFs!
WHEN I FOUND OUT ABOUT MILES BEING SPIDER-MAN I WAS SHOCKED BUT NOT SURPRISED.
IT SCARED ME. BUT IT ALSO MADE SENSE THAT MY LITTLE MAN SPENDS HIS TIME SAVING OTHER PEOPLE'S LIVES. *HELPING* OTHER PEOPLE.
BUT NOW MY SON IS MISSING AND I'M AFRAID *HE* NEEDS HELP.
AND I HAVEN'T BEEN ABLE TO DO A DAMN THING.
YOU'RE SITTING HERE STARING AT *PICTURES?* WE NEED TO GET BACK OUT THERE LOOKING. HE'S BEEN GONE *THREE DAYS,* JEFF!
WE'VE *BEEN* OUT THERE. WE'VE BEEN EVERYWHERE, RI
I'VE PUT OUT SO
EYES AND EARS
WE'VE GOT TO WAIT FOR--

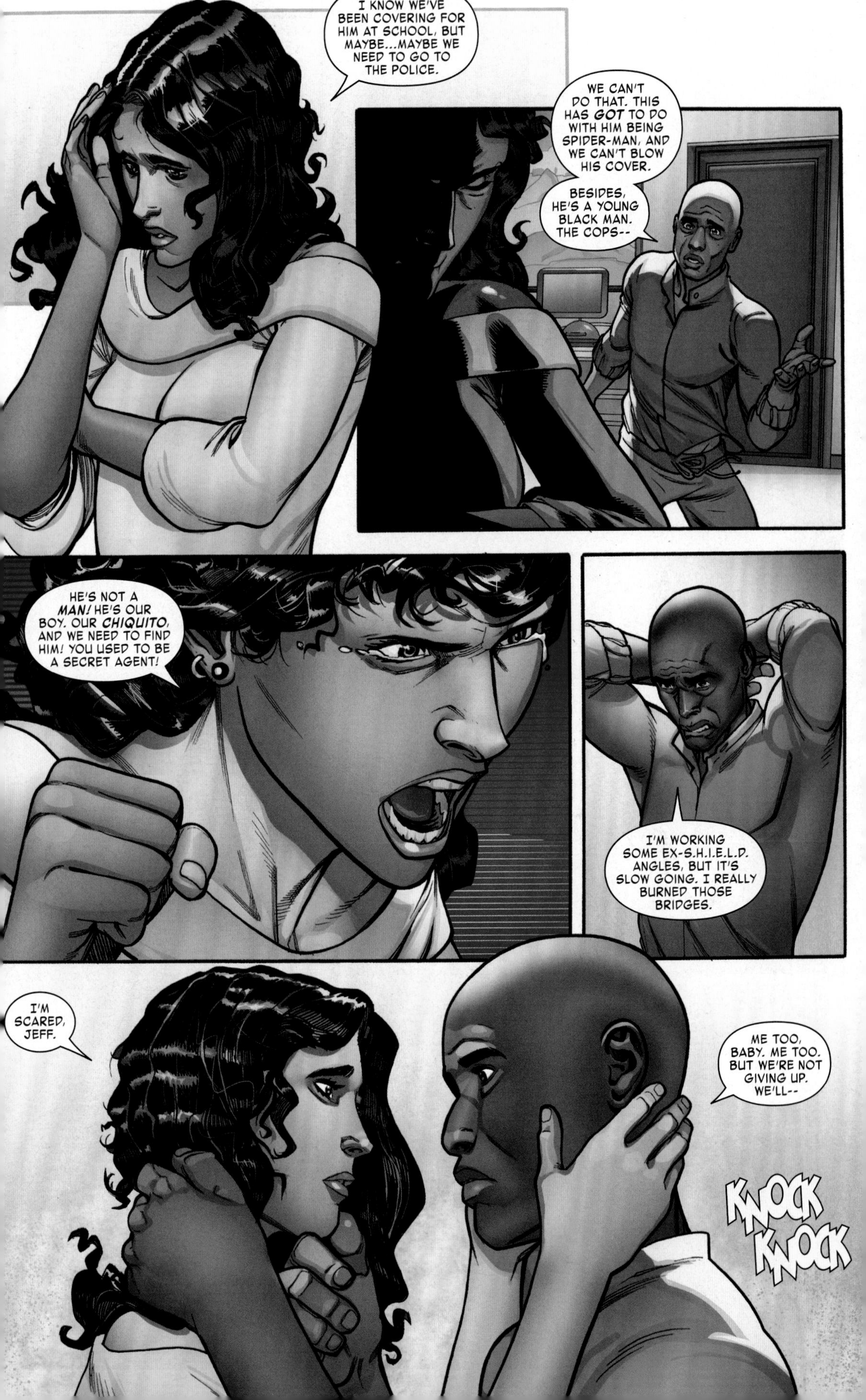
I KNOW WE'VE BEEN COVERING FOR HIM AT SCHOOL, BUT MAYBE...MAYBE WE NEED TO GO TO THE POLICE.
WE CAN'T DO THAT. THIS HAS GOT TO DO WITH HIM BEING SPIDER-MAN, AND WE CAN'T BLOW HIS COVER.
BESIDES, HE'S A YOUNG BLACK MAN. THE COPS--
HE'S NOT A MAN! HE'S OUR BOY. OUR CHIQUITO, AND WE NEED TO FIND HIM! YOU USED TO BE A SECRET AGENT!
I'M WORKING SOME EX-S.H.I.E.L.D. ANGLES, BUT IT'S SLOW GOING. I REALLY BURNED THOSE BRIDGES.
I'M SCARED, JEFF.
ME TOO, BABY. ME TOO. BUT WE'RE NOT GIVING UP. WE'LL--
KNOCK KNOCK

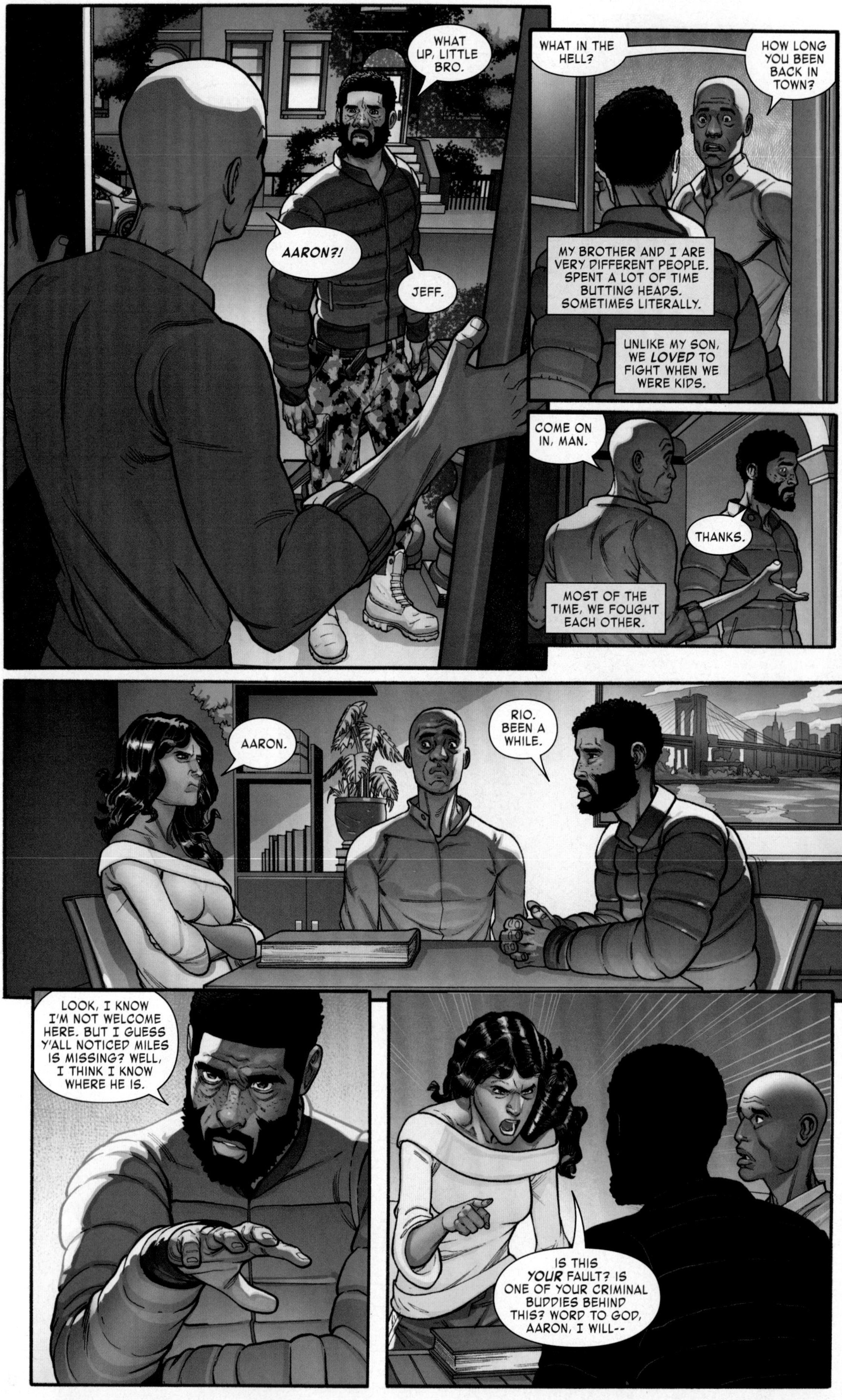
WHAT UP, LITTLE BRO.
AARON?!
JEFF.
WHAT IN THE HELL?
HOW LONG YOU BEEN BACK IN TOWN?
MY BROTHER AND I ARE VERY DIFFERENT PEOPLE. SPENT A LOT OF TIME BUTTING HEADS. SOMETIMES LITERALLY.
UNLIKE MY SON, WE LOVED TO FIGHT WHEN WE WERE KIDS.
COME ON IN, MAN.
THANKS.
MOST OF THE TIME, WE FOUGHT EACH OTHER.
AARON.
RIO. BEEN A WHILE.
LOOK, I KNOW I'M NOT WELCOME HERE. BUT I GUESS Y'ALL NOTICED MILES IS MISSING? WELL, I THINK I KNOW WHERE HE IS.
IS THIS YOUR FAULT? IS ONE OF YOUR CRIMINAL BUDDIES BEHIND THIS? WORD TO GOD, AARON, I WILL--

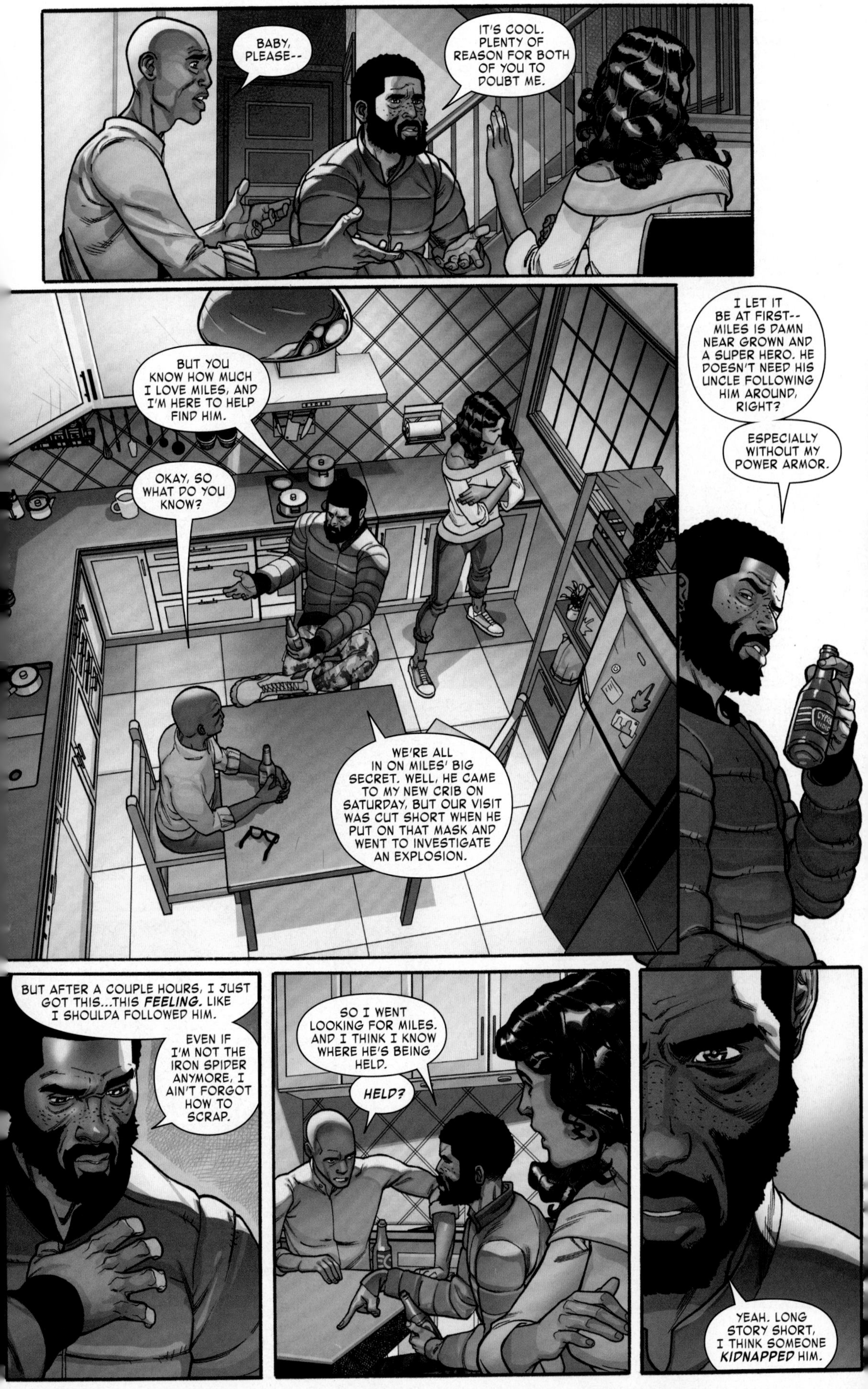
BABY, PLEASE--
IT'S COOL. PLENTY OF REASON FOR BOTH OF YOU TO DOUBT ME.
BUT YOU KNOW HOW MUCH I LOVE MILES, AND I'M HERE TO HELP FIND HIM.
OKAY, SO WHAT DO YOU KNOW?
WE'RE ALL IN ON MILES' BIG SECRET. WELL, HE CAME TO MY NEW CRIB ON SATURDAY, BUT OUR VISIT WAS CUT SHORT WHEN HE PUT ON THAT MASK AND WENT TO INVESTIGATE AN EXPLOSION.
I LET IT BE AT FIRST-- MILES IS DAMN NEAR GROWN AND A SUPER HERO. HE DOESN'T NEED HIS UNCLE FOLLOWING HIM AROUND, RIGHT?
ESPECIALLY WITHOUT MY POWER ARMOR.
BUT AFTER A COUPLE HOURS, I JUST GOT THIS...THIS FEELING. LIKE I SHOULDA FOLLOWED HIM.
EVEN IF I'M NOT THE IRON SPIDER ANYMORE, I AIN'T FORGOT HOW TO SCRAP.
SO I WENT LOOKING FOR MILES. AND I THINK I KNOW WHERE HE'S BEING HELD.
HELD?
YEAH. LONG STORY SHORT, I THINK SOMEONE KIDNAPPED HIM.

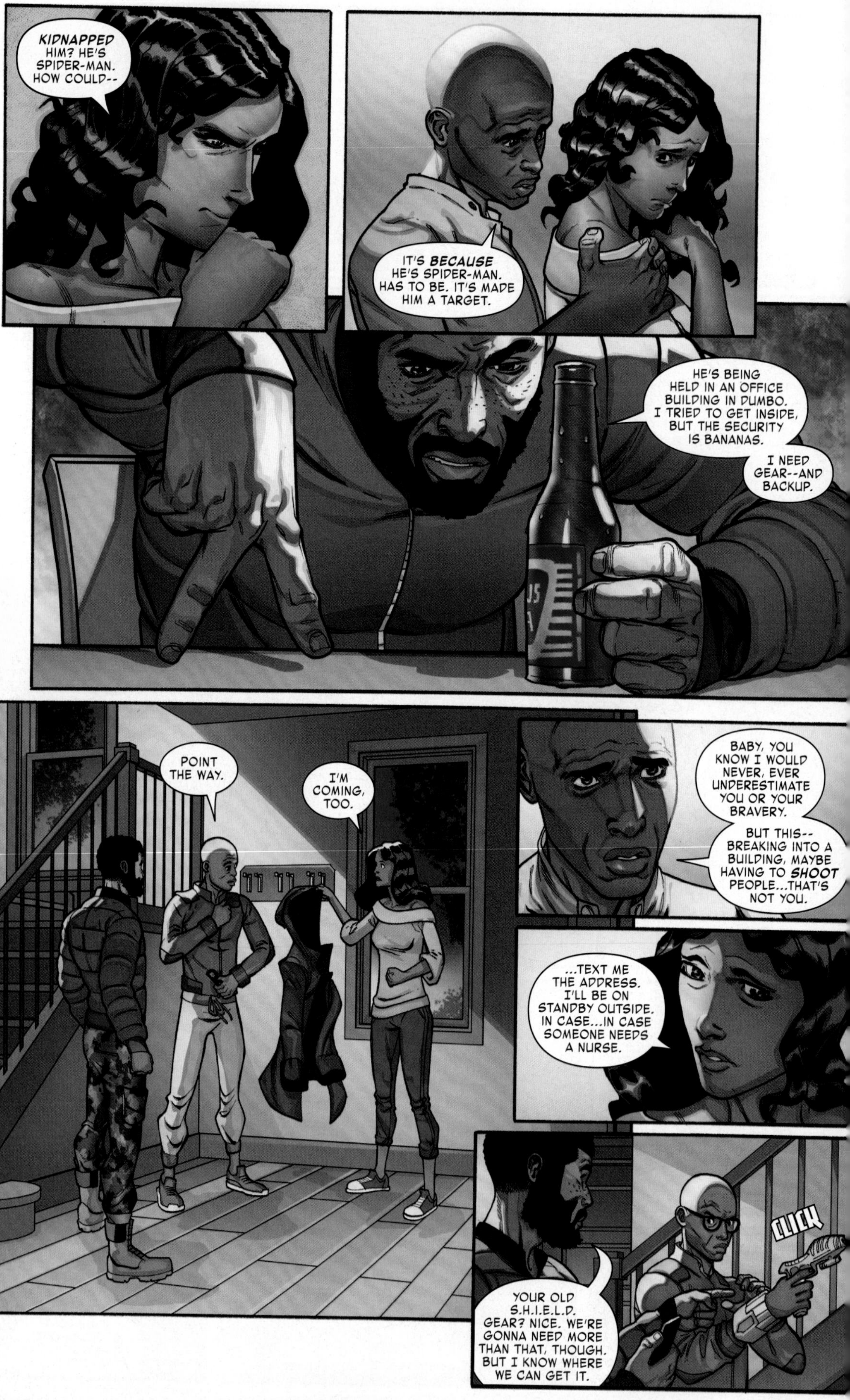

KIDNAPPED HIM? HE'S SPIDER-MAN. HOW COULD--
IT'S BECAUSE HE'S SPIDER-MAN. HAS TO BE. IT'S MADE HIM A TARGET.
HE'S BEING HELD IN AN OFFICE BUILDING IN DUMBO. I TRIED TO GET INSIDE, BUT THE SECURITY IS BANANAS.
I NEED GEAR--AND BACKUP.
POINT THE WAY.
I'M COMING, TOO.
BABY, YOU KNOW I WOULD NEVER, EVER UNDERESTIMATE YOU OR YOUR BRAVERY.
BUT THIS--BREAKING INTO A BUILDING, MAYBE HAVING TO SHOOT PEOPLE...THAT'S NOT YOU.
...TEXT ME THE ADDRESS. I'LL BE ON STANDBY OUTSIDE. IN CASE...IN CASE SOMEONE NEEDS A NURSE.
CLICK
YOUR OLD S.H.I.E.L.D. GEAR? NICE. WE'RE GONNA NEED MORE THAN THAT, THOUGH. BUT I KNOW WHERE WE CAN GET IT.

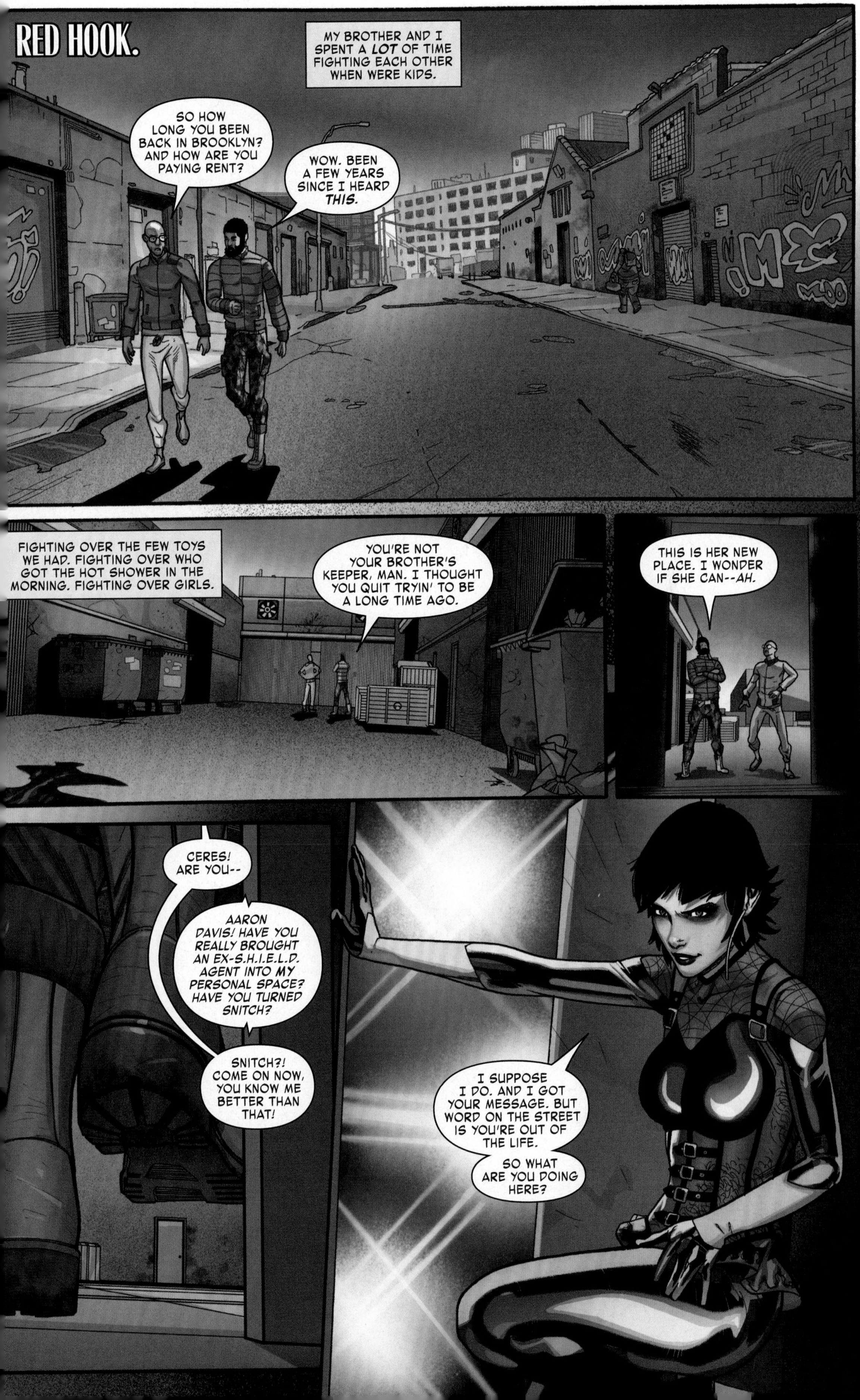
RED HOOK.
MY BROTHER AND I SPENT A LOT OF TIME FIGHTING EACH OTHER WHEN WERE KIDS.
SO HOW LONG YOU BEEN BACK IN BROOKLYN? AND HOW ARE YOU PAYING RENT?
WOW. BEEN A FEW YEARS SINCE I HEARD THIS.
FIGHTING OVER THE FEW TOYS WE HAD. FIGHTING OVER WHO GOT THE HOT SHOWER IN THE MORNING. FIGHTING OVER GIRLS.
YOU'RE NOT YOUR BROTHER'S KEEPER, MAN. I THOUGHT YOU QUIT TRYIN' TO BE A LONG TIME AGO.
THIS IS HER NEW PLACE. I WONDER IF SHE CAN--AH.
CERES! ARE YOU--
AARON DAVIS! HAVE YOU REALLY BROUGHT AN EX-S.H.I.E.L.D. AGENT INTO MY PERSONAL SPACE? HAVE YOU TURNED SNITCH?
SNITCH?! COME ON NOW, YOU KNOW ME BETTER THAN THAT!
I SUPPOSE I DO. AND I GOT YOUR MESSAGE. BUT WORD ON THE STREET IS YOU'RE OUT OF THE LIFE.
SO WHAT ARE YOU DOING HERE?

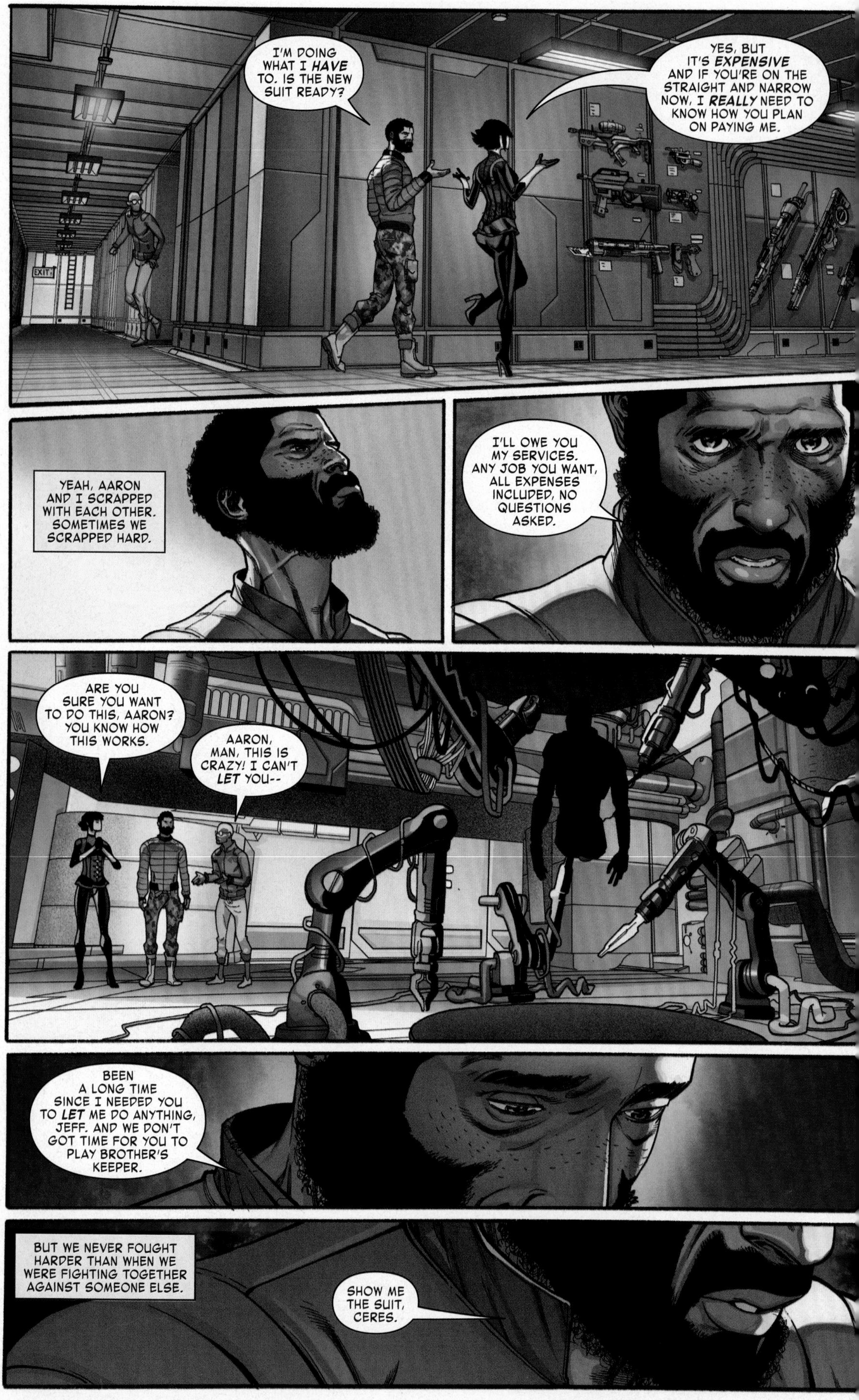

I'M DOING WHAT I *HAVE* TO. IS THE NEW SUIT READY?
YES, BUT IT'S ***EXPENSIVE*** AND IF YOU'RE ON THE STRAIGHT AND NARROW NOW, I ***REALLY*** NEED TO KNOW HOW YOU PLAN ON PAYING ME.
EXIT
YEAH, AARON AND I SCRAPPED WITH EACH OTHER. SOMETIMES WE SCRAPPED HARD.
I'LL OWE YOU MY SERVICES. ANY JOB YOU WANT, ALL EXPENSES INCLUDED, NO QUESTIONS ASKED.
ARE YOU SURE YOU WANT TO DO THIS, AARON? YOU KNOW HOW THIS WORKS.
AARON, MAN, THIS IS CRAZY! I CAN'T ***LET*** YOU--
BEEN A LONG TIME SINCE I NEEDED YOU TO ***LET*** ME DO ANYTHING, JEFF. AND WE DON'T GOT TIME FOR YOU TO PLAY BROTHER'S KEEPER.
BUT WE NEVER FOUGHT HARDER THAN WHEN WE WERE FIGHTING TOGETHER AGAINST SOMEONE ELSE.
SHOW ME THE SUIT, CERES.

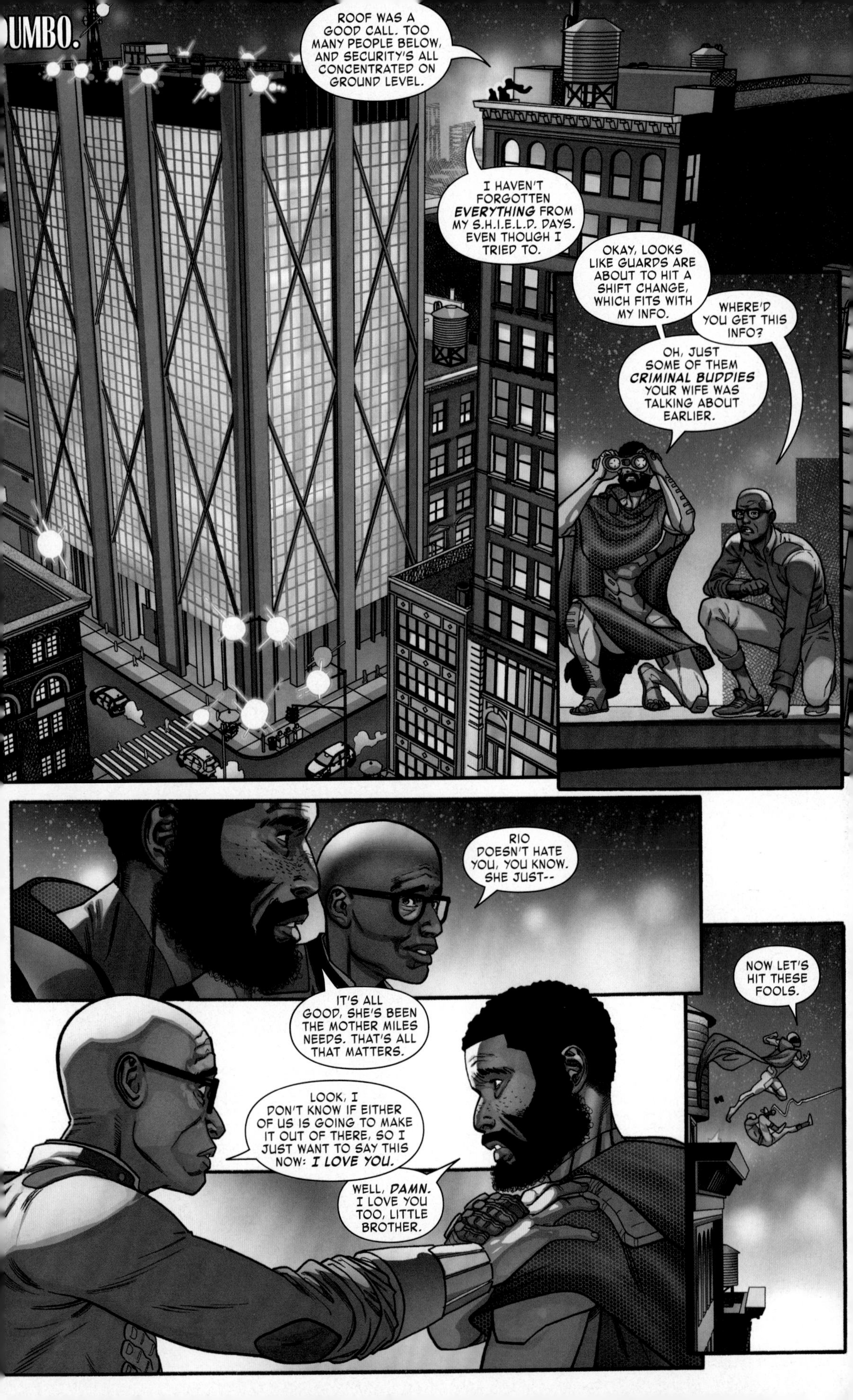

UMBO.
ROOF WAS A GOOD CALL. TOO MANY PEOPLE BELOW, AND SECURITY'S ALL CONCENTRATED ON GROUND LEVEL.
I HAVEN'T FORGOTTEN EVERYTHING FROM MY S.H.I.E.L.D. DAYS. EVEN THOUGH I TRIED TO.
OKAY, LOOKS LIKE GUARDS ARE ABOUT TO HIT A SHIFT CHANGE, WHICH FITS WITH MY INFO.
WHERE'D YOU GET THIS INFO?
OH, JUST SOME OF THEM CRIMINAL BUDDIES YOUR WIFE WAS TALKING ABOUT EARLIER.
RIO DOESN'T HATE YOU, YOU KNOW. SHE JUST--
IT'S ALL GOOD, SHE'S BEEN THE MOTHER MILES NEEDS. THAT'S ALL THAT MATTERS.
LOOK, I DON'T KNOW IF EITHER OF US IS GOING TO MAKE IT OUT OF THERE, SO I JUST WANT TO SAY THIS NOW: I LOVE YOU.
WELL, DAMN. I LOVE YOU TOO, LITTLE BROTHER.
NOW LET'S HIT THESE FOOLS.

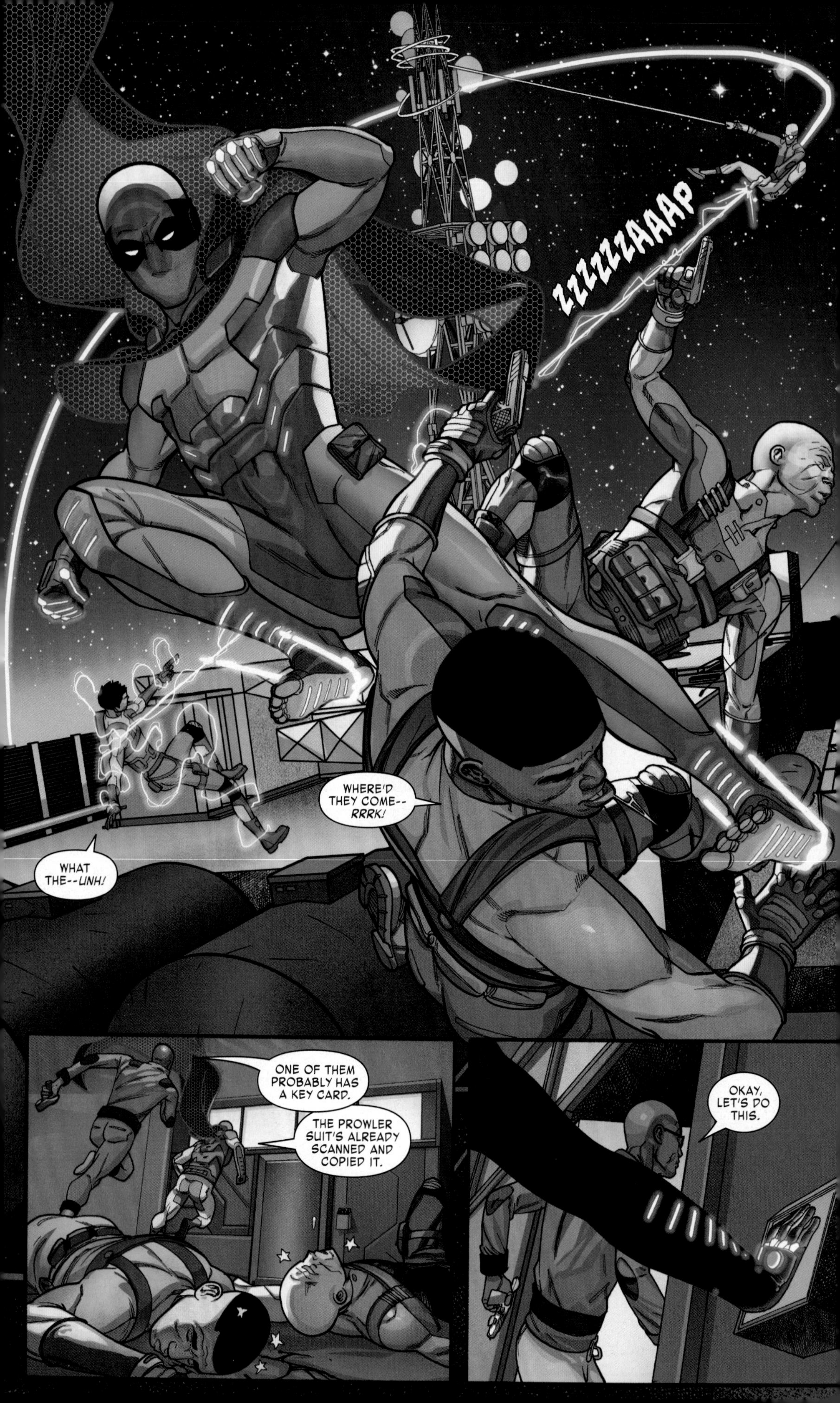
ZZZZZZAAAP
WHERE'D THEY COME-- RRRK!
WHAT THE--UNH!
ONE OF THEM PROBABLY HAS A KEY CARD.
THE PROWLER SUIT'S ALREADY SCANNED AND COPIED IT.
OKAY, LET'S DO THIS.

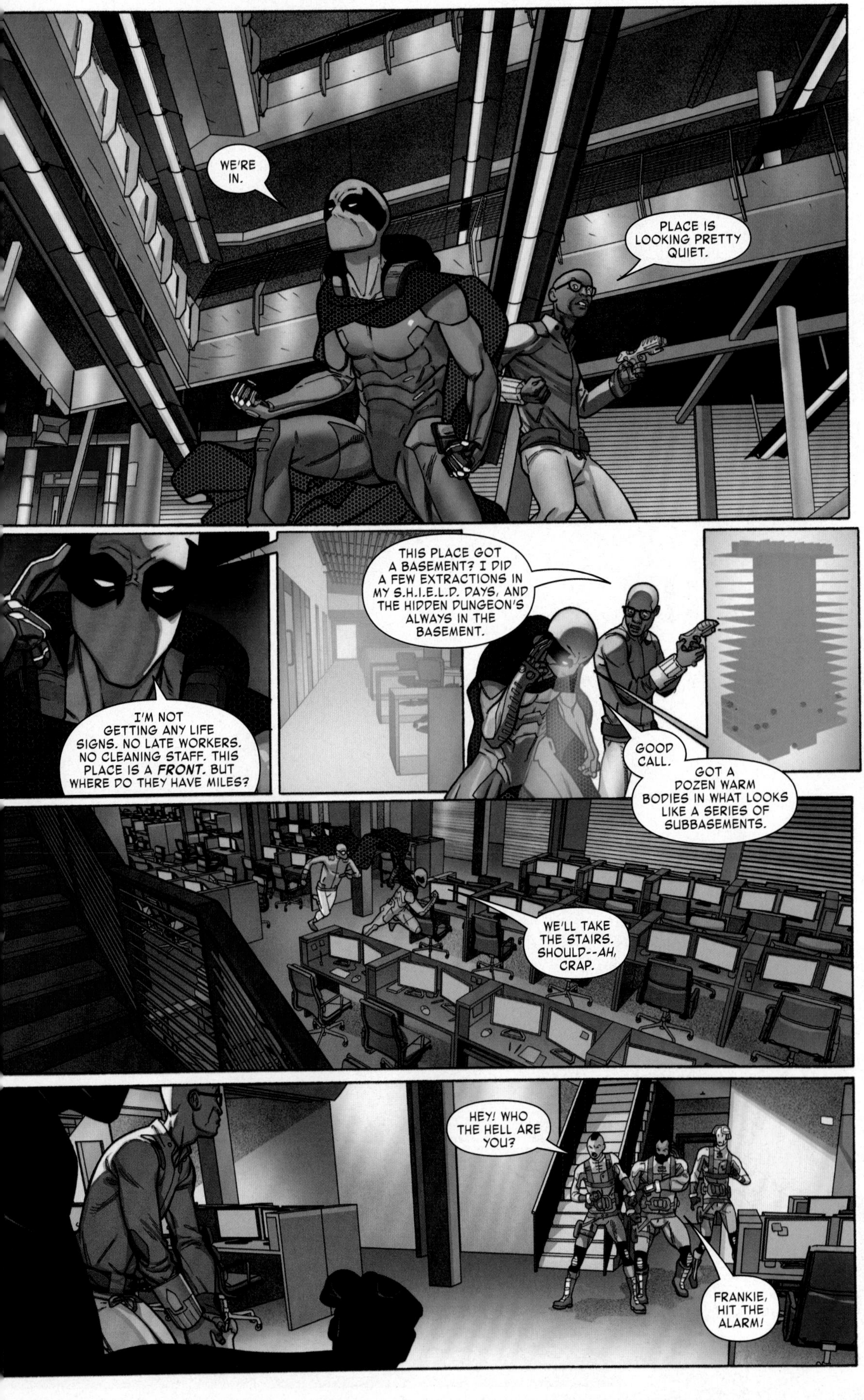

WE'RE IN.
PLACE IS LOOKING PRETTY QUIET.
I'M NOT GETTING ANY LIFE SIGNS. NO LATE WORKERS. NO CLEANING STAFF. THIS PLACE IS A *FRONT.* BUT WHERE DO THEY HAVE MILES?
THIS PLACE GOT A BASEMENT? I DID A FEW EXTRACTIONS IN MY S.H.I.E.L.D. DAYS, AND THE HIDDEN DUNGEON'S ALWAYS IN THE BASEMENT.
GOOD CALL.
GOT A DOZEN WARM BODIES IN WHAT LOOKS LIKE A SERIES OF SUBBASEMENTS.
WE'LL TAKE THE STAIRS. SHOULD--AH, CRAP.
HEY! WHO THE HELL ARE YOU?
FRANKIE, HIT THE ALARM!

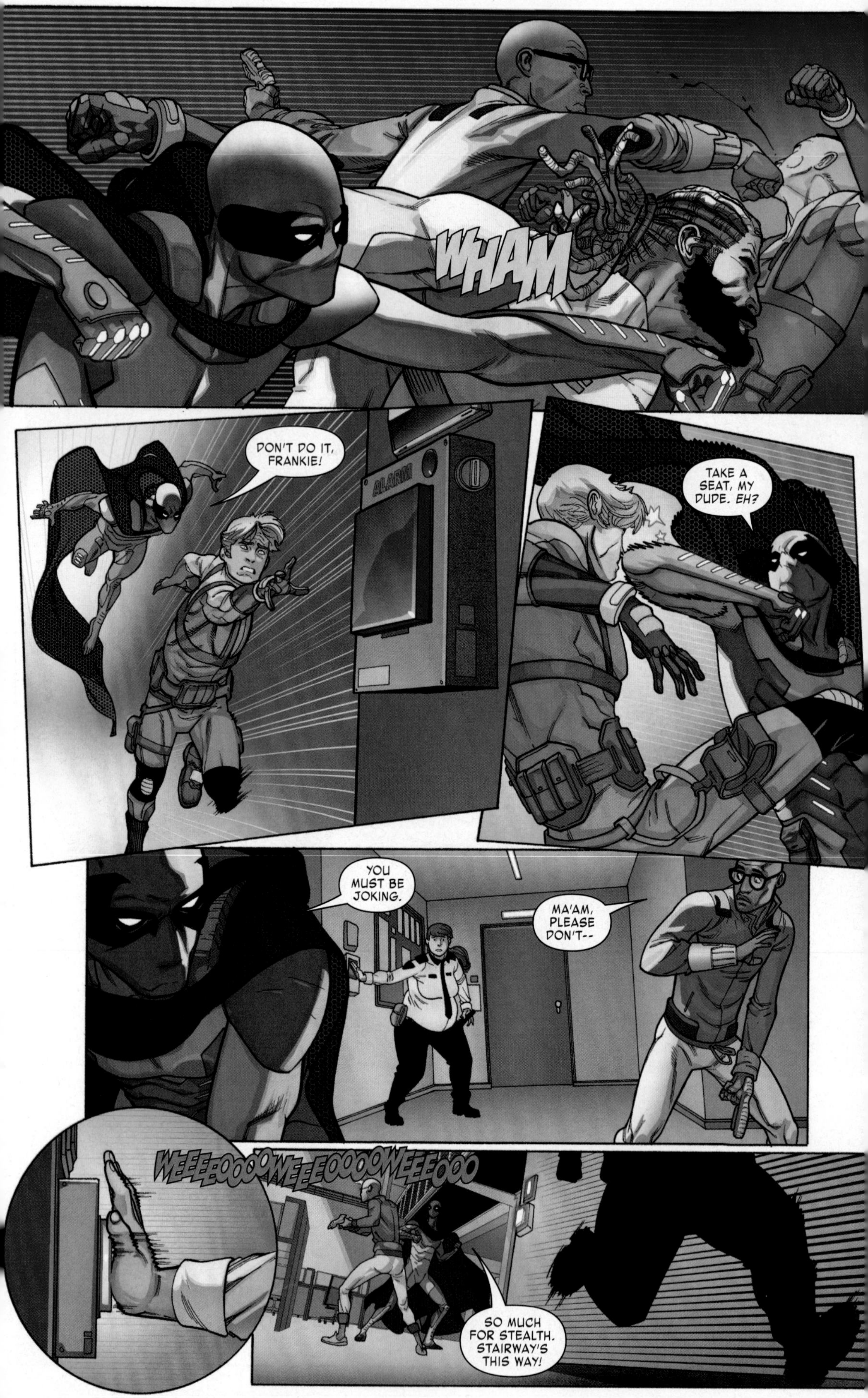
WHAM
DON'T DO IT, FRANKIE!
ALARM!
TAKE A SEAT, MY DUDE. EH?
YOU MUST BE JOKING.
MA'AM, PLEASE DON'T--
WEEEEOOOOWEEEEOOOOWEEEEOOO
SO MUCH FOR STEALTH. STAIRWAY'S THIS WAY!

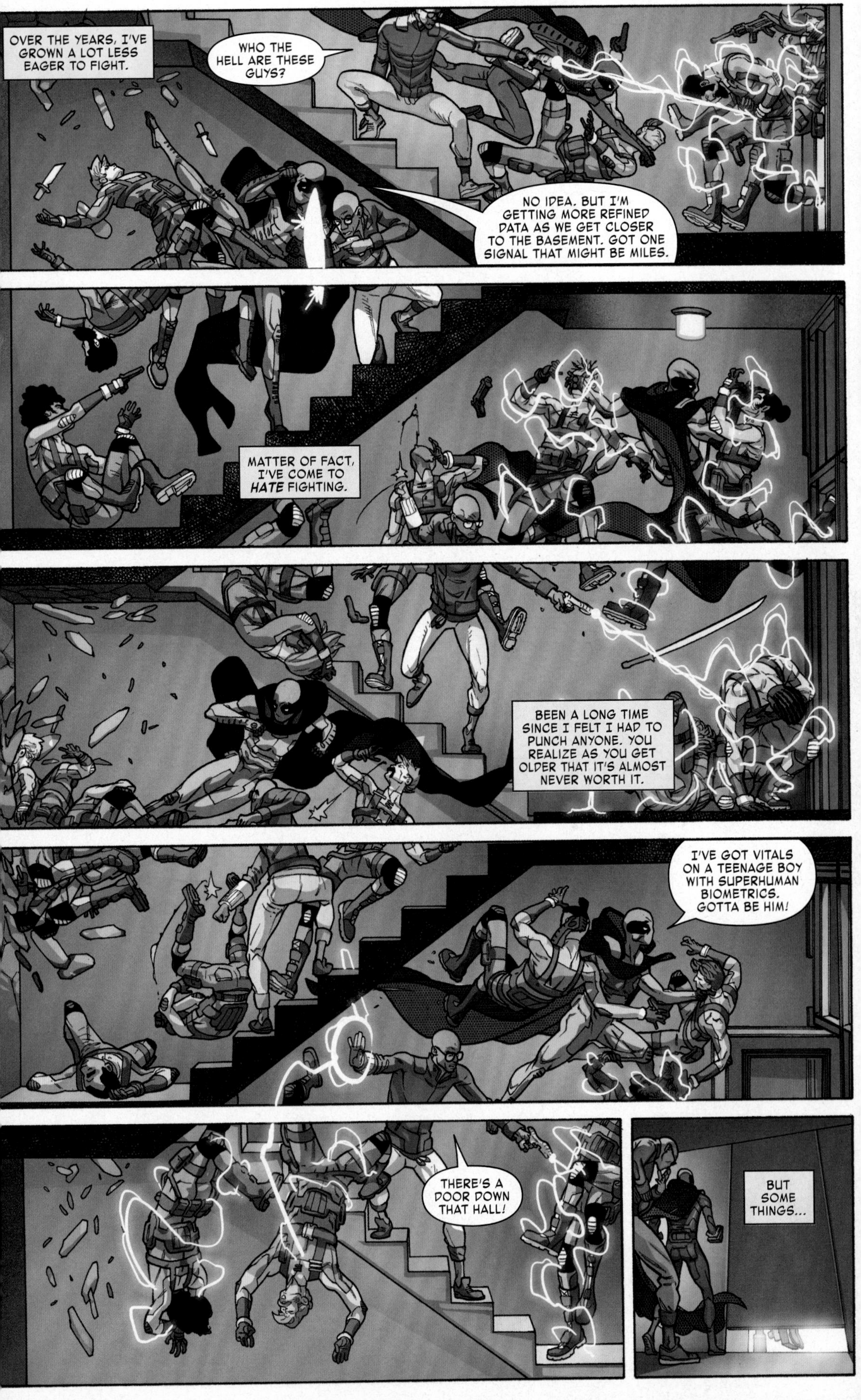

OVER THE YEARS, I'VE GROWN A LOT LESS EAGER TO FIGHT.
WHO THE HELL ARE THESE GUYS?
NO IDEA. BUT I'M GETTING MORE REFINED DATA AS WE GET CLOSER TO THE BASEMENT. GOT ONE SIGNAL THAT MIGHT BE MILES.
MATTER OF FACT, I'VE COME TO HATE FIGHTING.
BEEN A LONG TIME SINCE I FELT I HAD TO PUNCH ANYONE. YOU REALIZE AS YOU GET OLDER THAT IT'S ALMOST NEVER WORTH IT.
I'VE GOT VITALS ON A TEENAGE BOY WITH SUPERHUMAN BIOMETRICS. GOTTA BE HIM!
THERE'S A DOOR DOWN THAT HALL!
BUT SOME THINGS...

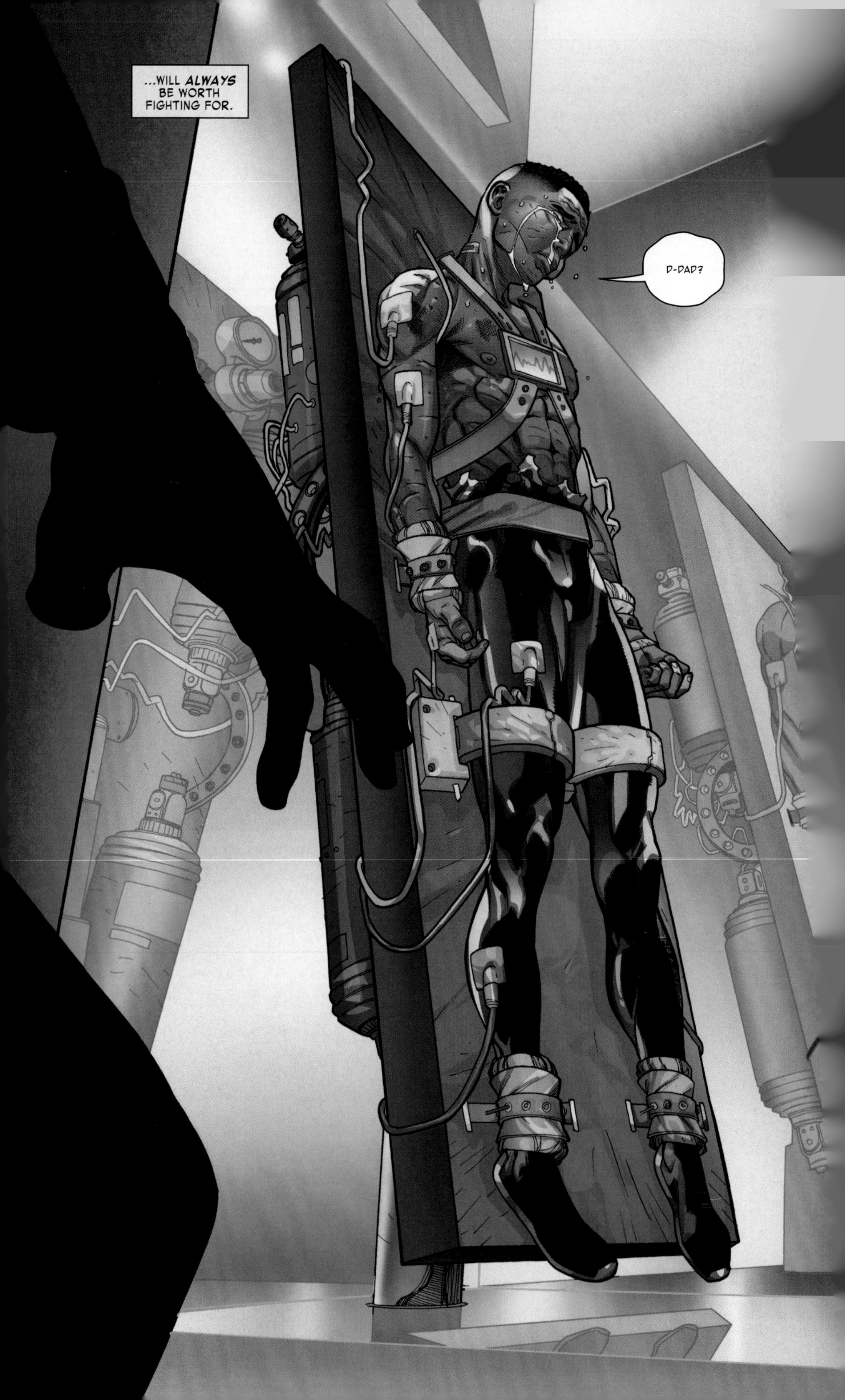
...WILL ALWAYS BE WORTH FIGHTING FOR.
D-DAD?

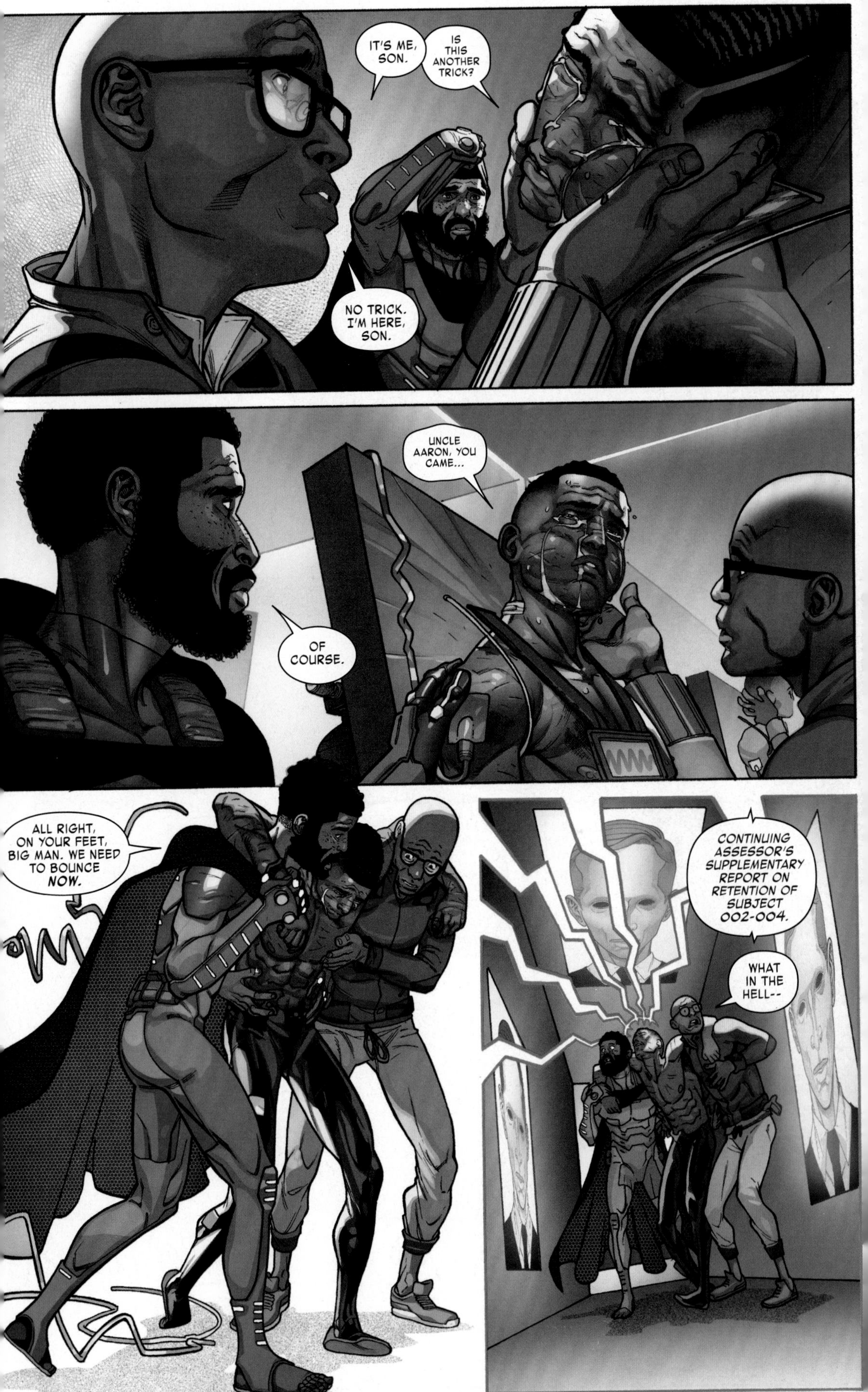

IT'S ME, SON.
IS THIS ANOTHER TRICK?
NO TRICK. I'M HERE, SON.
UNCLE AARON, YOU CAME...
OF COURSE.
ALL RIGHT, ON YOUR FEET, BIG MAN. WE NEED TO BOUNCE NOW.
CONTINUING ASSESSOR'S SUPPLEMENTARY REPORT ON RETENTION OF SUBJECT 002-004.
WHAT IN THE HELL--

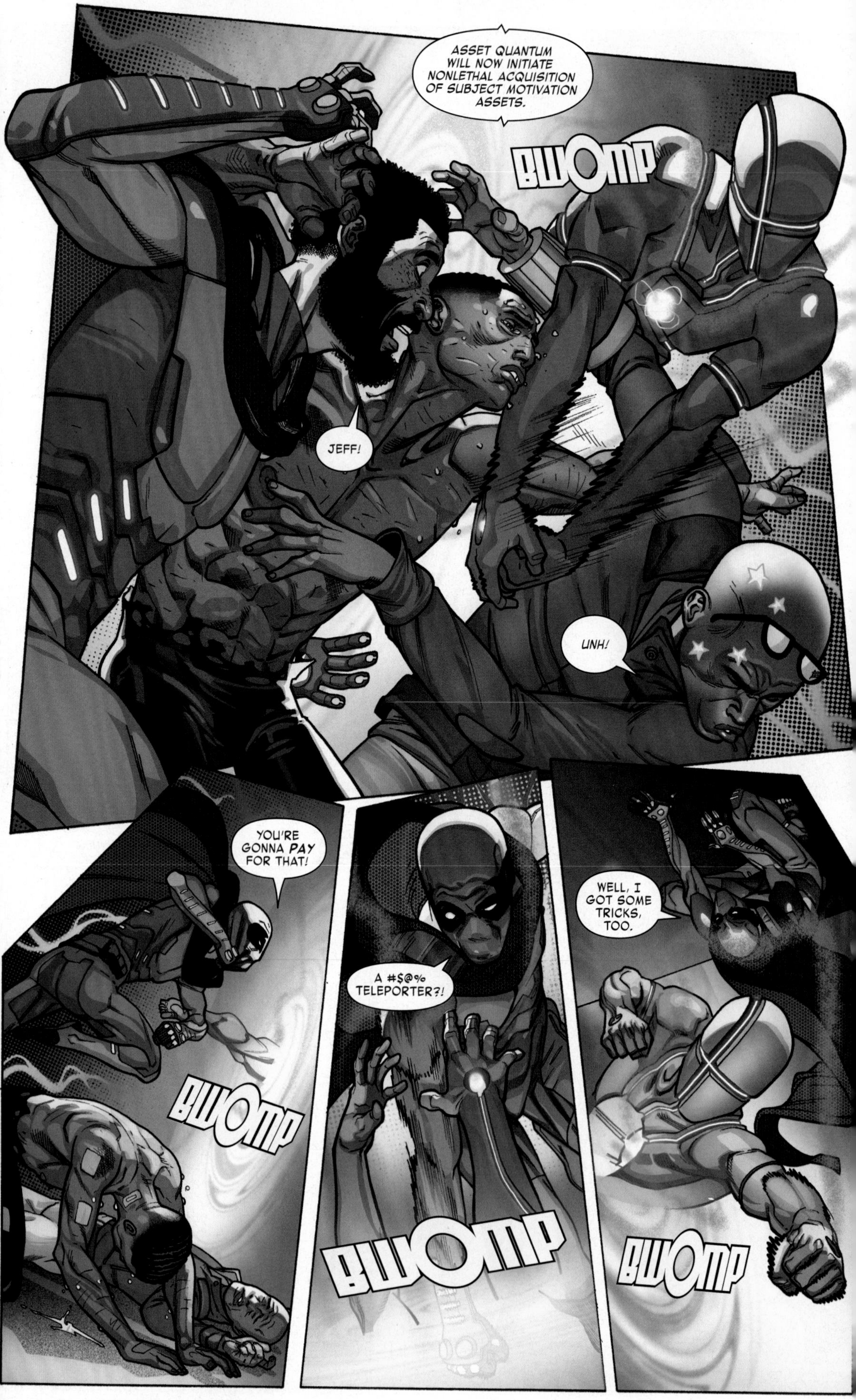

ASSET QUANTUM WILL NOW INITIATE NONLETHAL ACQUISITION OF SUBJECT MOTIVATION ASSETS.
BWOMP
JEFF!
UNH!
YOU'RE GONNA PAY FOR THAT!
BWOMP
A #$@% TELEPORTER?!
BWOMP
WELL, I GOT SOME TRICKS, TOO.
BWOMP

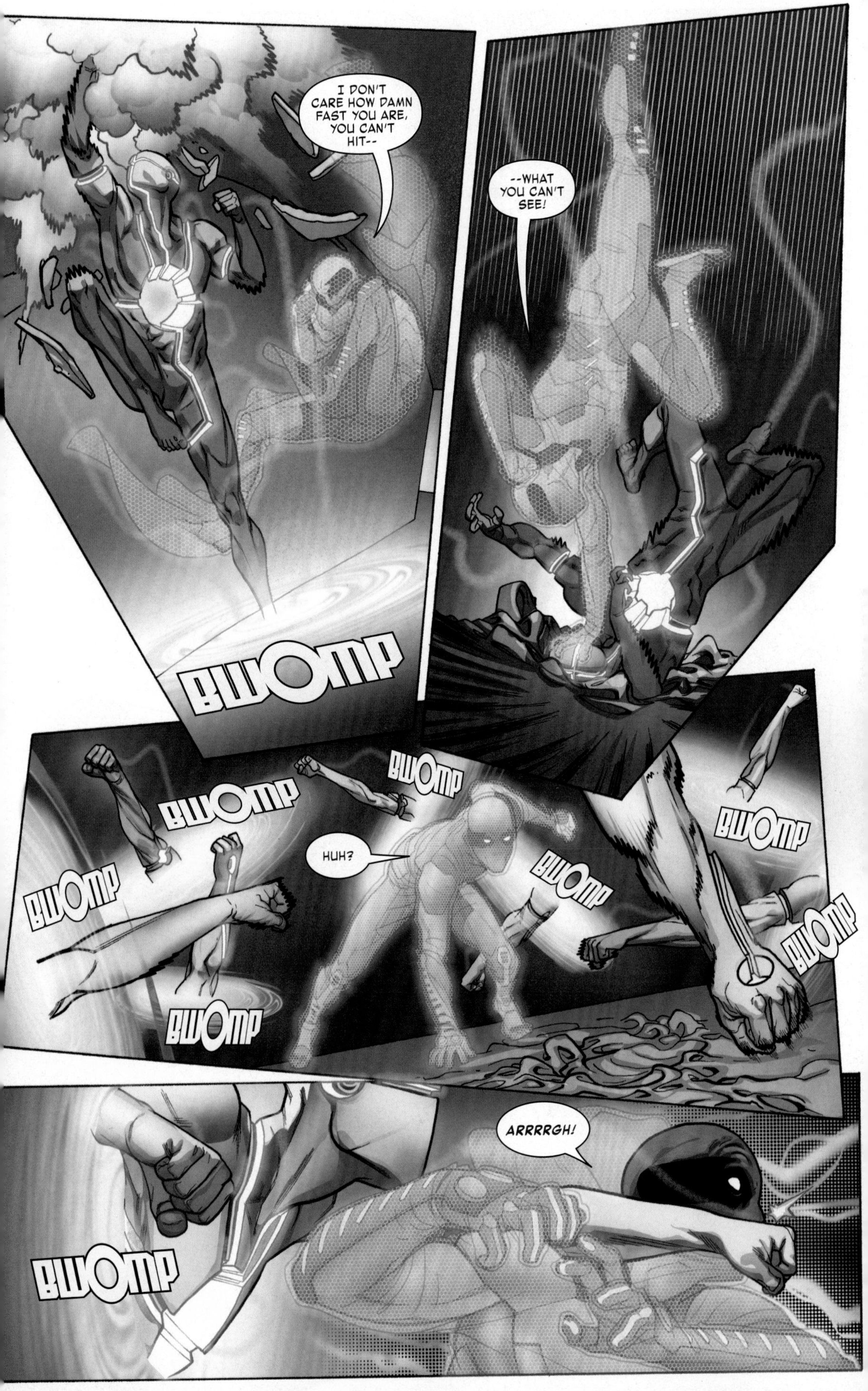
I DON'T CARE HOW DAMN FAST YOU ARE, YOU CAN'T HIT--
--WHAT YOU CAN'T SEE!
BWOMP
BWOMP
BWOMP
BWOMP
HUH?
BWOMP
BWOMP
BWOMP
BWOMP
ARRRRGH!
BWOMP

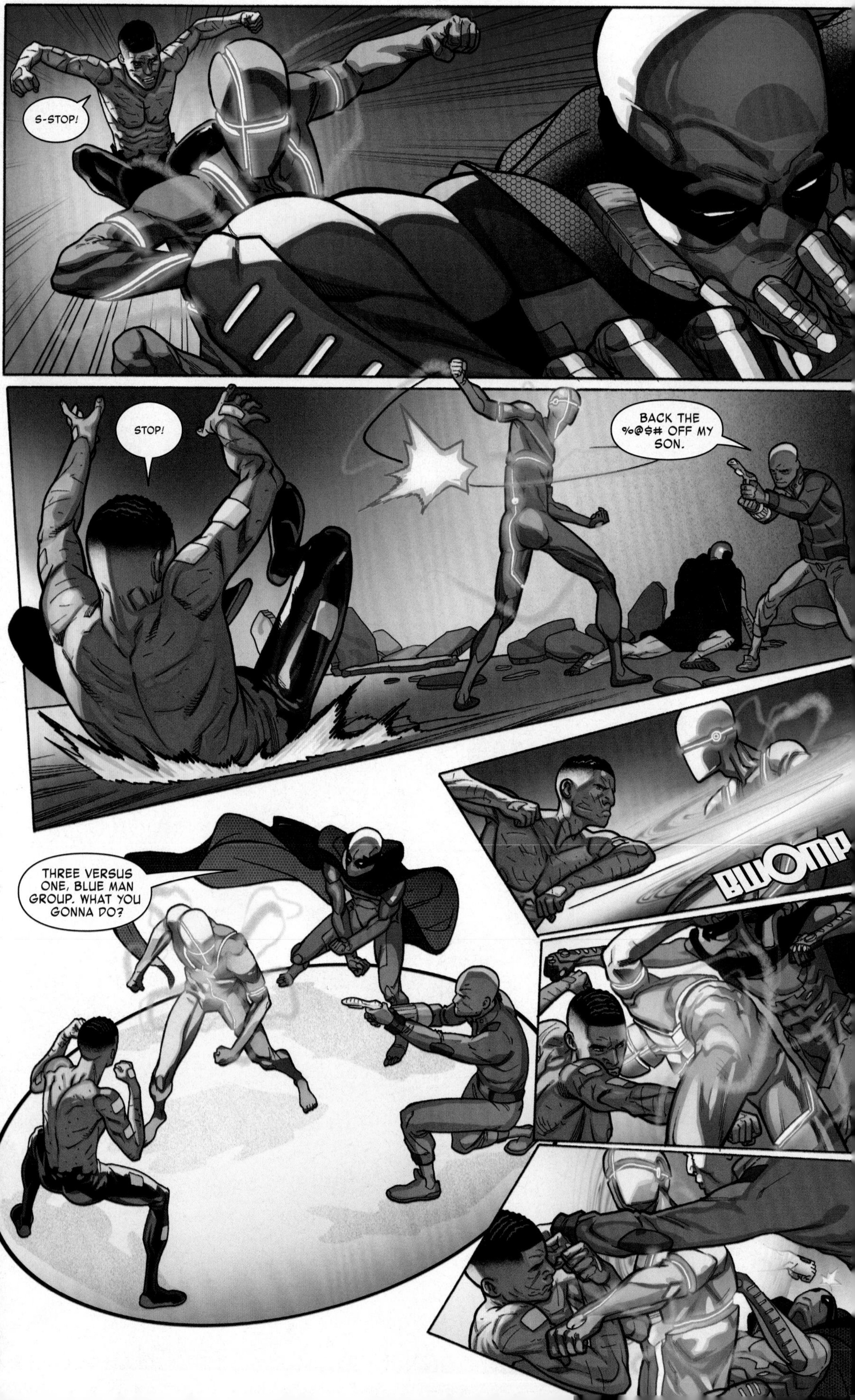

S-STOP!
STOP!
BACK THE %@$# OFF MY SON.
BWOMP
THREE VERSUS ONE, BLUE MAN GROUP. WHAT YOU GONNA DO?

ASSESSOR'S EXECUTIVE COMMITTEE REPORT: WE HAVE COMPLETED REVIEW OF SUBJECT 002-004. ASSET QUANTUM WILL NOW WITHDRAW TO AVOID FURTHER ASSET EXPENDITURES.

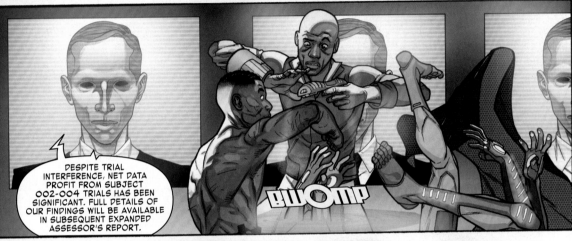

DESPITE TRIAL INTERFERENCE, NET DATA PROFIT FROM SUBJECT 002-004 TRIALS HAS BEEN SIGNIFICANT. FULL DETAILS OF OUR FINDINGS WILL BE AVAILABLE IN SUBSEQUENT EXPANDED ASSESSOR'S REPORT.

BWOMP

I DON'T KNOW *WHAT* THE HELL THAT WAS, BUT THE TELEPORTER IS GONE. NOW'S OUR CHANCE.

CAN'T LEAVE... GOT TO STOP THEM...COULD HURT OTHER FOLKS.

RIGHT NOW, SON...

...WE JUST NEED TO GET YOU HOME.

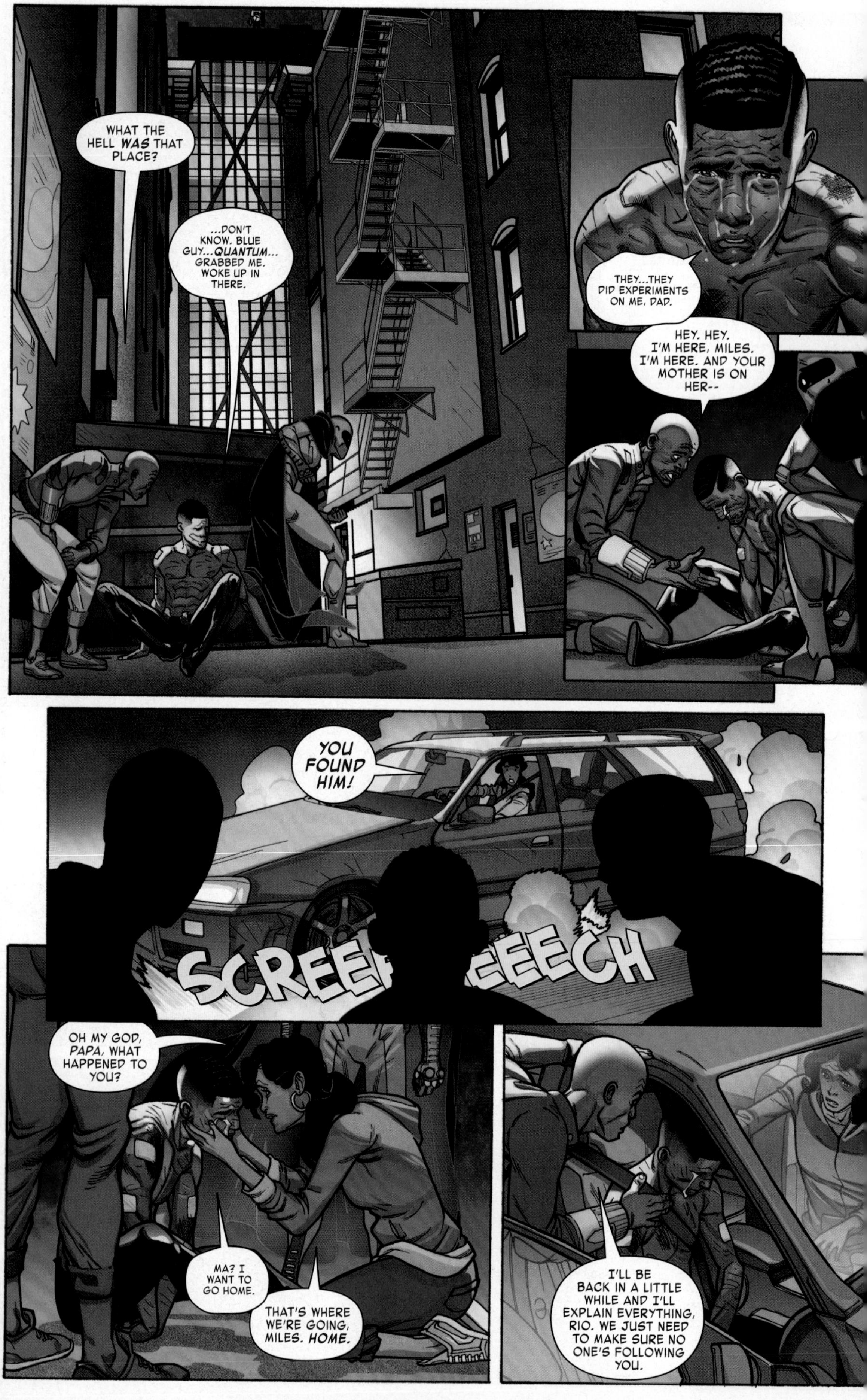
WHAT THE HELL **WAS** THAT PLACE?
...DON'T KNOW. BLUE GUY...**QUANTUM**... GRABBED ME. WOKE UP IN THERE.
THEY...THEY DID EXPERIMENTS ON ME, DAD.
HEY. HEY. I'M HERE, MILES. I'M HERE. AND YOUR MOTHER IS ON HER--
YOU FOUND HIM!
SCREEEEEEECH
OH MY GOD, *PAPA*, WHAT HAPPENED TO YOU?
MA? I WANT TO GO HOME.
THAT'S WHERE WE'RE GOING, MILES. **HOME.**
I'LL BE BACK IN A LITTLE WHILE AND I'LL EXPLAIN EVERYTHING, RIO. WE JUST NEED TO MAKE SURE NO ONE'S FOLLOWING YOU.

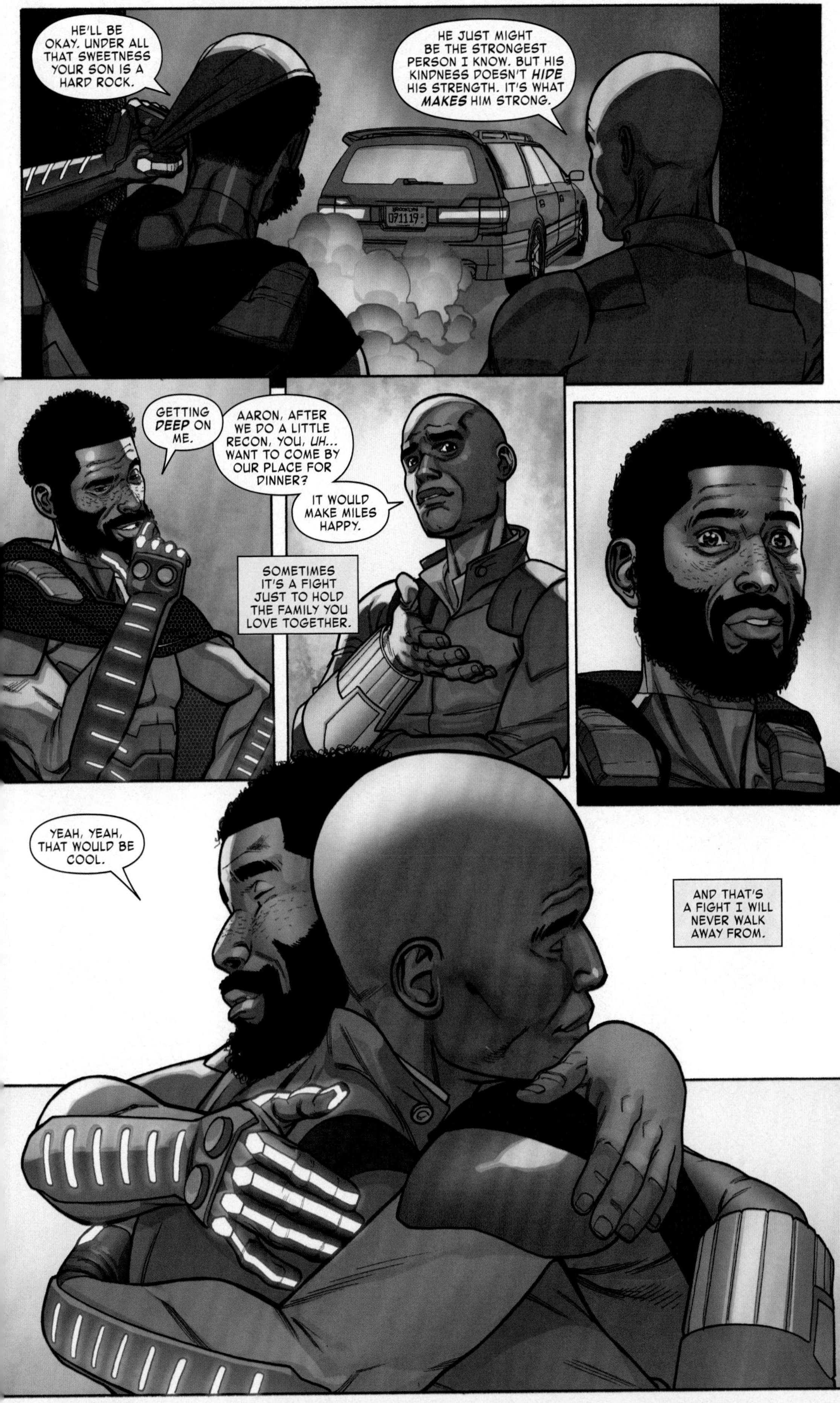
HE'LL BE OKAY. UNDER ALL THAT SWEETNESS YOUR SON IS A HARD ROCK.
HE JUST MIGHT BE THE STRONGEST PERSON I KNOW. BUT HIS KINDNESS DOESN'T HIDE HIS STRENGTH. IT'S WHAT MAKES HIM STRONG.
BROOKLYN
071119
GETTING DEEP ON ME.
AARON, AFTER WE DO A LITTLE RECON, YOU, UH... WANT TO COME BY OUR PLACE FOR DINNER?
IT WOULD MAKE MILES HAPPY.
SOMETIMES IT'S A FIGHT JUST TO HOLD THE FAMILY YOU LOVE TOGETHER.
YEAH, YEAH, THAT WOULD BE COOL.
AND THAT'S A FIGHT I WILL NEVER WALK AWAY FROM.

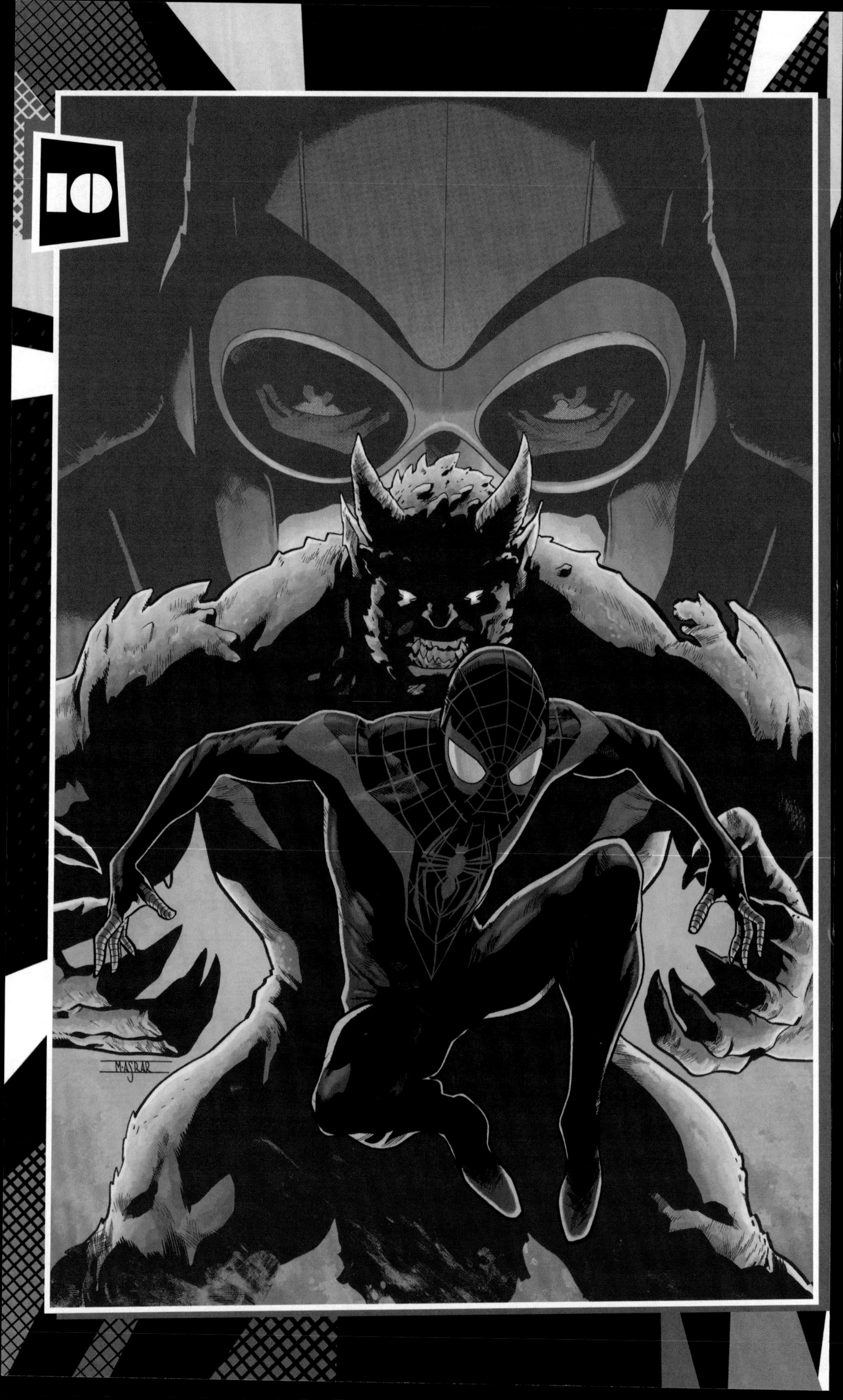
10
M.ASRAR

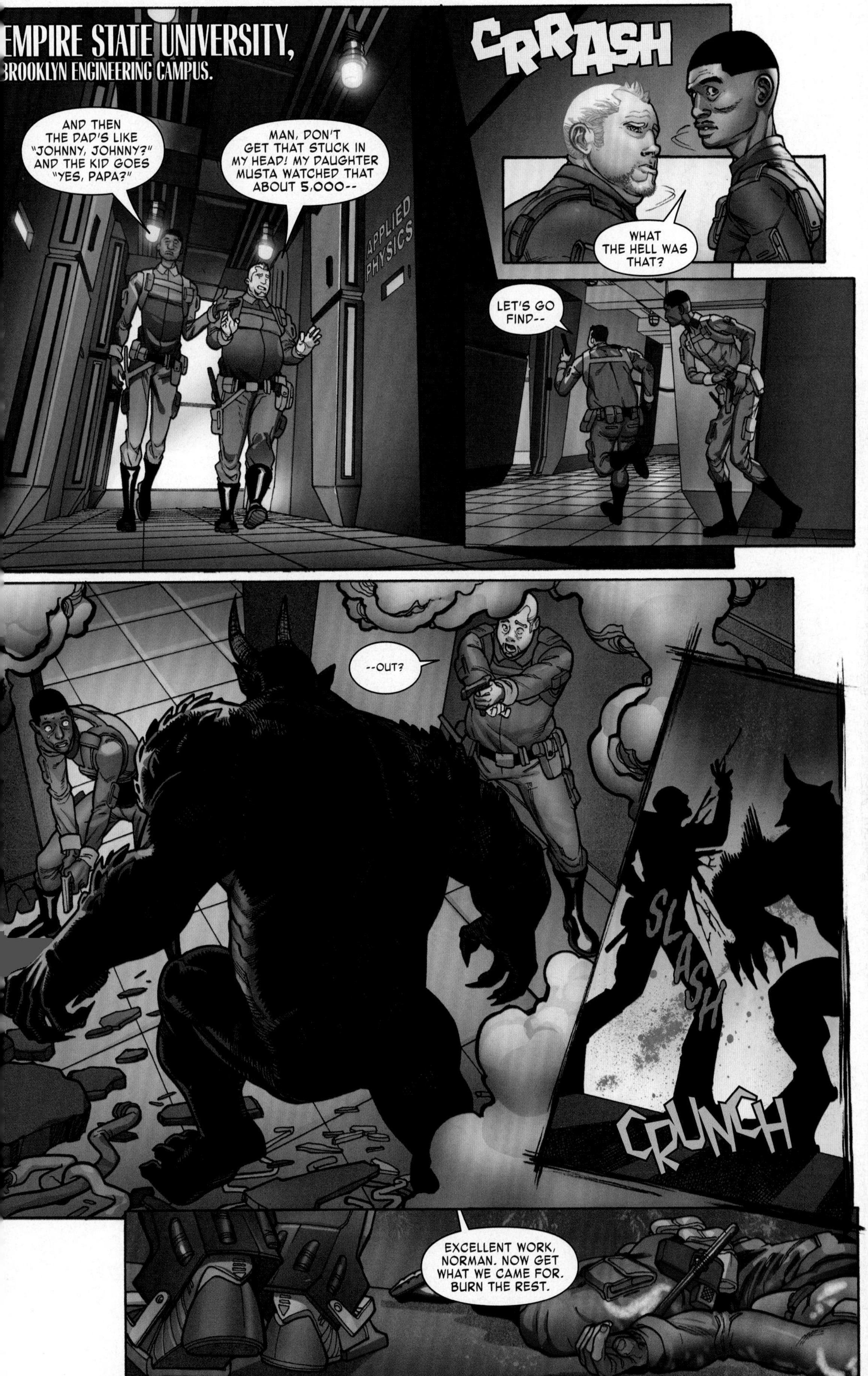

EMPIRE STATE UNIVERSITY,
BROOKLYN ENGINEERING CAMPUS.
AND THEN THE DAD'S LIKE "JOHNNY, JOHNNY?" AND THE KID GOES "YES, PAPA?"
MAN, DON'T GET THAT STUCK IN MY HEAD! MY DAUGHTER MUSTA WATCHED THAT ABOUT 5,000--
APPLIED PHYSICS
CRRASH
WHAT THE HELL WAS THAT?
LET'S GO FIND--
--OUT?
SLASH
CRUNCH
EXCELLENT WORK, NORMAN. NOW GET WHAT WE CAME FOR. BURN THE REST.

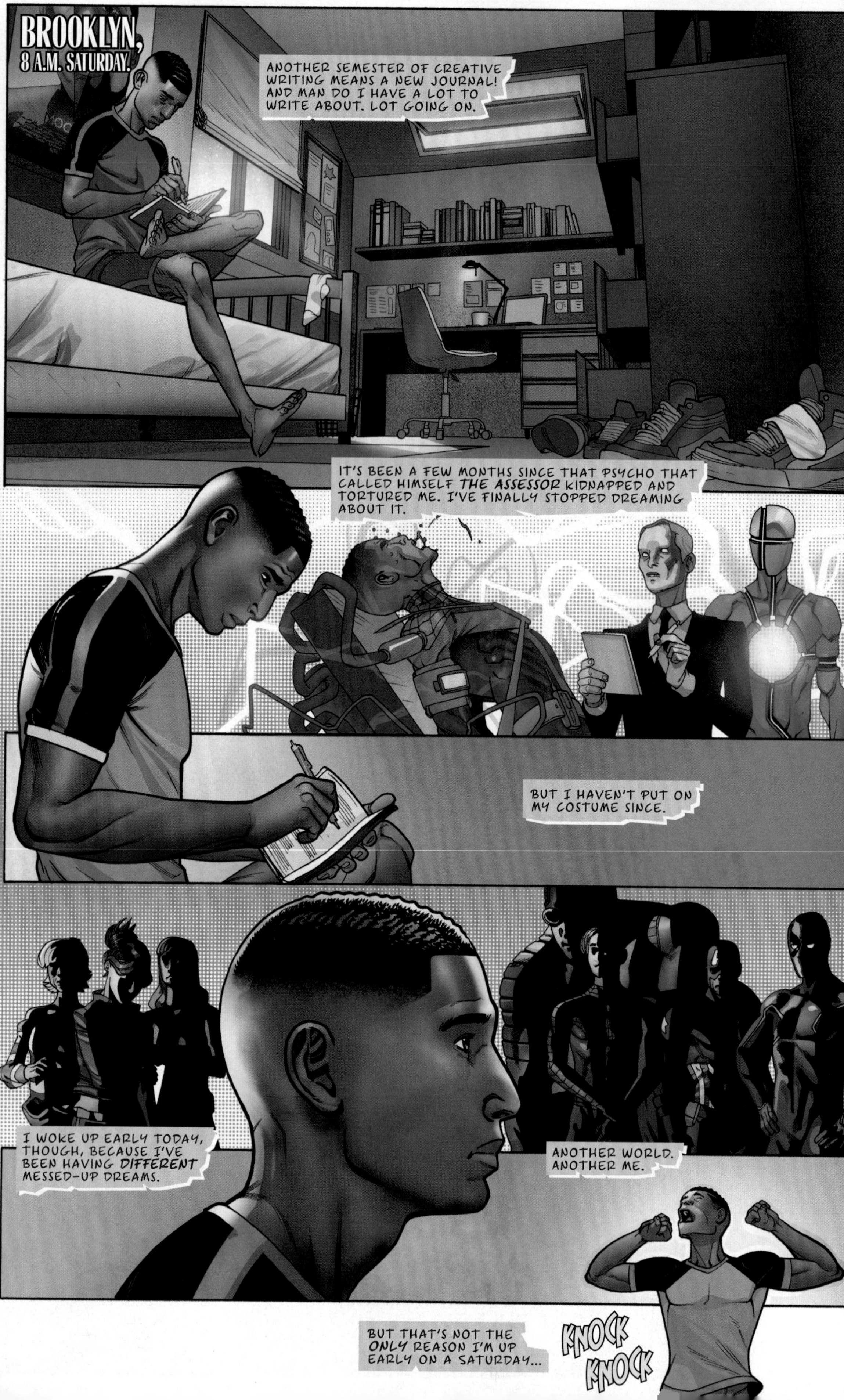
BROOKLYN, 8 A.M. SATURDAY.
ANOTHER SEMESTER OF CREATIVE WRITING MEANS A NEW JOURNAL! AND MAN DO I HAVE A LOT TO WRITE ABOUT. LOT GOING ON.
IT'S BEEN A FEW MONTHS SINCE THAT PSYCHO THAT CALLED HIMSELF THE ASSESSOR KIDNAPPED AND TORTURED ME. I'VE FINALLY STOPPED DREAMING ABOUT IT.
BUT I HAVEN'T PUT ON MY COSTUME SINCE.
I WOKE UP EARLY TODAY, THOUGH, BECAUSE I'VE BEEN HAVING DIFFERENT MESSED-UP DREAMS.
ANOTHER WORLD. ANOTHER ME.
BUT THAT'S NOT THE ONLY REASON I'M UP EARLY ON A SATURDAY...
KNOCK
KNOCK

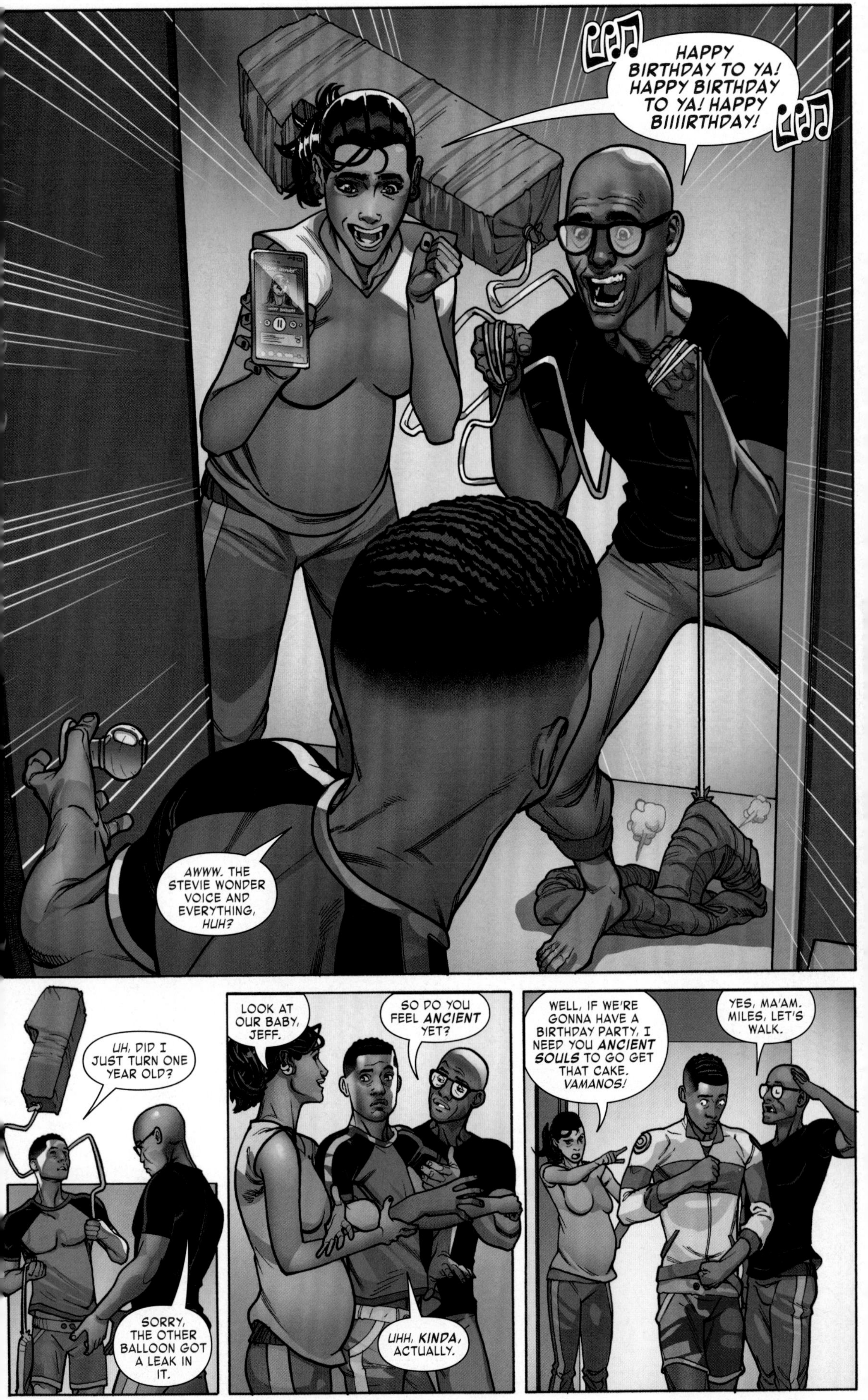
HAPPY BIRTHDAY TO YA! HAPPY BIRTHDAY TO YA! HAPPY BIIIIRTHDAY!
AWWW. THE STEVIE WONDER VOICE AND EVERYTHING, HUH?
UH, DID I JUST TURN ONE YEAR OLD?
SORRY, THE OTHER BALLOON GOT A LEAK IN IT.
LOOK AT OUR BABY, JEFF.
SO DO YOU FEEL ANCIENT YET?
UHH, KINDA, ACTUALLY.
WELL, IF WE'RE GONNA HAVE A BIRTHDAY PARTY, I NEED YOU ANCIENT SOULS TO GO GET THAT CAKE. VAMANOS!
YES, MA'AM. MILES, LET'S WALK.

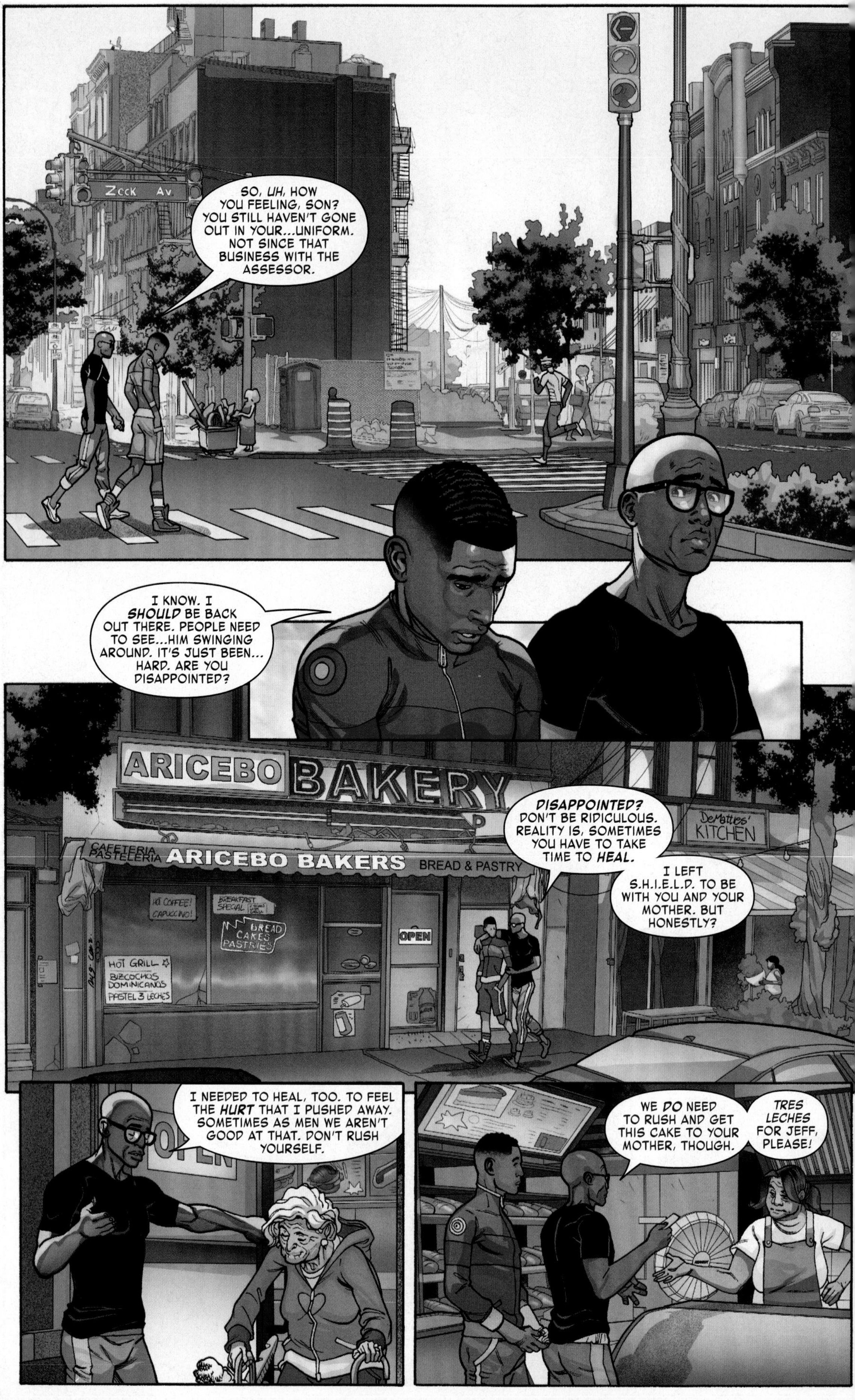

Zeck Av.
SO, UH, HOW YOU FEELING, SON? YOU STILL HAVEN'T GONE OUT IN YOUR...UNIFORM. NOT SINCE THAT BUSINESS WITH THE ASSESSOR.
I KNOW. I SHOULD BE BACK OUT THERE. PEOPLE NEED TO SEE...HIM SWINGING AROUND. IT'S JUST BEEN... HARD. ARE YOU DISAPPOINTED?
ARICEBO BAKERY
CAFETERIA PASTELERIA ARICEBO BAKERS BREAD & PASTRY
HOT COFFEE! CAPUCCINO!
BREAKFAST SPECIAL
BREAD CAKES PASTRIES
HOT GRILL
BIZCOCHOS DOMINICANOS
PASTEL 3 LECHES
OPEN
DeMatteis' KITCHEN
DISAPPOINTED? DON'T BE RIDICULOUS. REALITY IS, SOMETIMES YOU HAVE TO TAKE TIME TO HEAL.
I LEFT S.H.I.E.L.D. TO BE WITH YOU AND YOUR MOTHER. BUT HONESTLY?
I NEEDED TO HEAL, TOO. TO FEEL THE HURT THAT I PUSHED AWAY. SOMETIMES AS MEN WE AREN'T GOOD AT THAT. DON'T RUSH YOURSELF.
WE DO NEED TO RUSH AND GET THIS CAKE TO YOUR MOTHER, THOUGH.
TRES LECHES FOR JEFF, PLEASE!

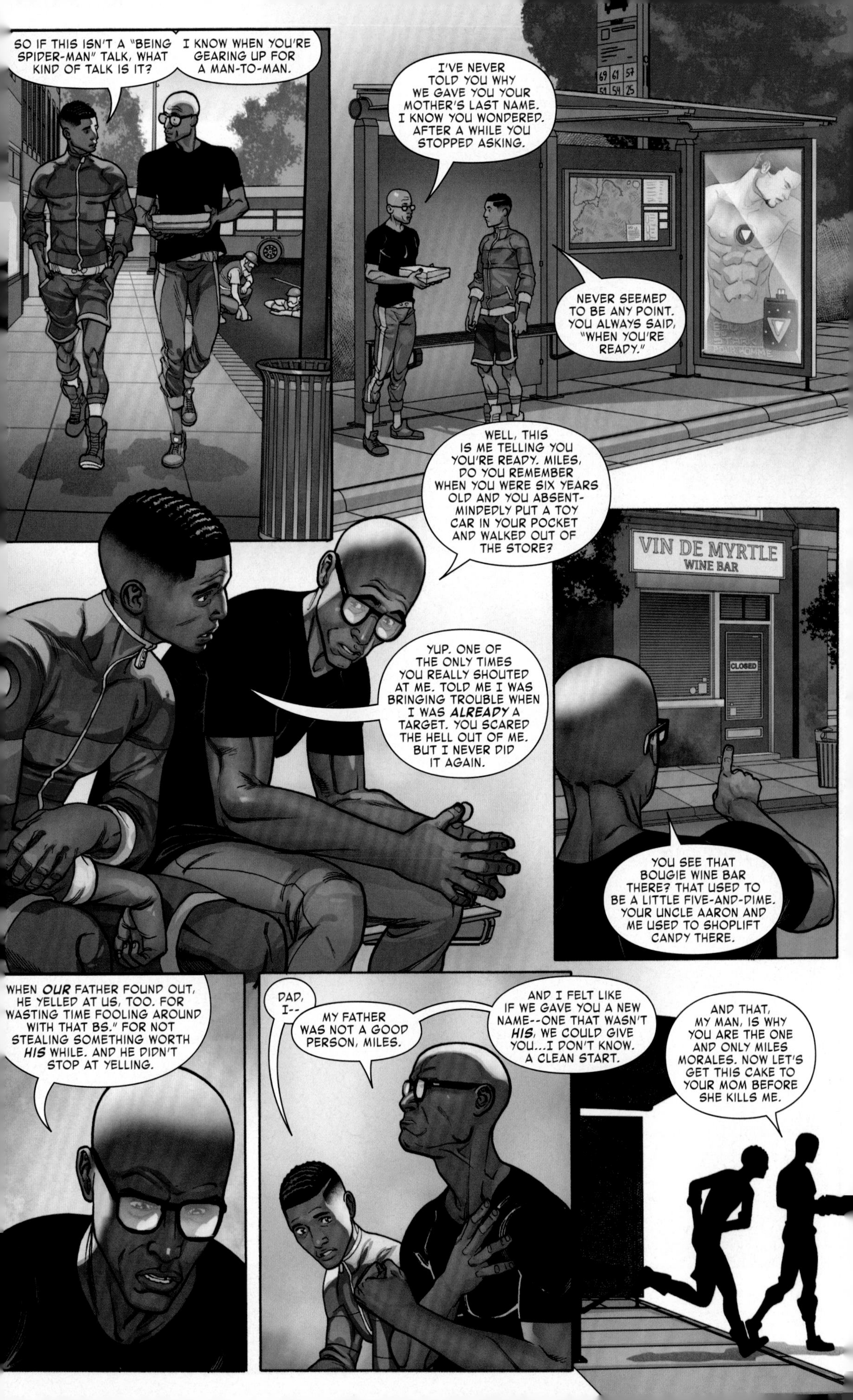
SO IF THIS ISN'T A "BEING SPIDER-MAN" TALK, WHAT KIND OF TALK IS IT?
I KNOW WHEN YOU'RE GEARING UP FOR A MAN-TO-MAN.
I'VE NEVER TOLD YOU WHY WE GAVE YOU YOUR MOTHER'S LAST NAME. I KNOW YOU WONDERED. AFTER A WHILE YOU STOPPED ASKING.
NEVER SEEMED TO BE ANY POINT. YOU ALWAYS SAID, "WHEN YOU'RE READY."
69 61 57
53 54 25
WELL, THIS IS ME TELLING YOU YOU'RE READY. MILES, DO YOU REMEMBER WHEN YOU WERE SIX YEARS OLD AND YOU ABSENT-MINDEDLY PUT A TOY CAR IN YOUR POCKET AND WALKED OUT OF THE STORE?
YUP. ONE OF THE ONLY TIMES YOU REALLY SHOUTED AT ME. TOLD ME I WAS BRINGING TROUBLE WHEN I WAS *ALREADY* A TARGET. YOU SCARED THE HELL OUT OF ME. BUT I NEVER DID IT AGAIN.
VIN DE MYRTLE
WINE BAR
CLOSED
YOU SEE THAT BOUGIE WINE BAR THERE? THAT USED TO BE A LITTLE FIVE-AND-DIME. YOUR UNCLE AARON AND ME USED TO SHOPLIFT CANDY THERE.
WHEN *OUR* FATHER FOUND OUT, HE YELLED AT US, TOO. FOR WASTING TIME FOOLING AROUND WITH THAT BS." FOR NOT STEALING SOMETHING WORTH *HIS* WHILE. AND HE DIDN'T STOP AT YELLING.
DAD, I--
MY FATHER WAS NOT A GOOD PERSON, MILES.
AND I FELT LIKE IF WE GAVE YOU A NEW NAME--ONE THAT WASN'T *HIS*, WE COULD GIVE YOU...I DON'T KNOW. A CLEAN START.
AND THAT, MY MAN, IS WHY YOU ARE THE ONE AND ONLY MILES MORALES. NOW LET'S GET THIS CAKE TO YOUR MOM BEFORE SHE KILLS ME.

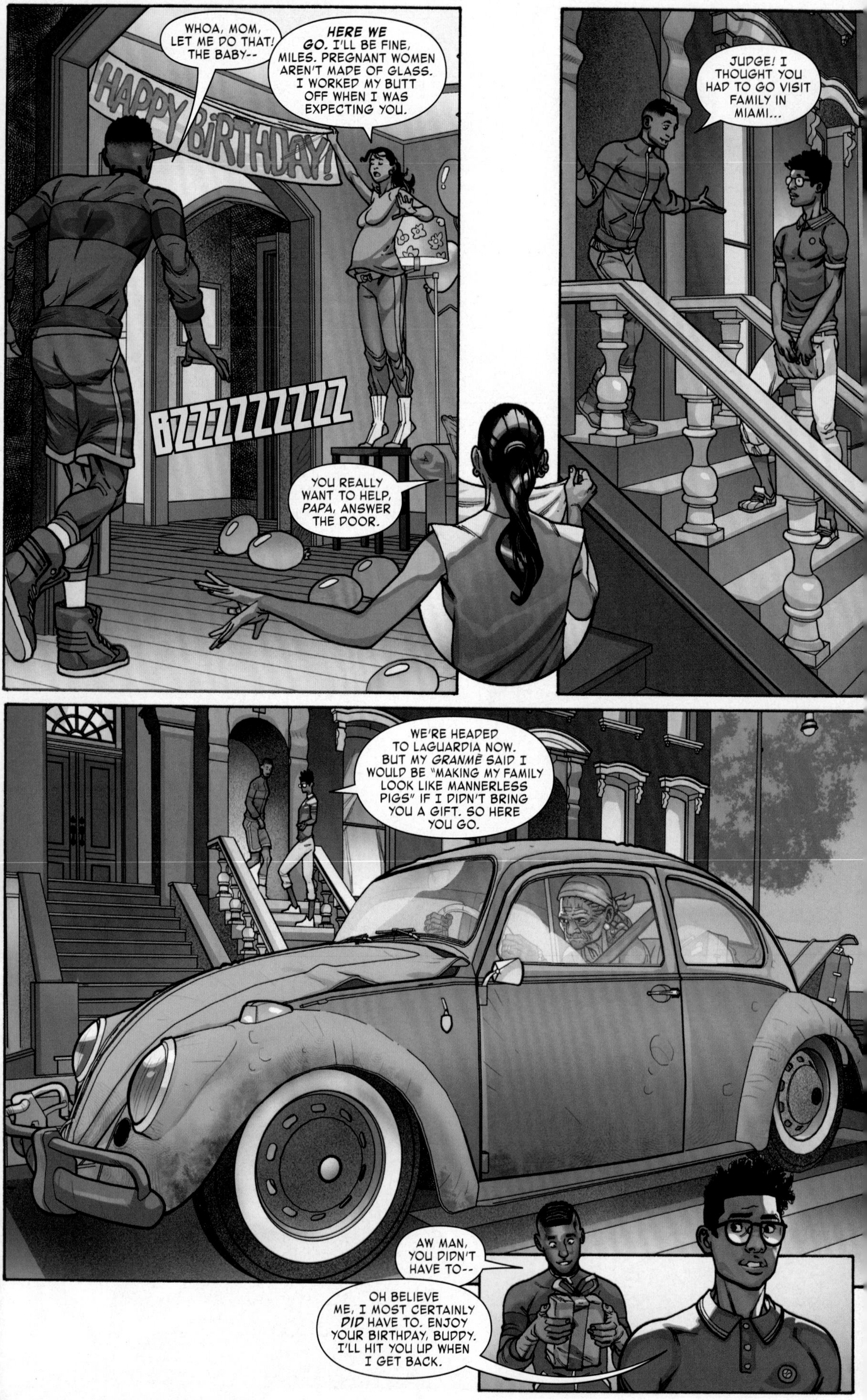
WHOA, MOM, LET ME DO THAT! THE BABY--
HAPPY BIRTHDAY!
HERE WE GO. I'LL BE FINE, MILES. PREGNANT WOMEN AREN'T MADE OF GLASS. I WORKED MY BUTT OFF WHEN I WAS EXPECTING YOU.
BZZZZZZZZZ
YOU REALLY WANT TO HELP, PAPA, ANSWER THE DOOR.
JUDGE! I THOUGHT YOU HAD TO GO VISIT FAMILY IN MIAMI...
WE'RE HEADED TO LAGUARDIA NOW. BUT MY GRANMÈ SAID I WOULD BE "MAKING MY FAMILY LOOK LIKE MANNERLESS PIGS" IF I DIDN'T BRING YOU A GIFT. SO HERE YOU GO.
AW MAN, YOU DIDN'T HAVE TO--
OH BELIEVE ME, I MOST CERTAINLY DID HAVE TO. ENJOY YOUR BIRTHDAY, BUDDY. I'LL HIT YOU UP WHEN I GET BACK.

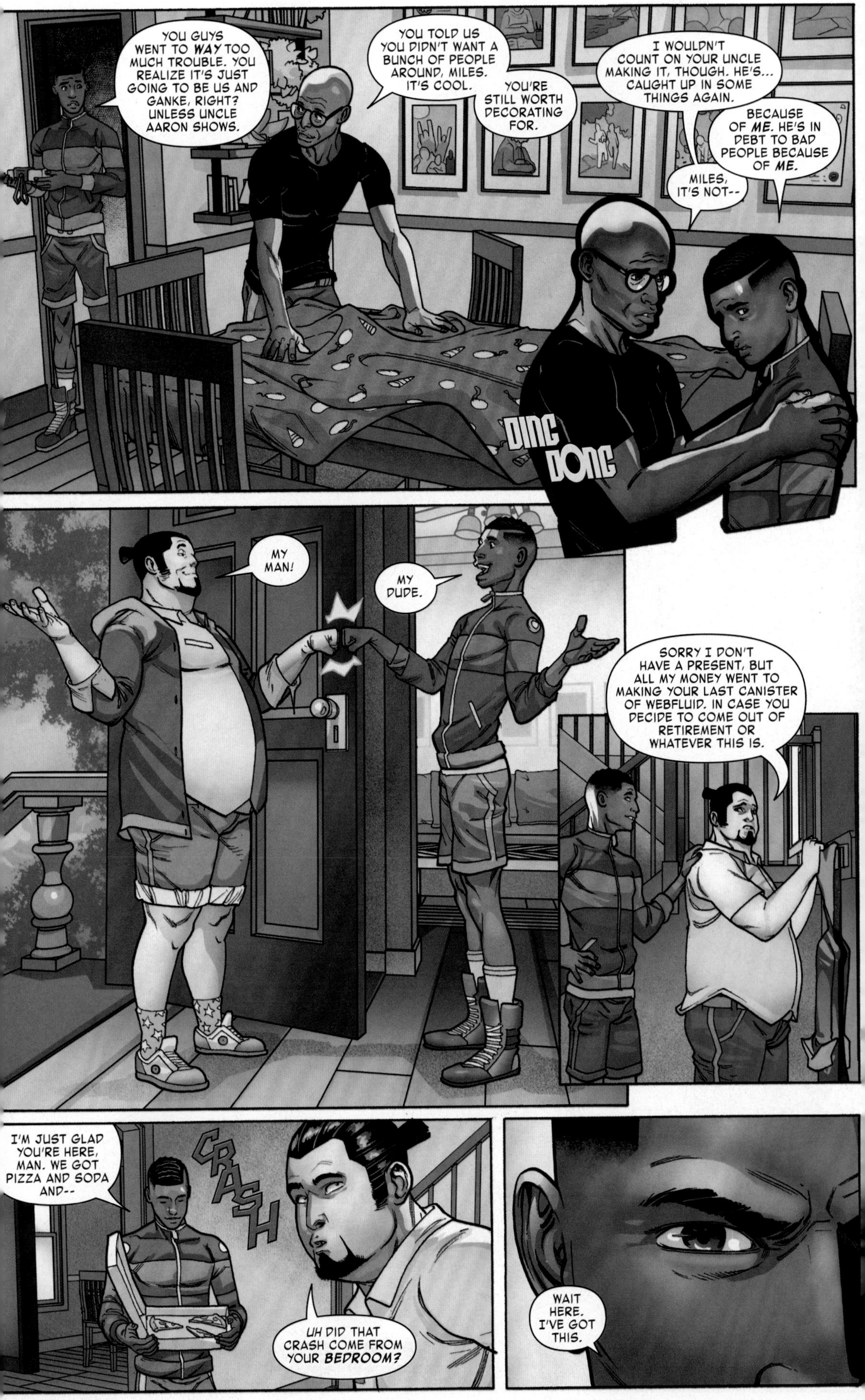
YOU GUYS WENT TO WAY TOO MUCH TROUBLE. YOU REALIZE IT'S JUST GOING TO BE US AND GANKE, RIGHT? UNLESS UNCLE AARON SHOWS.
YOU TOLD US YOU DIDN'T WANT A BUNCH OF PEOPLE AROUND, MILES. IT'S COOL.
YOU'RE STILL WORTH DECORATING FOR.
I WOULDN'T COUNT ON YOUR UNCLE MAKING IT, THOUGH. HE'S... CAUGHT UP IN SOME THINGS AGAIN.
BECAUSE OF ME. HE'S IN DEBT TO BAD PEOPLE BECAUSE OF ME.
MILES, IT'S NOT--
DING DONG
MY MAN!
MY DUDE.
SORRY I DON'T HAVE A PRESENT, BUT ALL MY MONEY WENT TO MAKING YOUR LAST CANISTER OF WEBFLUID. IN CASE YOU DECIDE TO COME OUT OF RETIREMENT OR WHATEVER THIS IS.
I'M JUST GLAD YOU'RE HERE, MAN. WE GOT PIZZA AND SODA AND--
CRASH
UH DID THAT CRASH COME FROM YOUR BEDROOM?
WAIT HERE. I'VE GOT THIS.

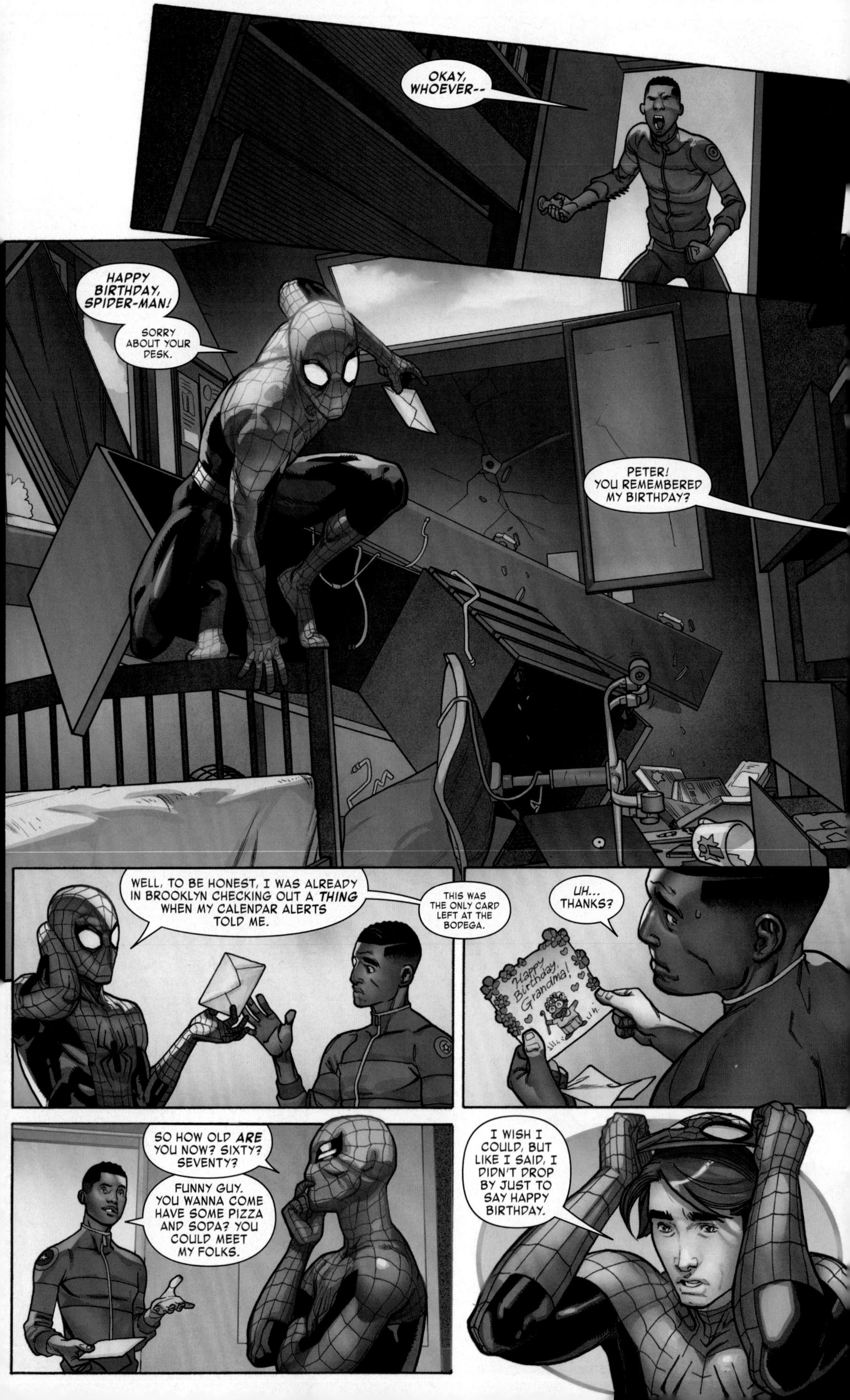

OKAY, WHOEVER--
HAPPY BIRTHDAY, SPIDER-MAN!
SORRY ABOUT YOUR DESK.
PETER! YOU REMEMBERED MY BIRTHDAY?
WELL, TO BE HONEST, I WAS ALREADY IN BROOKLYN CHECKING OUT A THING WHEN MY CALENDAR ALERTS TOLD ME.
THIS WAS THE ONLY CARD LEFT AT THE BODEGA.
Happy Birthday, Grandma!
UH... THANKS?
SO HOW OLD ARE YOU NOW? SIXTY? SEVENTY?
FUNNY GUY. YOU WANNA COME HAVE SOME PIZZA AND SODA? YOU COULD MEET MY FOLKS.
I WISH I COULD, BUT LIKE I SAID, I DIDN'T DROP BY JUST TO SAY HAPPY BIRTHDAY.

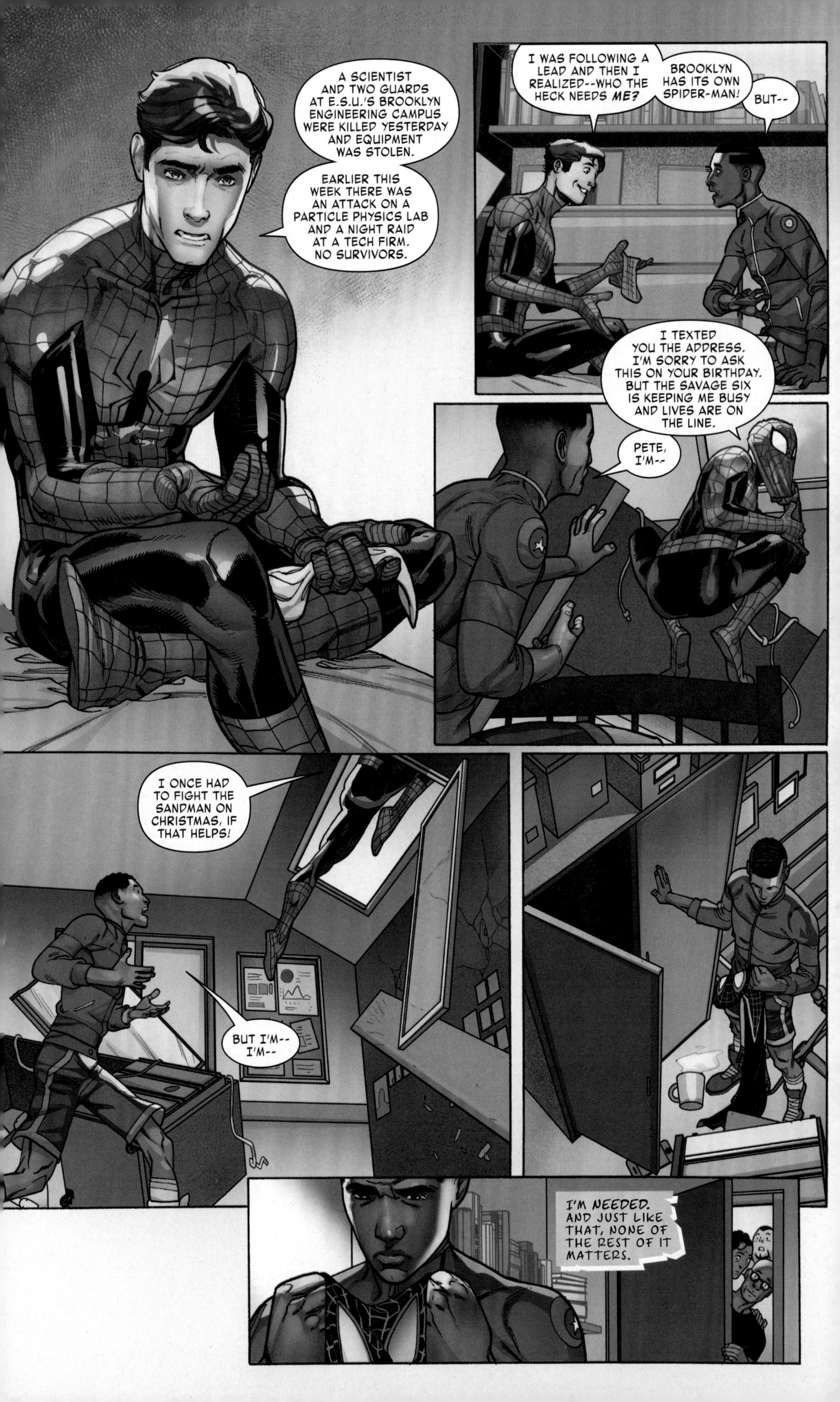
A SCIENTIST AND TWO GUARDS AT E.S.U.'S BROOKLYN ENGINEERING CAMPUS WERE KILLED YESTERDAY AND EQUIPMENT WAS STOLEN.
EARLIER THIS WEEK THERE WAS AN ATTACK ON A PARTICLE PHYSICS LAB AND A NIGHT RAID AT A TECH FIRM. NO SURVIVORS.
I WAS FOLLOWING A LEAD AND THEN I REALIZED--WHO THE HECK NEEDS *ME?*
BROOKLYN HAS ITS OWN SPIDER-MAN!
BUT--
I TEXTED YOU THE ADDRESS. I'M SORRY TO ASK THIS ON YOUR BIRTHDAY. BUT THE SAVAGE SIX IS KEEPING ME BUSY AND LIVES ARE ON THE LINE.
PETE, I'M--
I ONCE HAD TO FIGHT THE SANDMAN ON CHRISTMAS, IF THAT HELPS!
BUT I'M-- I'M--
I'M NEEDED. AND JUST LIKE THAT, NONE OF THE REST OF IT MATTERS.

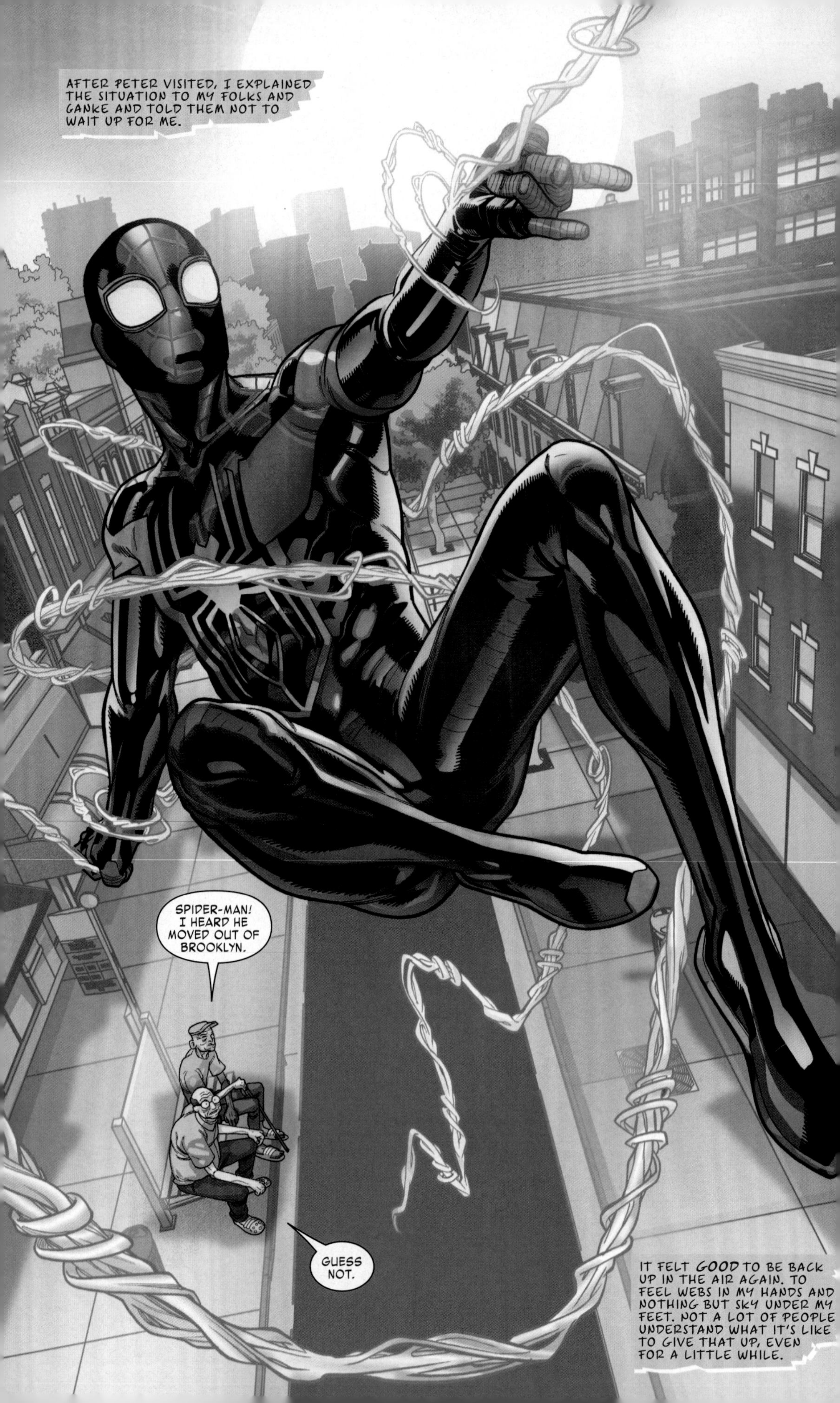
AFTER PETER VISITED, I EXPLAINED THE SITUATION TO MY FOLKS AND GANKE AND TOLD THEM NOT TO WAIT UP FOR ME.
SPIDER-MAN! I HEARD HE MOVED OUT OF BROOKLYN.
GUESS NOT.
IT FELT *GOOD* TO BE BACK UP IN THE AIR AGAIN. TO FEEL WEBS IN MY HANDS AND NOTHING BUT SKY UNDER MY FEET. NOT A LOT OF PEOPLE UNDERSTAND WHAT IT'S LIKE TO GIVE THAT UP, EVEN FOR A LITTLE WHILE.

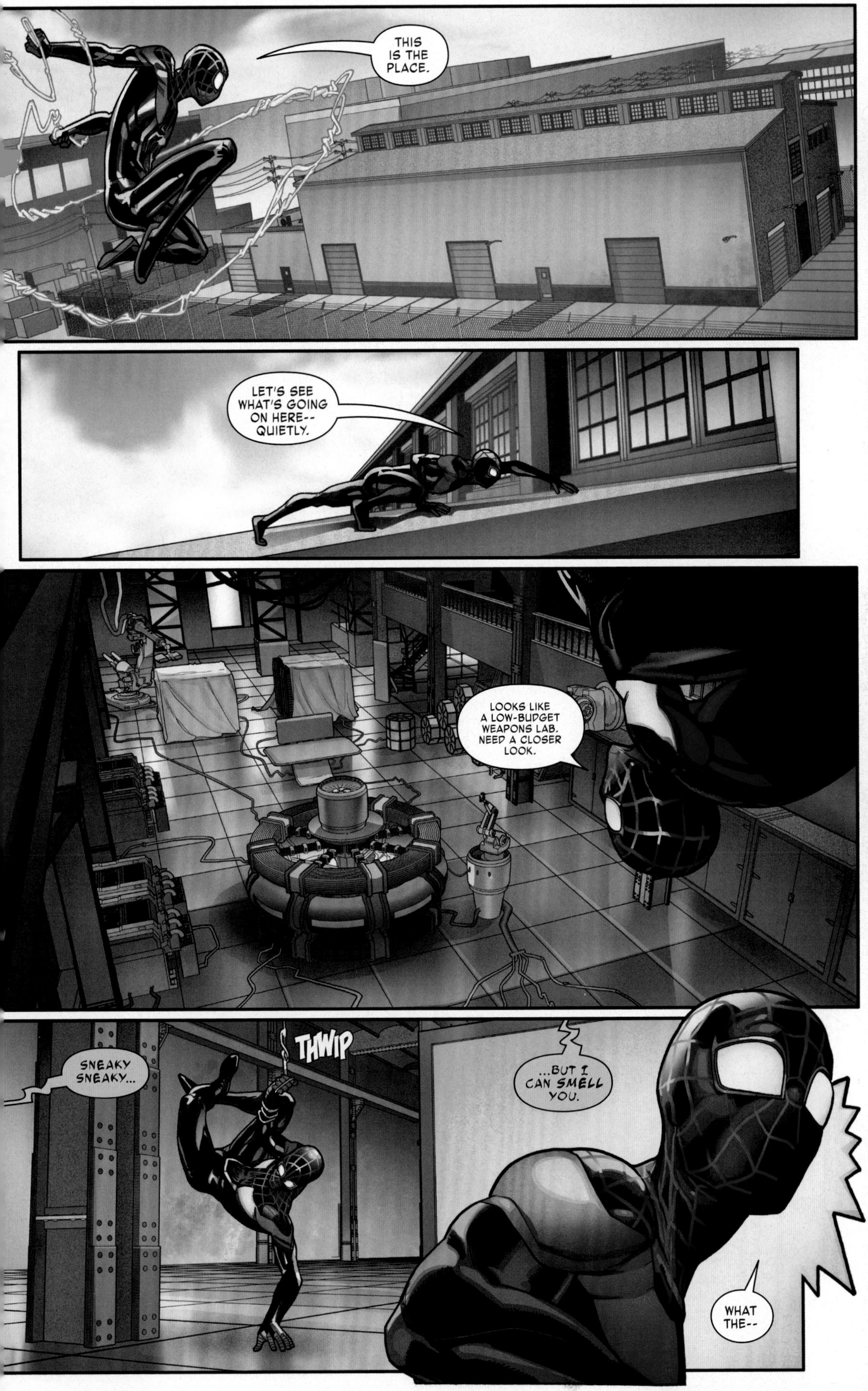
THIS IS THE PLACE.
LET'S SEE WHAT'S GOING ON HERE-- QUIETLY.
LOOKS LIKE A LOW-BUDGET WEAPONS LAB. NEED A CLOSER LOOK.
SNEAKY SNEAKY...
THWIP
...BUT I CAN SMELL YOU.
WHAT THE--

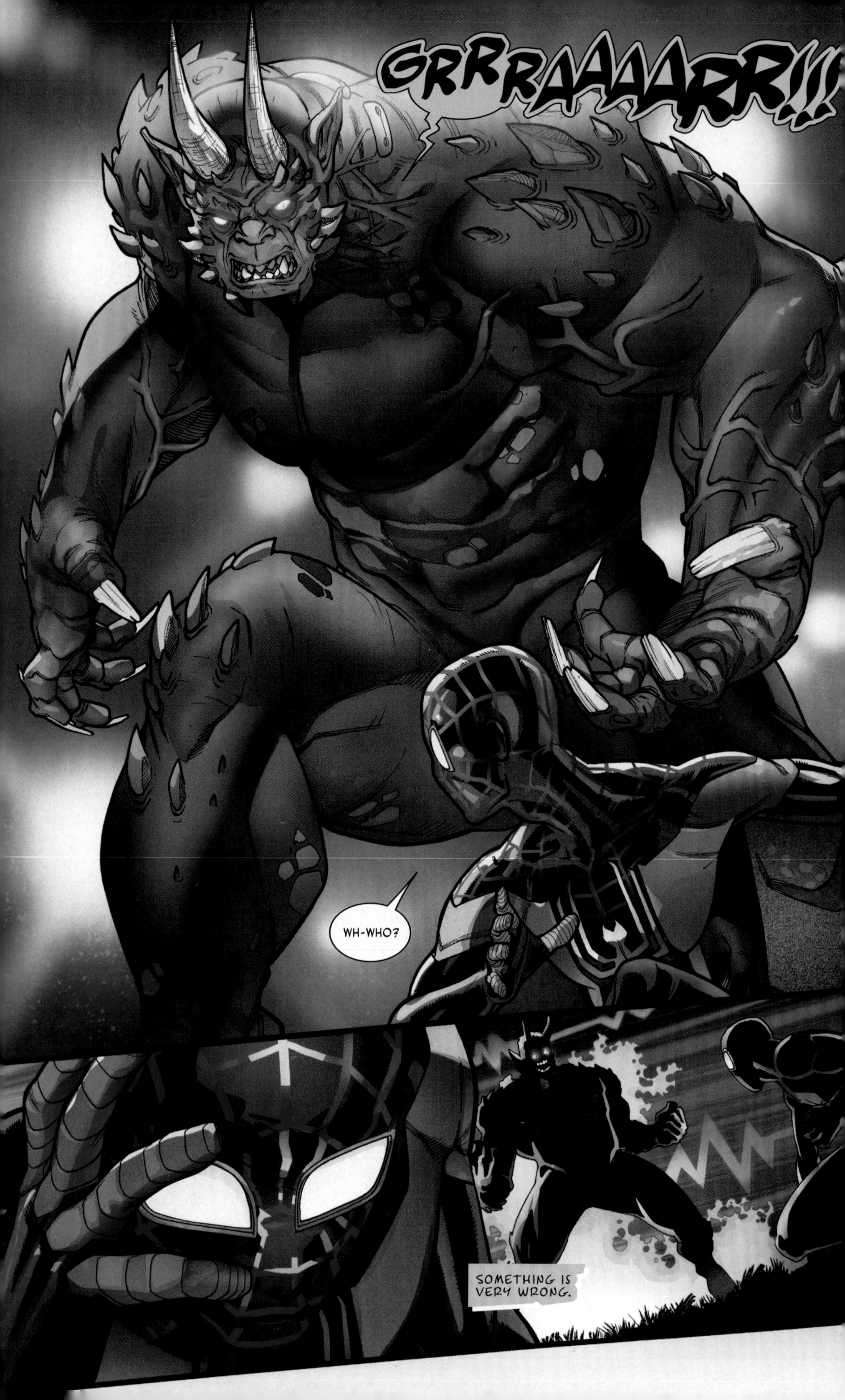
GRRRAAAAARR!!
WH-WHO?
SOMETHING IS VERY WRONG.

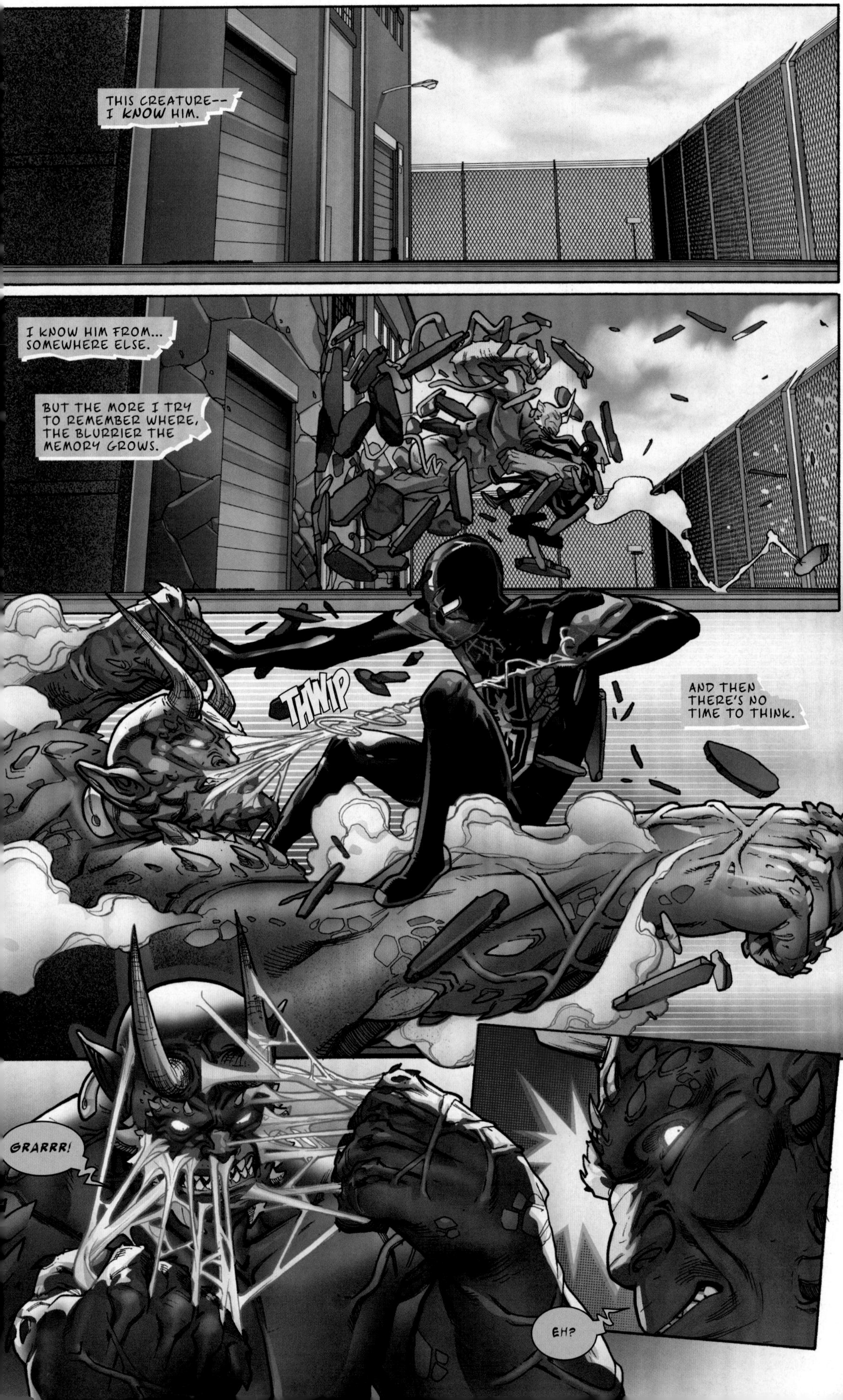

THIS CREATURE-- I KNOW HIM.
I KNOW HIM FROM... SOMEWHERE ELSE.
BUT THE MORE I TRY TO REMEMBER WHERE, THE BLURRIER THE MEMORY GROWS.
THWIP
AND THEN THERE'S NO TIME TO THINK.
GRARRR!
EH?

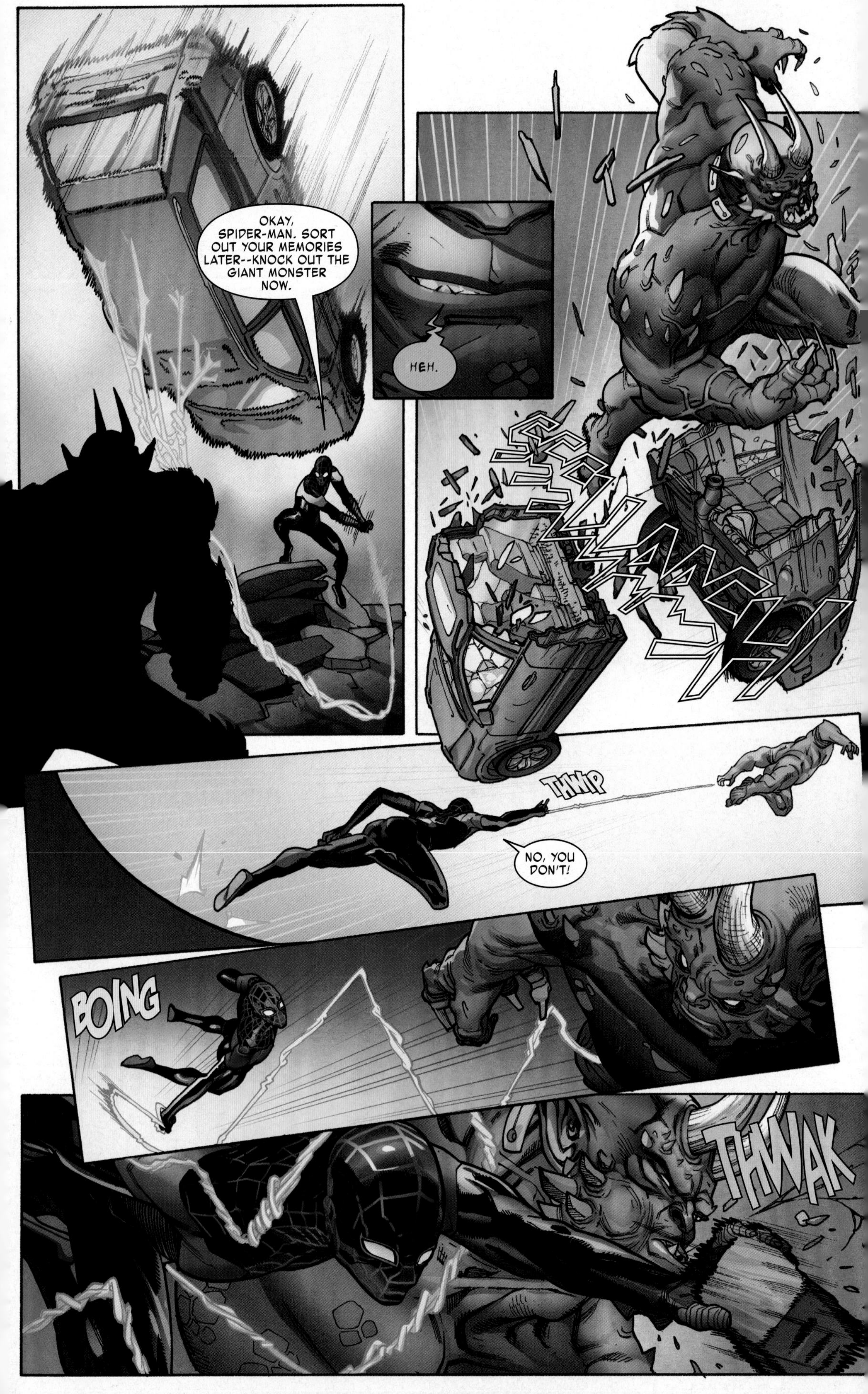
OKAY, SPIDER-MAN. SORT OUT YOUR MEMORIES LATER--KNOCK OUT THE GIANT MONSTER NOW.
HEH.
SCHLAMMM!
THWIP
NO, YOU DON'T!
BOING
THWAK

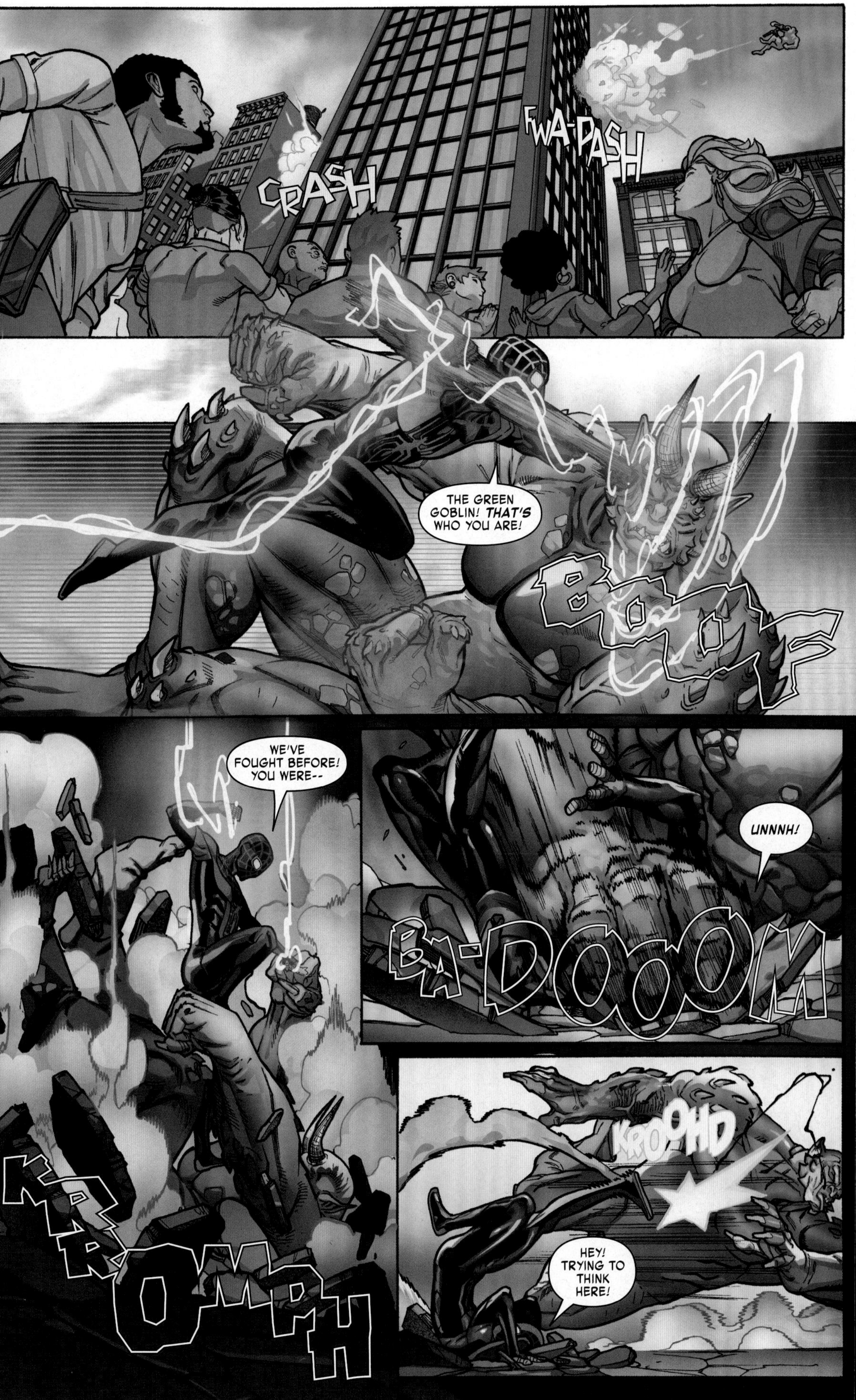
CRASH
FWA-PASH
THE GREEN GOBLIN! THAT'S WHO YOU ARE!
BOOF
WE'VE FOUGHT BEFORE! YOU WERE--
KRROMPH
UNNNH!
BA-DOOOOM
KROOHD
HEY! TRYING TO THINK HERE!

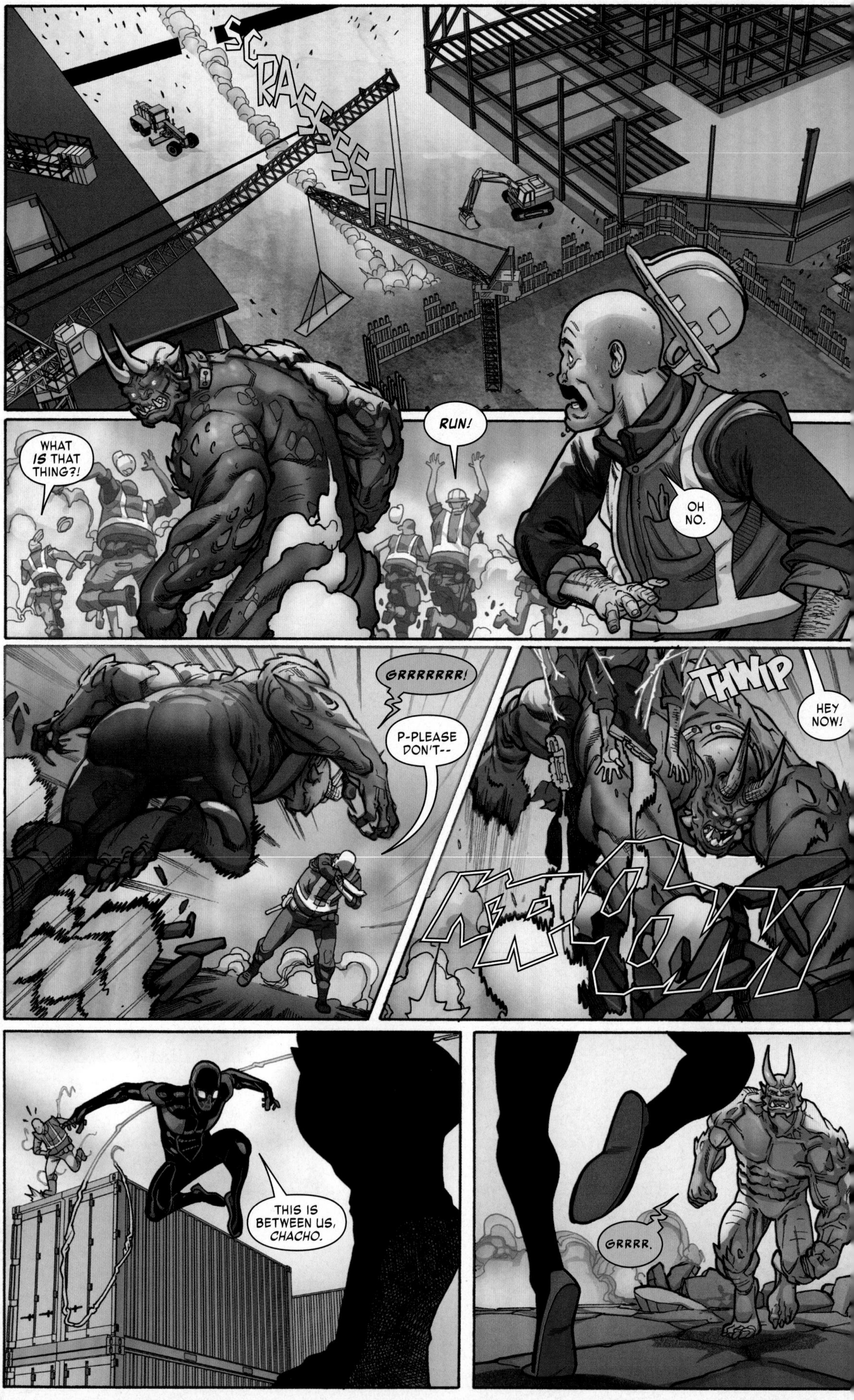
SCRASSSSH
WHAT IS THAT THING?!
RUN!
OH NO.
GRRRRRRR!
P-PLEASE DON'T--
THWIP
HEY NOW!
THIS IS BETWEEN US, CHACHO.
GRRRR.

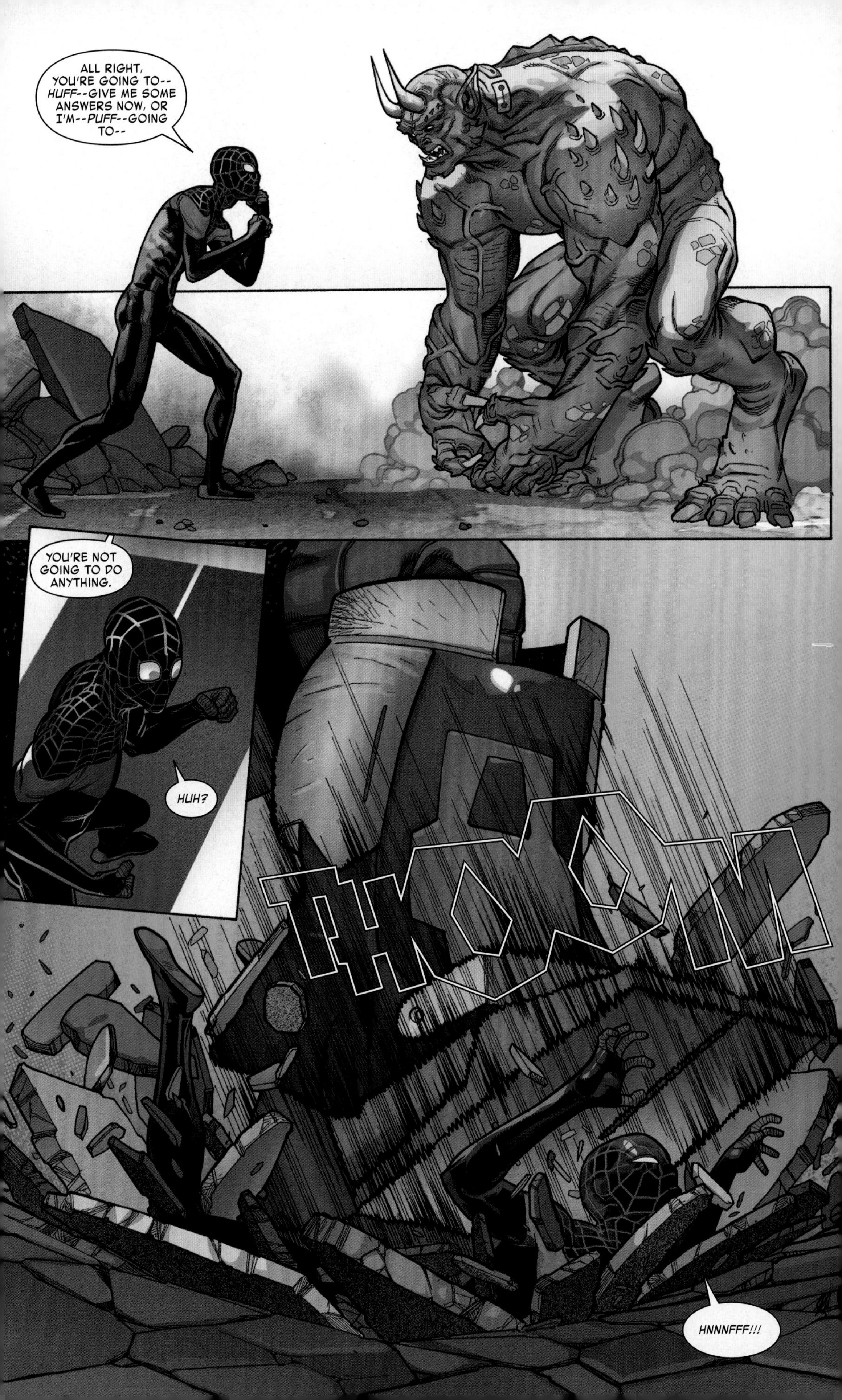
ALL RIGHT, YOU'RE GOING TO-- HUFF--GIVE ME SOME ANSWERS NOW, OR I'M--PUFF--GOING TO--
YOU'RE NOT GOING TO DO ANYTHING.
HUH?
THOOM
HNNNFFF!!!

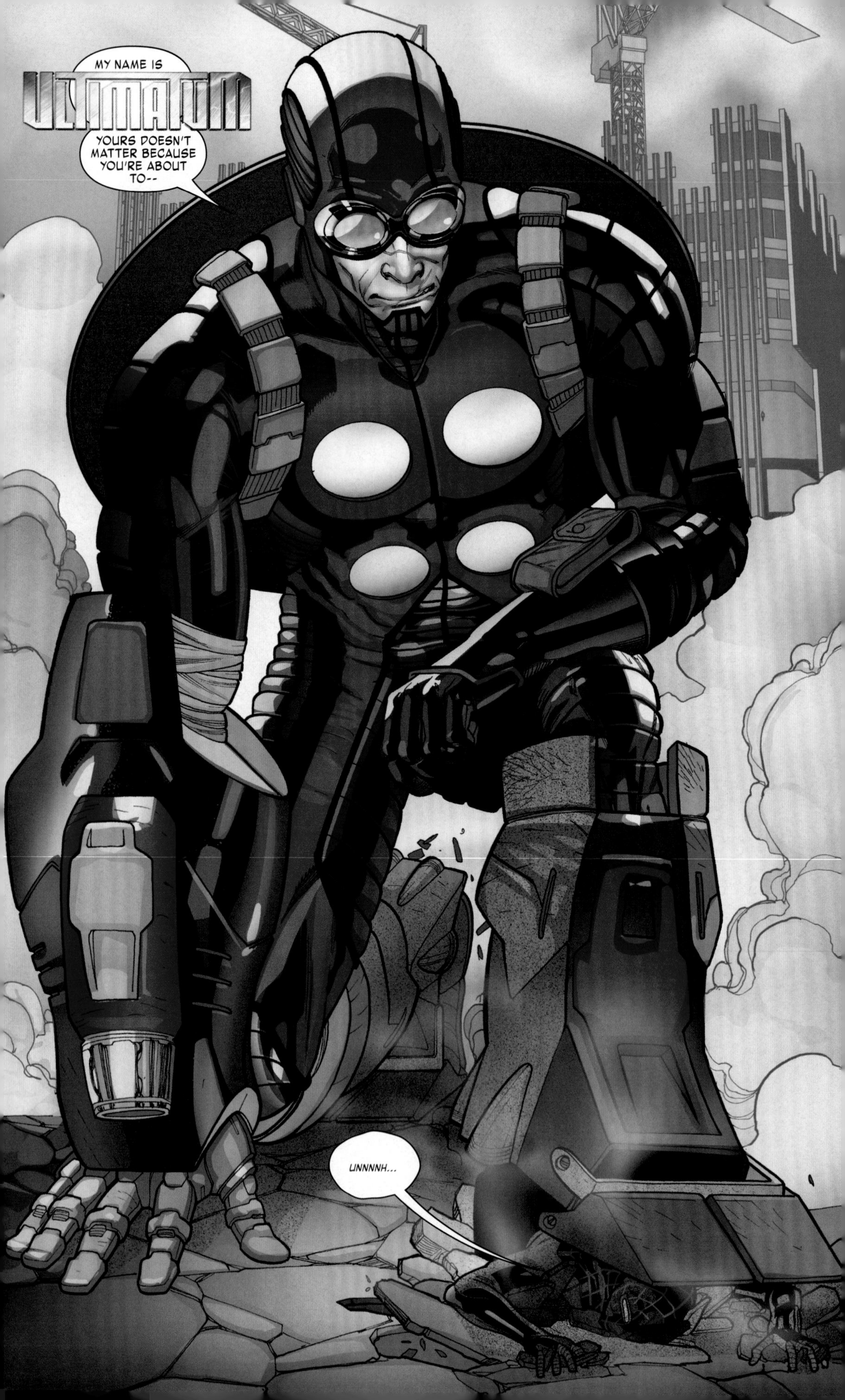
MY NAME IS
ULTIMATUM
YOURS DOESN'T MATTER BECAUSE YOU'RE ABOUT TO--
UNNNNH...

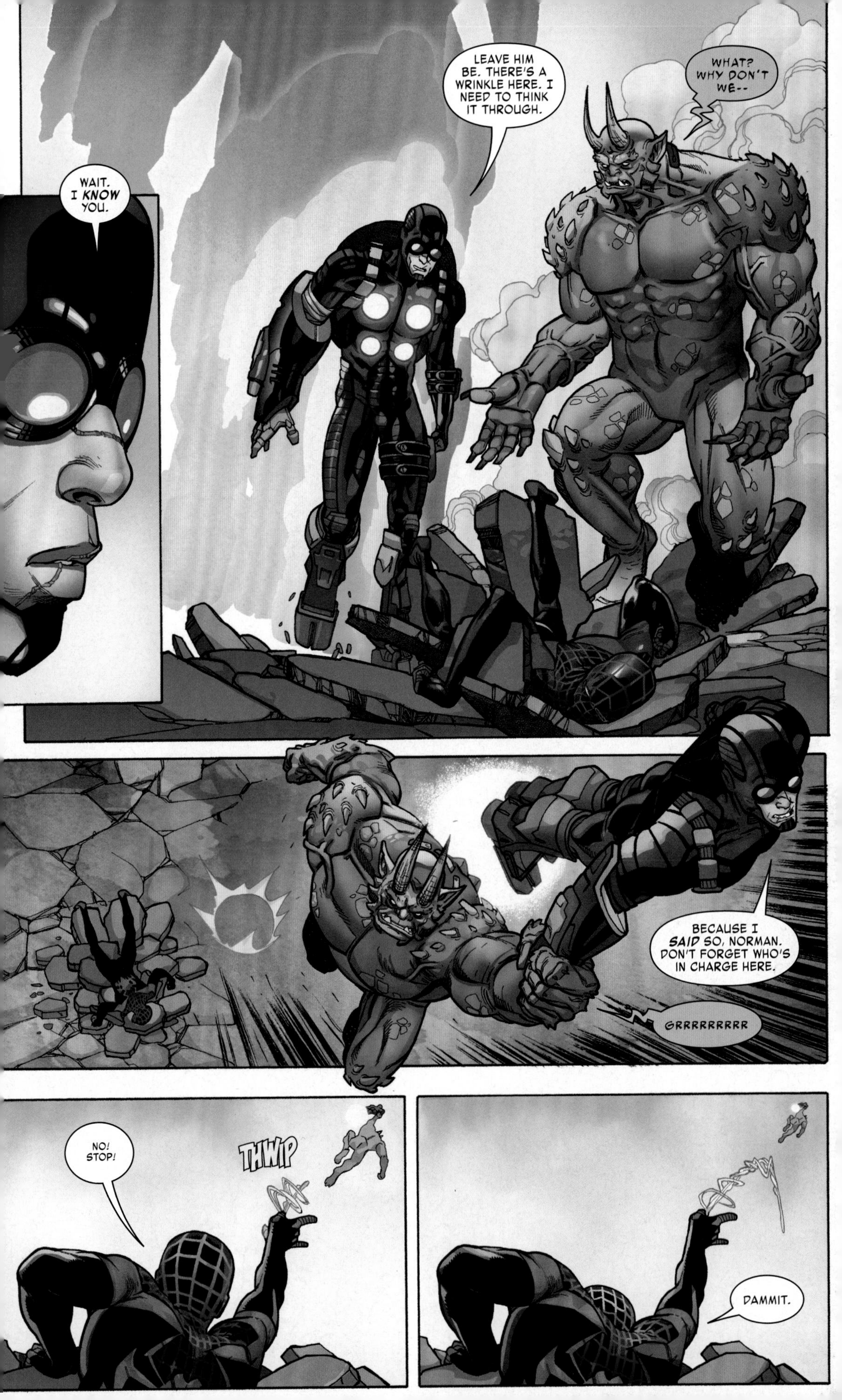
WAIT. I *KNOW* YOU.
LEAVE HIM BE. THERE'S A WRINKLE HERE. I NEED TO THINK IT THROUGH.
WHAT? WHY DON'T WE--
BECAUSE I *SAID* SO, NORMAN. DON'T FORGET WHO'S IN CHARGE HERE.
GRRRRRRRRR
NO! STOP!
THWIP
DAMMIT.

THE GIANT ONE KNEW ME, JOURNAL. BUT WHO WAS HE?

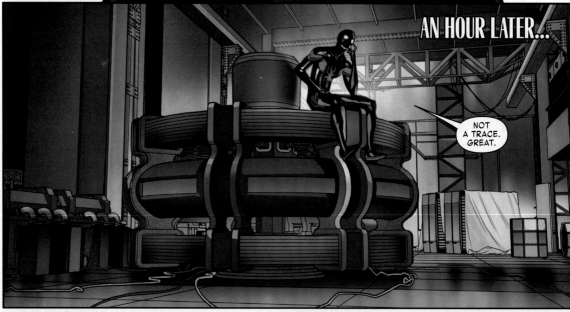

AN HOUR LATER...

NOT A TRACE. GREAT.

NO ANSWERS. NO TRAIL. NO CAKE. THIS BIRTHDAY TURNED OUT TO BE SOME BUNK.

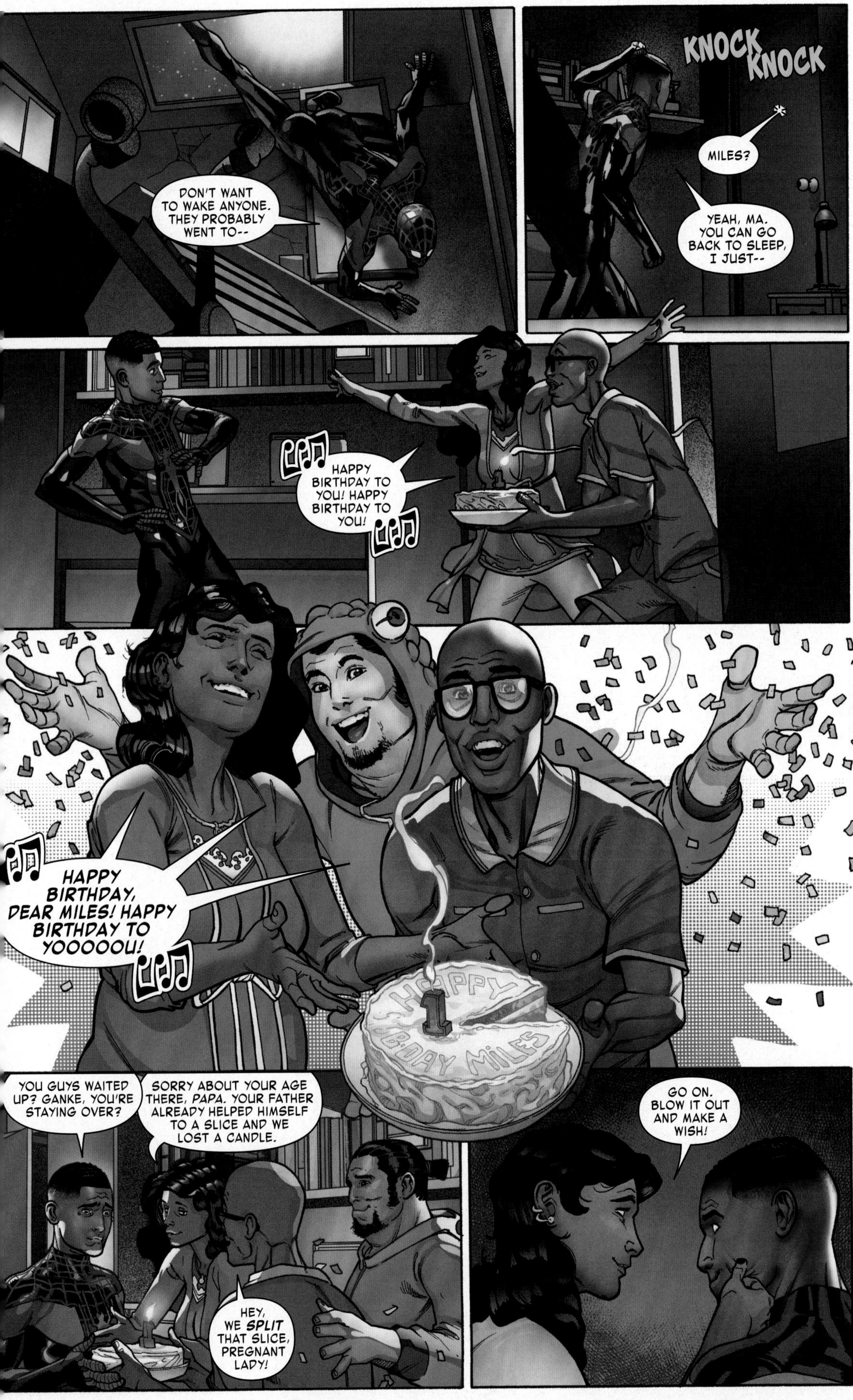
DON'T WANT TO WAKE ANYONE. THEY PROBABLY WENT TO--
KNOCK KNOCK
MILES?
YEAH, MA. YOU CAN GO BACK TO SLEEP, I JUST--
HAPPY BIRTHDAY TO YOU! HAPPY BIRTHDAY TO YOU!
HAPPY BIRTHDAY, DEAR MILES! HAPPY BIRTHDAY TO YOOOOOU!
HAPPY B-DAY MILES
YOU GUYS WAITED UP? GANKE, YOU'RE STAYING OVER?
SORRY ABOUT YOUR AGE THERE, *PAPA*. YOUR FATHER ALREADY HELPED HIMSELF TO A SLICE AND WE LOST A CANDLE.
HEY, WE *SPLIT* THAT SLICE, PREGNANT LADY!
GO ON. BLOW IT OUT AND MAKE A WISH!

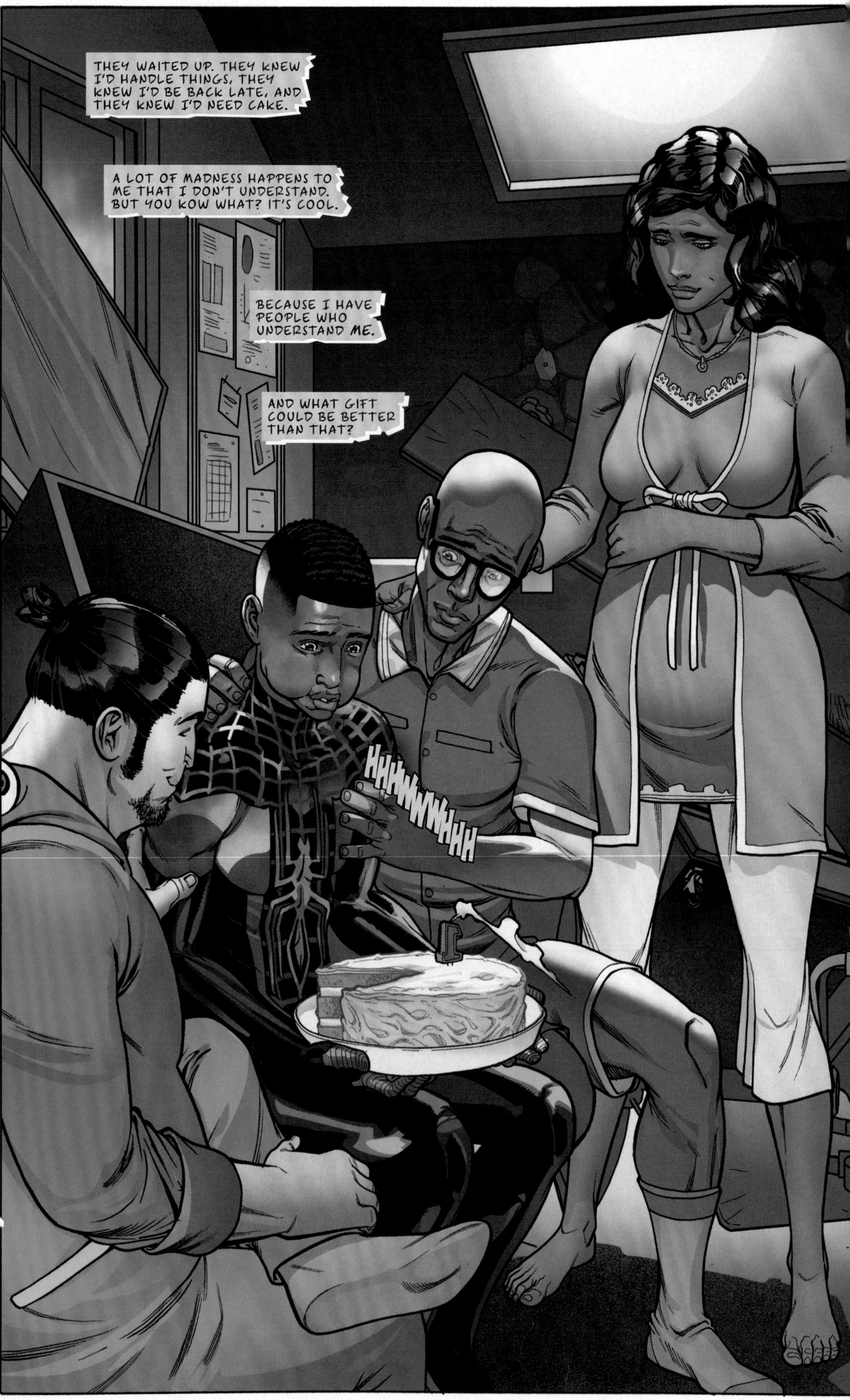
THEY WAITED UP. THEY KNEW I'D HANDLE THINGS, THEY KNEW I'D BE BACK LATE, AND THEY KNEW I'D NEED CAKE.
A LOT OF MADNESS HAPPENS TO ME THAT I DON'T UNDERSTAND. BUT YOU KOW WHAT? IT'S COOL.
BECAUSE I HAVE PEOPLE WHO UNDERSTAND ME.
AND WHAT GIFT COULD BE BETTER THAN THAT?
HHHWWWHHH

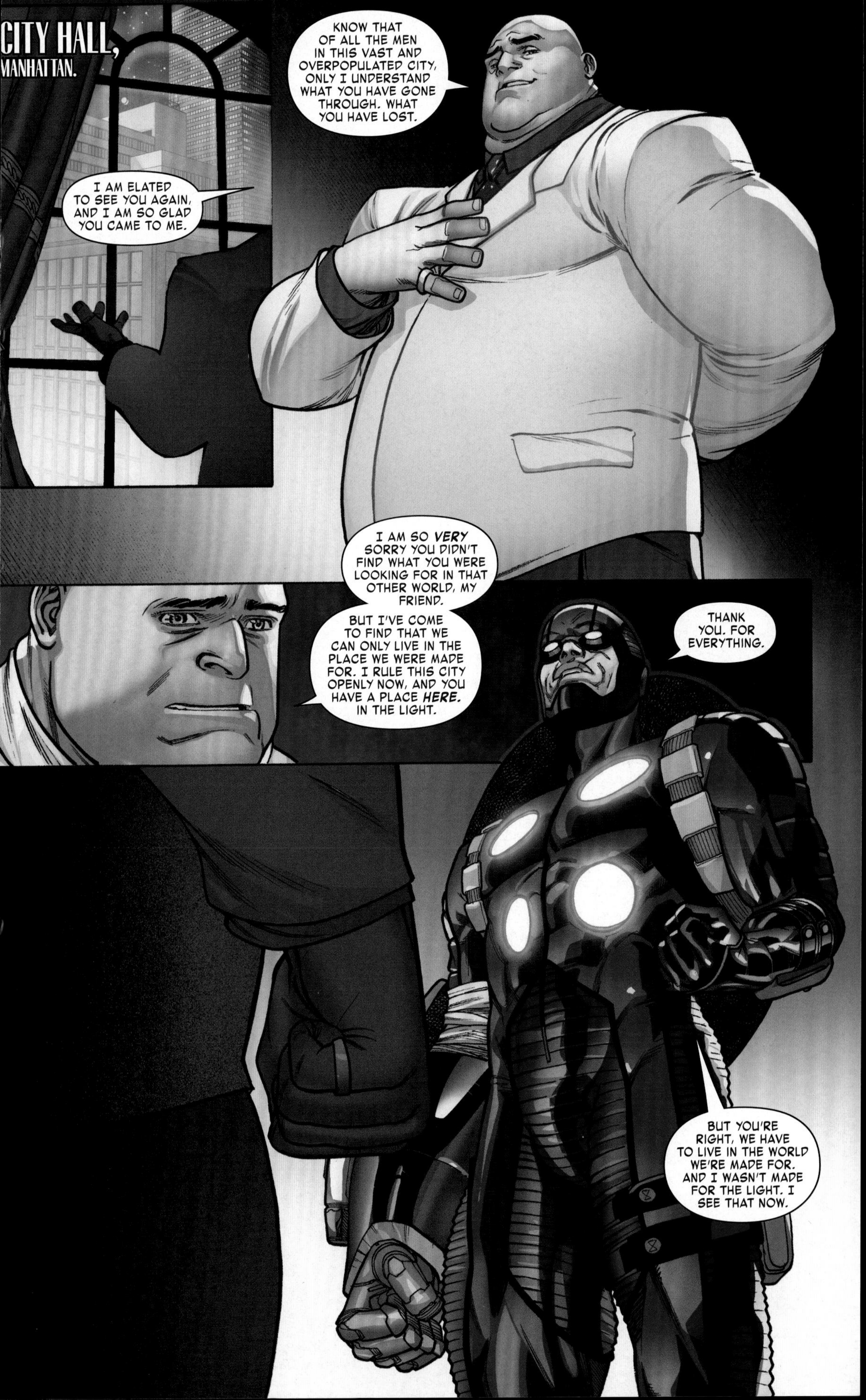
CITY HALL, MANHATTAN.
KNOW THAT OF ALL THE MEN IN THIS VAST AND OVERPOPULATED CITY, ONLY I UNDERSTAND WHAT YOU HAVE GONE THROUGH. WHAT YOU HAVE LOST.
I AM ELATED TO SEE YOU AGAIN, AND I AM SO GLAD YOU CAME TO ME.
I AM SO VERY SORRY YOU DIDN'T FIND WHAT YOU WERE LOOKING FOR IN THAT OTHER WORLD, MY FRIEND.
BUT I'VE COME TO FIND THAT WE CAN ONLY LIVE IN THE PLACE WE WERE MADE FOR. I RULE THIS CITY OPENLY NOW, AND YOU HAVE A PLACE HERE. IN THE LIGHT.
THANK YOU. FOR EVERYTHING.
BUT YOU'RE RIGHT, WE HAVE TO LIVE IN THE WORLD WE'RE MADE FOR. AND I WASN'T MADE FOR THE LIGHT. I SEE THAT NOW.

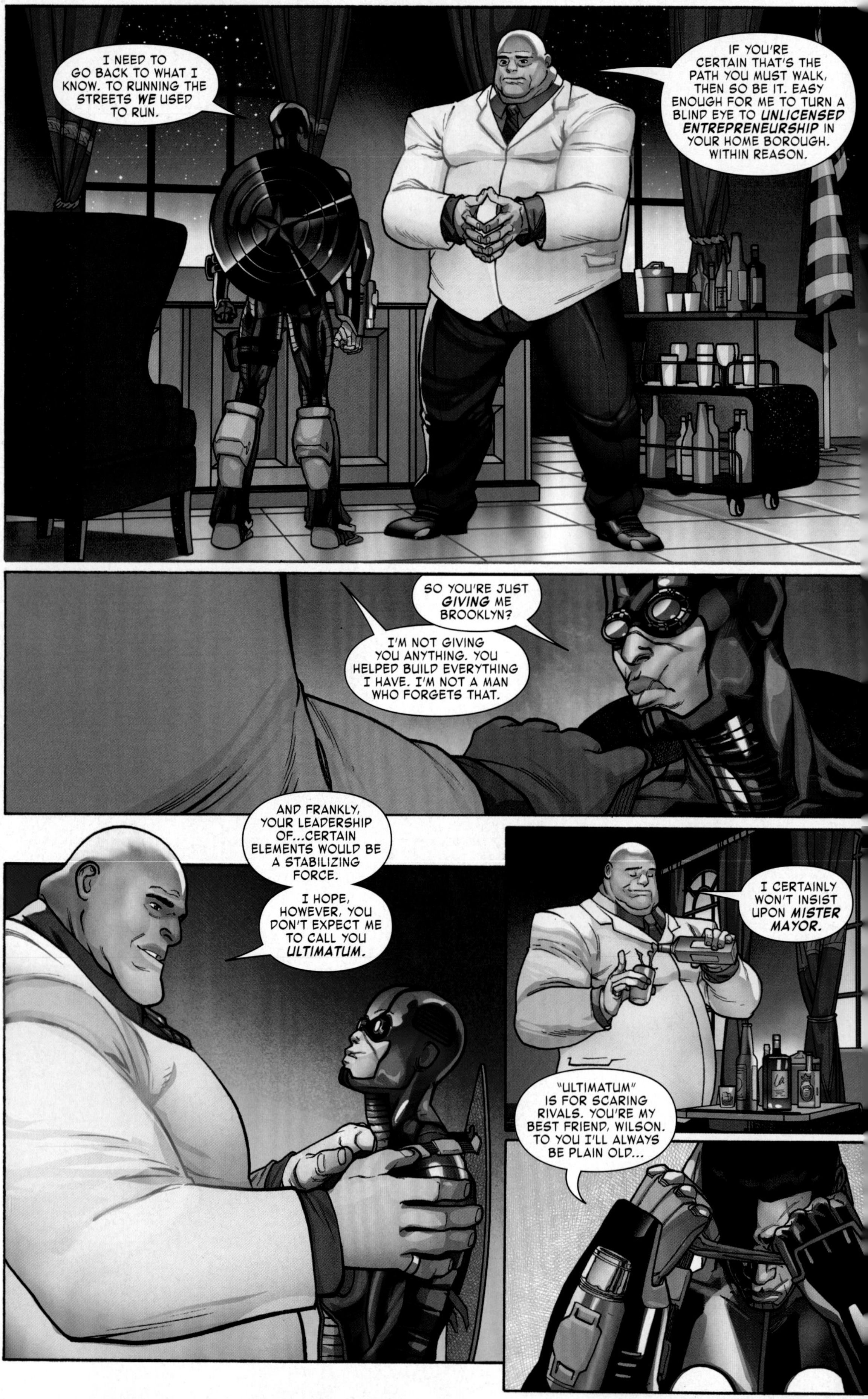
I NEED TO GO BACK TO WHAT I KNOW. TO RUNNING THE STREETS *WE* USED TO RUN.
IF YOU'RE CERTAIN THAT'S THE PATH YOU MUST WALK, THEN SO BE IT. EASY ENOUGH FOR ME TO TURN A BLIND EYE TO *UNLICENSED ENTREPRENEURSHIP* IN YOUR HOME BOROUGH. WITHIN REASON.
SO YOU'RE JUST *GIVING* ME BROOKLYN?
I'M NOT GIVING YOU ANYTHING. YOU HELPED BUILD EVERYTHING I HAVE. I'M NOT A MAN WHO FORGETS THAT.
AND FRANKLY, YOUR LEADERSHIP OF...CERTAIN ELEMENTS WOULD BE A STABILIZING FORCE.
I HOPE, HOWEVER, YOU DON'T EXPECT ME TO CALL YOU *ULTIMATUM.*
I CERTAINLY WON'T INSIST UPON *MISTER MAYOR.*
"ULTIMATUM" IS FOR SCARING RIVALS. YOU'RE MY BEST FRIEND, WILSON. TO YOU I'LL ALWAYS BE PLAIN OLD...

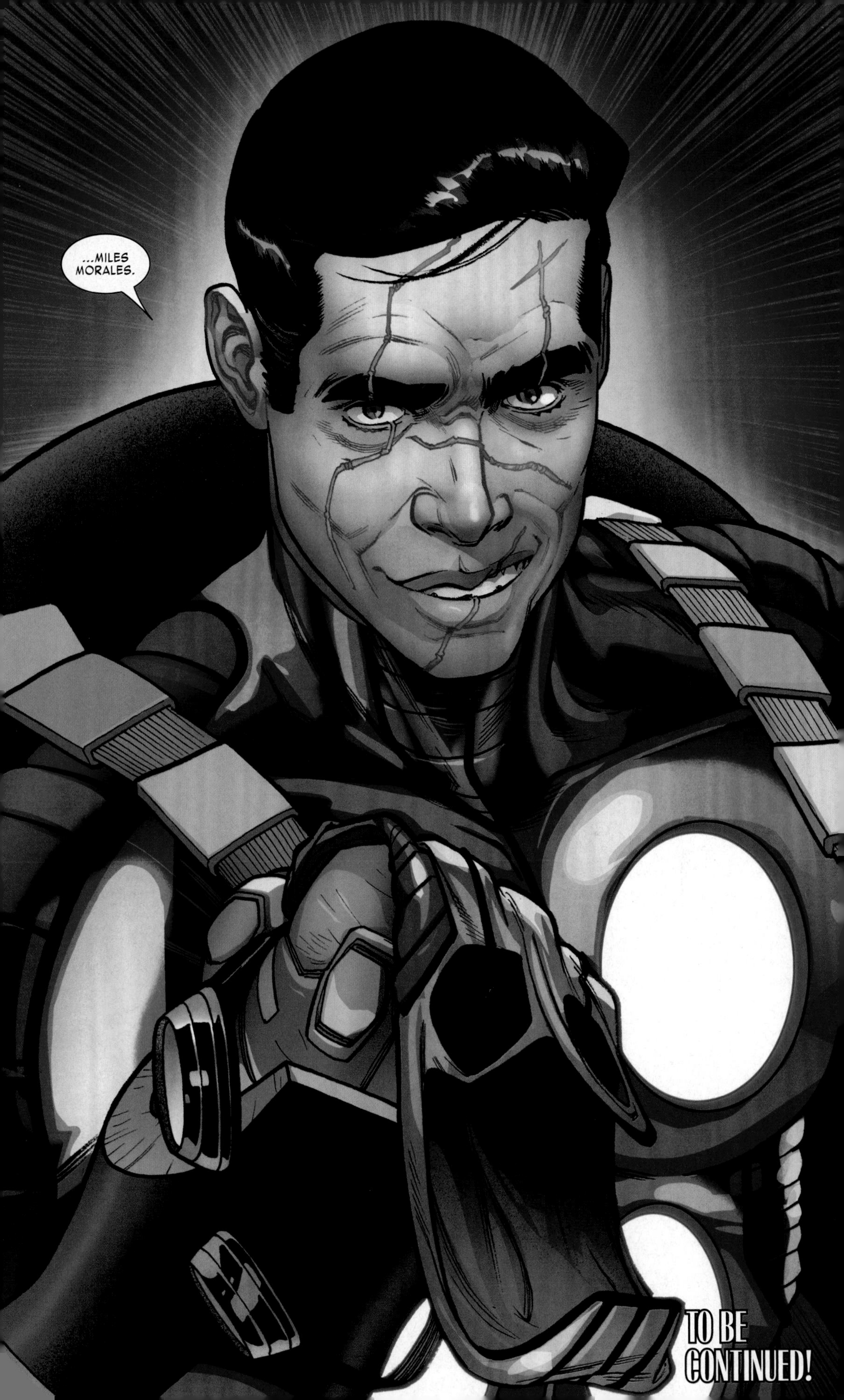
...MILES MORALES.
TO BE CONTINUED!

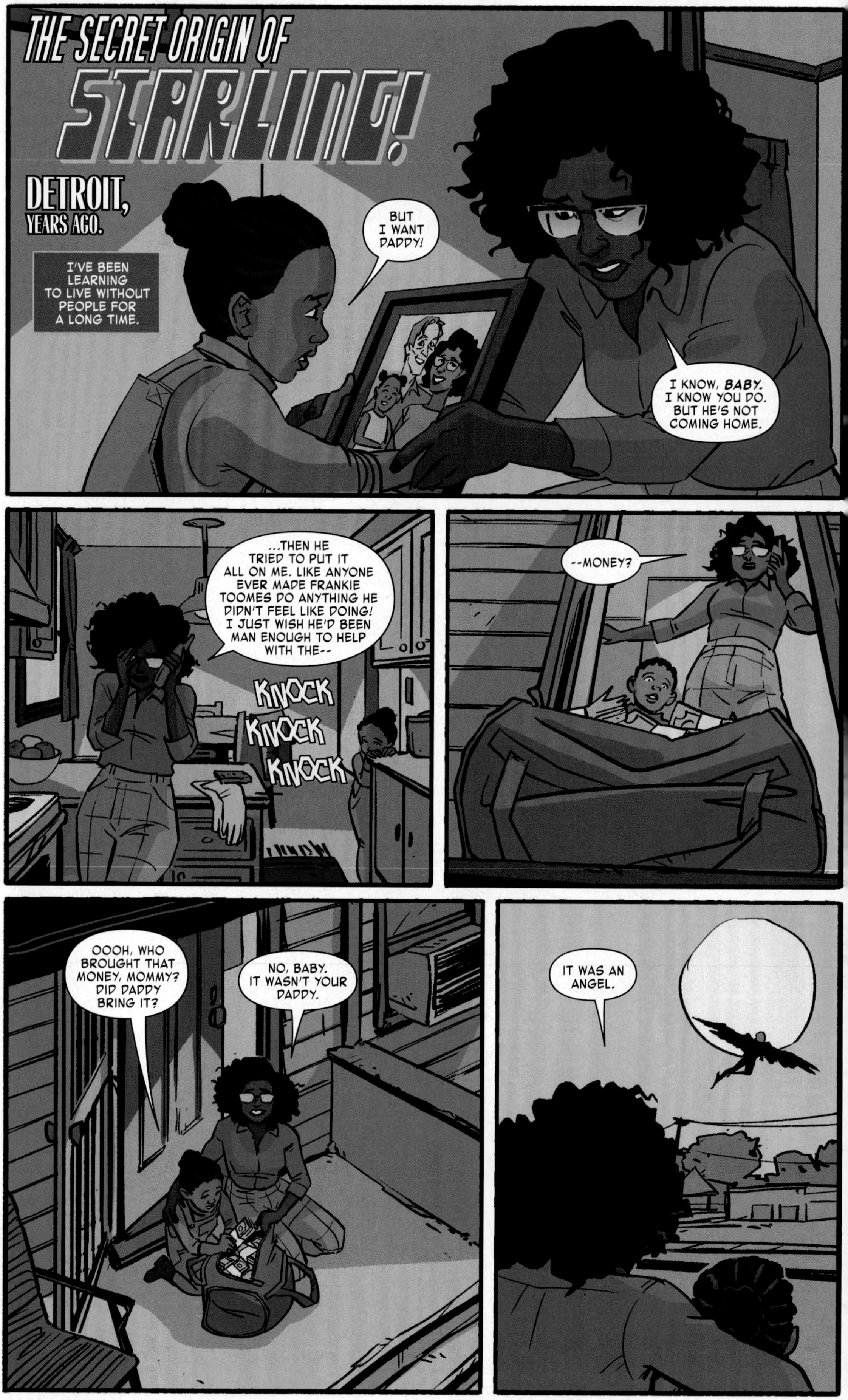
THE SECRET ORIGIN OF
STARLING!
DETROIT, YEARS AGO.
I'VE BEEN LEARNING TO LIVE WITHOUT PEOPLE FOR A LONG TIME.
BUT I WANT DADDY!
I KNOW, BABY. I KNOW YOU DO. BUT HE'S NOT COMING HOME.
...THEN HE TRIED TO PUT IT ALL ON ME. LIKE ANYONE EVER MADE FRANKIE TOOMES DO ANYTHING HE DIDN'T FEEL LIKE DOING! I JUST WISH HE'D BEEN MAN ENOUGH TO HELP WITH THE--
KNOCK KNOCK KNOCK
--MONEY?
OOOH, WHO BROUGHT THAT MONEY, MOMMY? DID DADDY BRING IT?
NO, BABY. IT WASN'T YOUR DADDY.
IT WAS AN ANGEL.

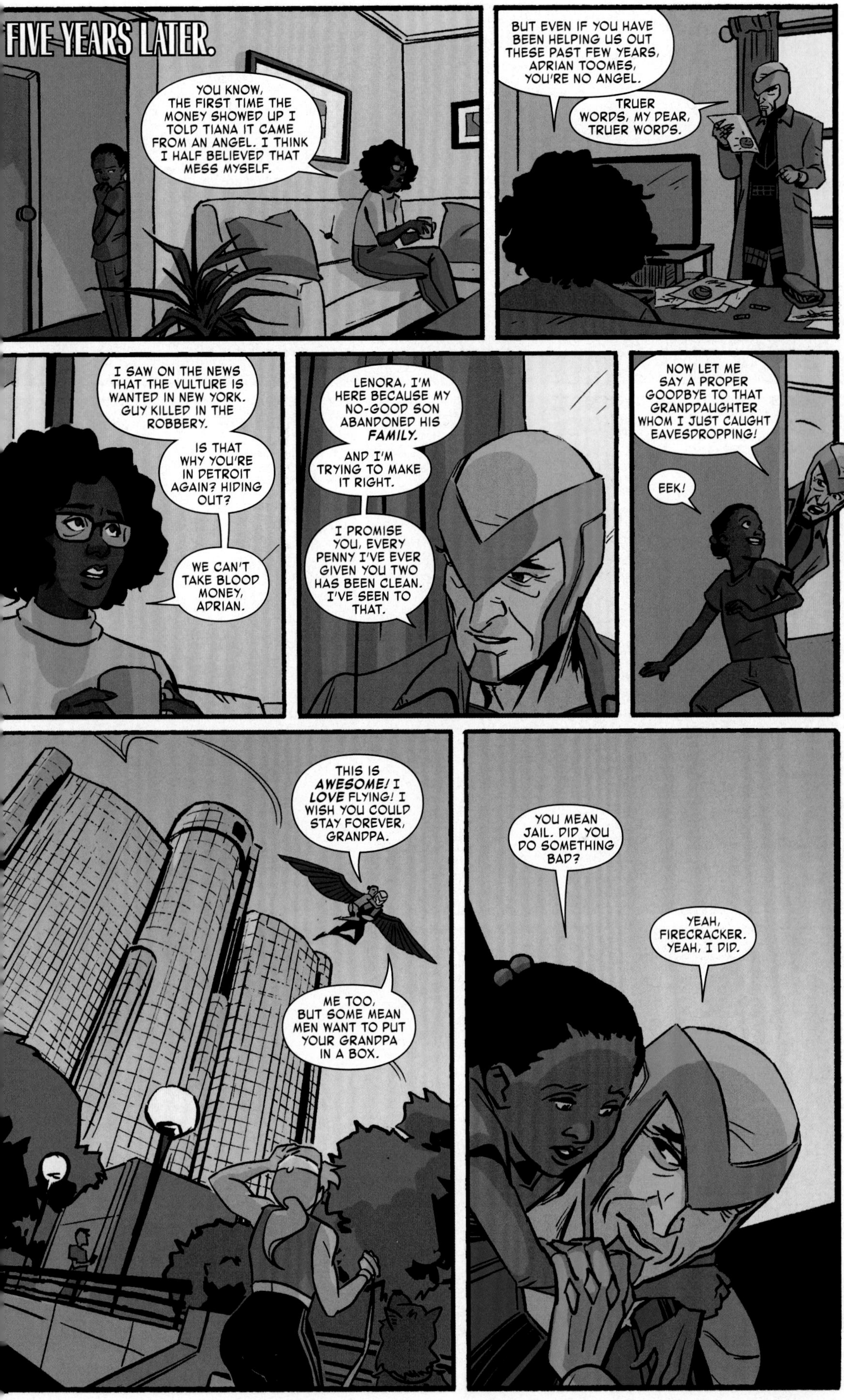

FIVE YEARS LATER.
YOU KNOW, THE FIRST TIME THE MONEY SHOWED UP I TOLD TIANA IT CAME FROM AN ANGEL. I THINK I HALF BELIEVED THAT MESS MYSELF.
BUT EVEN IF YOU HAVE BEEN HELPING US OUT THESE PAST FEW YEARS, ADRIAN TOOMES, YOU'RE NO ANGEL.
TRUER WORDS, MY DEAR, TRUER WORDS.
I SAW ON THE NEWS THAT THE VULTURE IS WANTED IN NEW YORK. GUY KILLED IN THE ROBBERY.
IS THAT WHY YOU'RE IN DETROIT AGAIN? HIDING OUT?
WE CAN'T TAKE BLOOD MONEY, ADRIAN.
LENORA, I'M HERE BECAUSE MY NO-GOOD SON ABANDONED HIS FAMILY.
AND I'M TRYING TO MAKE IT RIGHT.
I PROMISE YOU, EVERY PENNY I'VE EVER GIVEN YOU TWO HAS BEEN CLEAN. I'VE SEEN TO THAT.
NOW LET ME SAY A PROPER GOODBYE TO THAT GRANDDAUGHTER WHOM I JUST CAUGHT EAVESDROPPING!
EEK!
THIS IS AWESOME! I LOVE FLYING! I WISH YOU COULD STAY FOREVER, GRANDPA.
ME TOO, BUT SOME MEAN MEN WANT TO PUT YOUR GRANDPA IN A BOX.
YOU MEAN JAIL. DID YOU DO SOMETHING BAD?
YEAH, FIRECRACKER. YEAH, I DID.

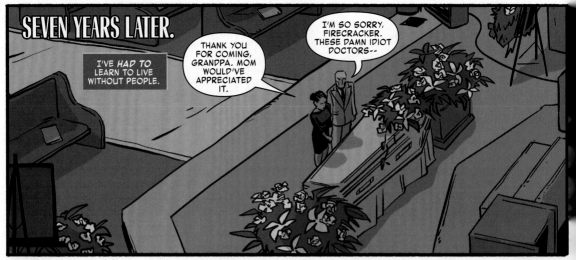

SEVEN YEARS LATER.

I'VE *HAD* TO LEARN TO LIVE WITHOUT PEOPLE.

THANK YOU FOR COMING, GRANDPA. MOM WOULD'VE APPRECIATED IT.

I'M SO SORRY, FIRECRACKER. THESE DAMN IDIOT DOCTORS--

SHE WAS SICK A LONG TIME. SHE'S HAPPIER NOW... DOES MY DAD EVEN KNOW? IS HE EVEN STILL ALIVE?

I...I DON'T KNOW. HE STOPPED TALKING TO ME A LONG TIME AGO.

I KNOW THE FEELING.

I CAN'T STICK AROUND TOO LONG. BUT WHEN YOU'RE READY-- AFTER THE SERVICE-- I HAVE SOMETHING TO SHOW YOU.

OH MY GOODNESS! IS IT...IS IT...

YOUR OWN SUIT. WANNA TEST IT OUT?

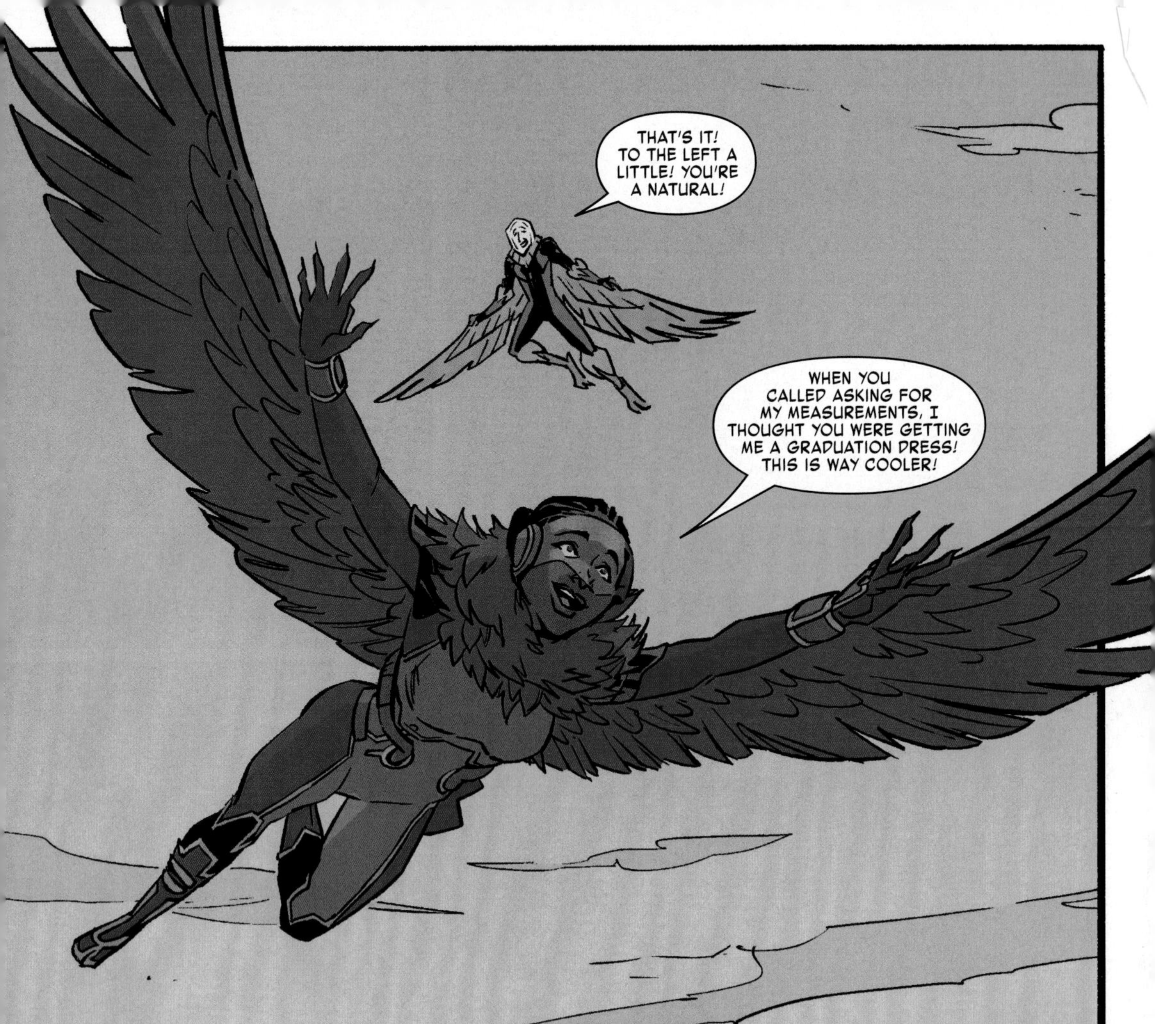
THAT'S IT! TO THE LEFT A LITTLE! YOU'RE A NATURAL!
WHEN YOU CALLED ASKING FOR MY MEASUREMENTS, I THOUGHT YOU WERE GETTING ME A GRADUATION DRESS! THIS IS WAY COOLER!

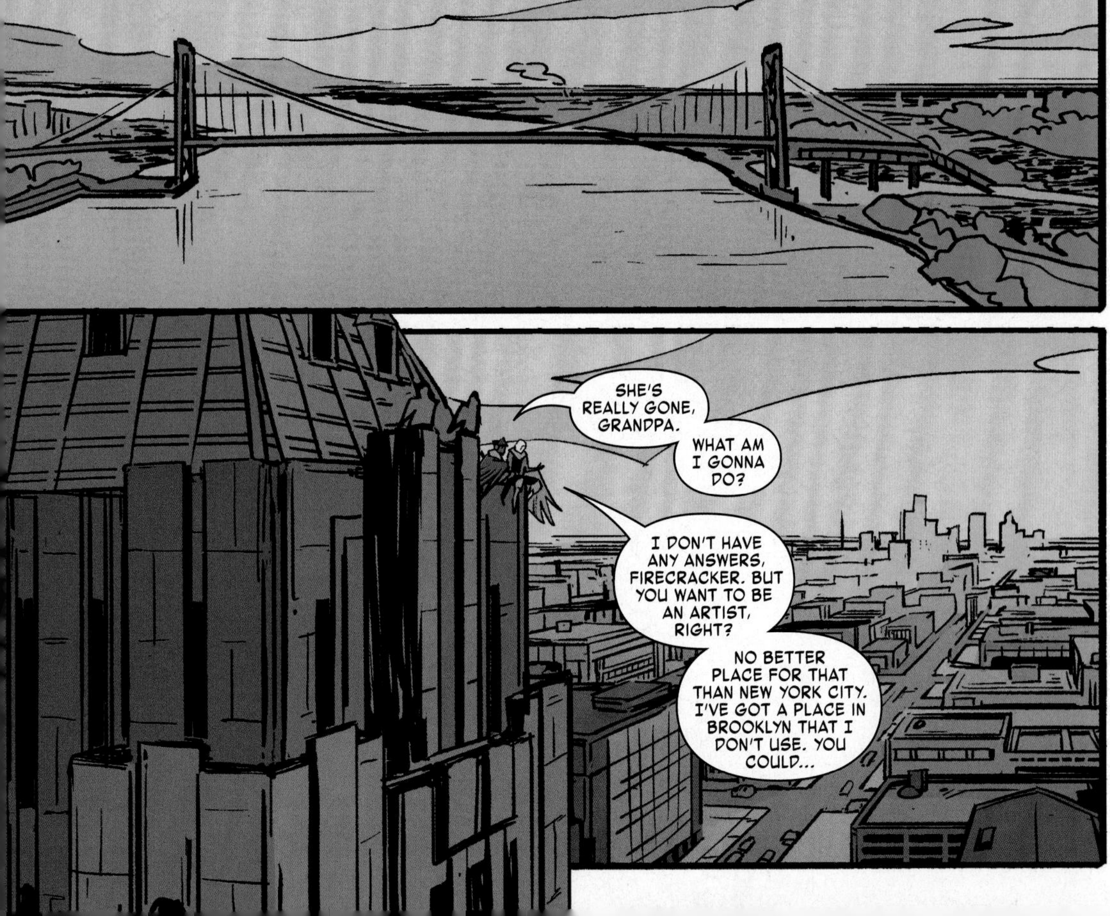
SHE'S REALLY GONE, GRANDPA.
WHAT AM I GONNA DO?
I DON'T HAVE ANY ANSWERS, FIRECRACKER. BUT YOU WANT TO BE AN ARTIST, RIGHT?
NO BETTER PLACE FOR THAT THAN NEW YORK CITY. I'VE GOT A PLACE IN BROOKLYN THAT I DON'T USE. YOU COULD...

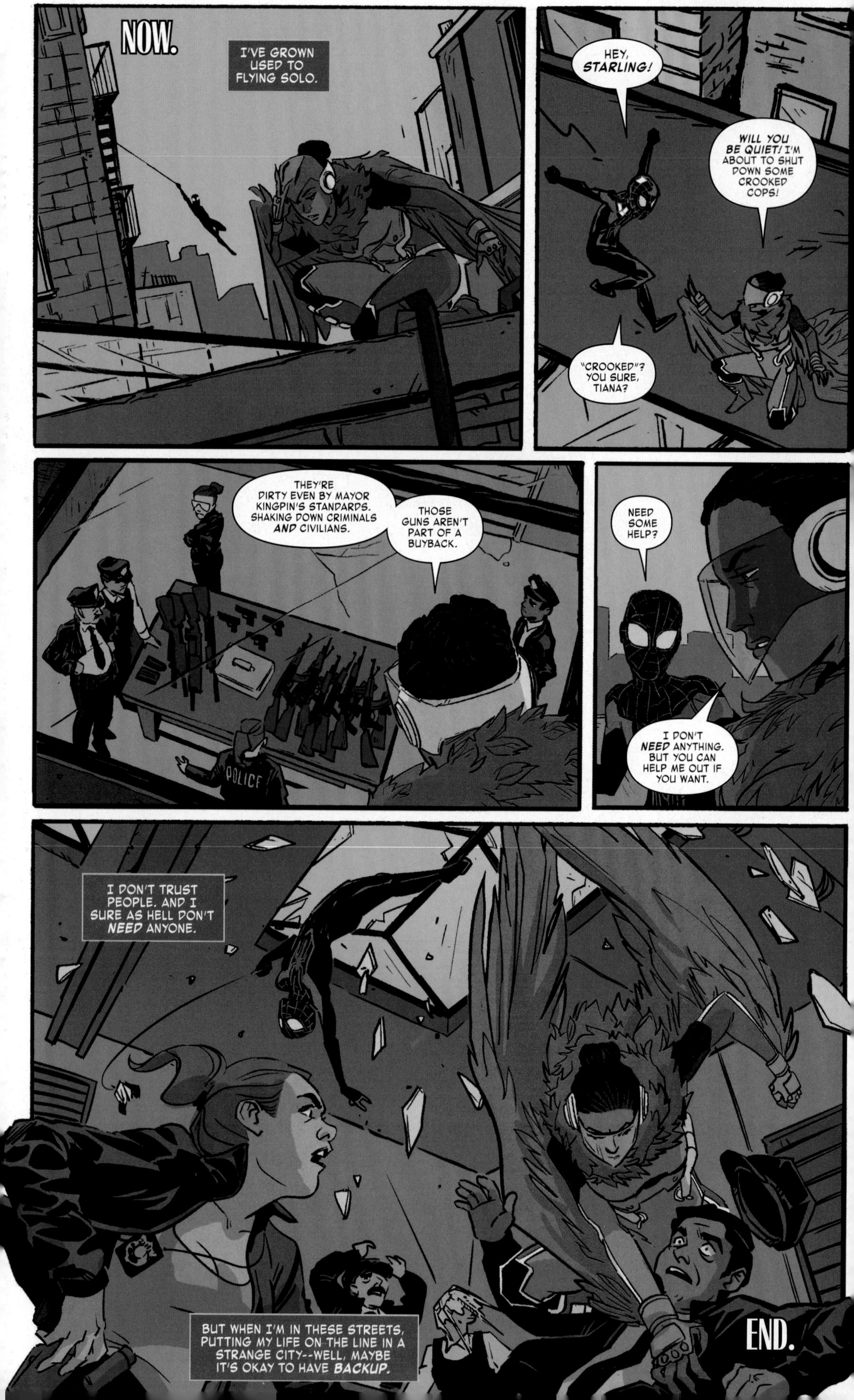
NOW.
I'VE GROWN USED TO FLYING SOLO.
HEY, STARLING!
WILL YOU BE QUIET! I'M ABOUT TO SHUT DOWN SOME CROOKED COPS!
"CROOKED"? YOU SURE, TIANA?
THEY'RE DIRTY EVEN BY MAYOR KINGPIN'S STANDARDS. SHAKING DOWN CRIMINALS AND CIVILIANS.
THOSE GUNS AREN'T PART OF A BUYBACK.
POLICE
NEED SOME HELP?
I DON'T NEED ANYTHING. BUT YOU CAN HELP ME OUT IF YOU WANT.
I DON'T TRUST PEOPLE. AND I SURE AS HELL DON'T NEED ANYONE.
BUT WHEN I'M IN THESE STREETS, PUTTING MY LIFE ON THE LINE IN A STRANGE CITY--WELL, MAYBE IT'S OKAY TO HAVE BACKUP.
END.

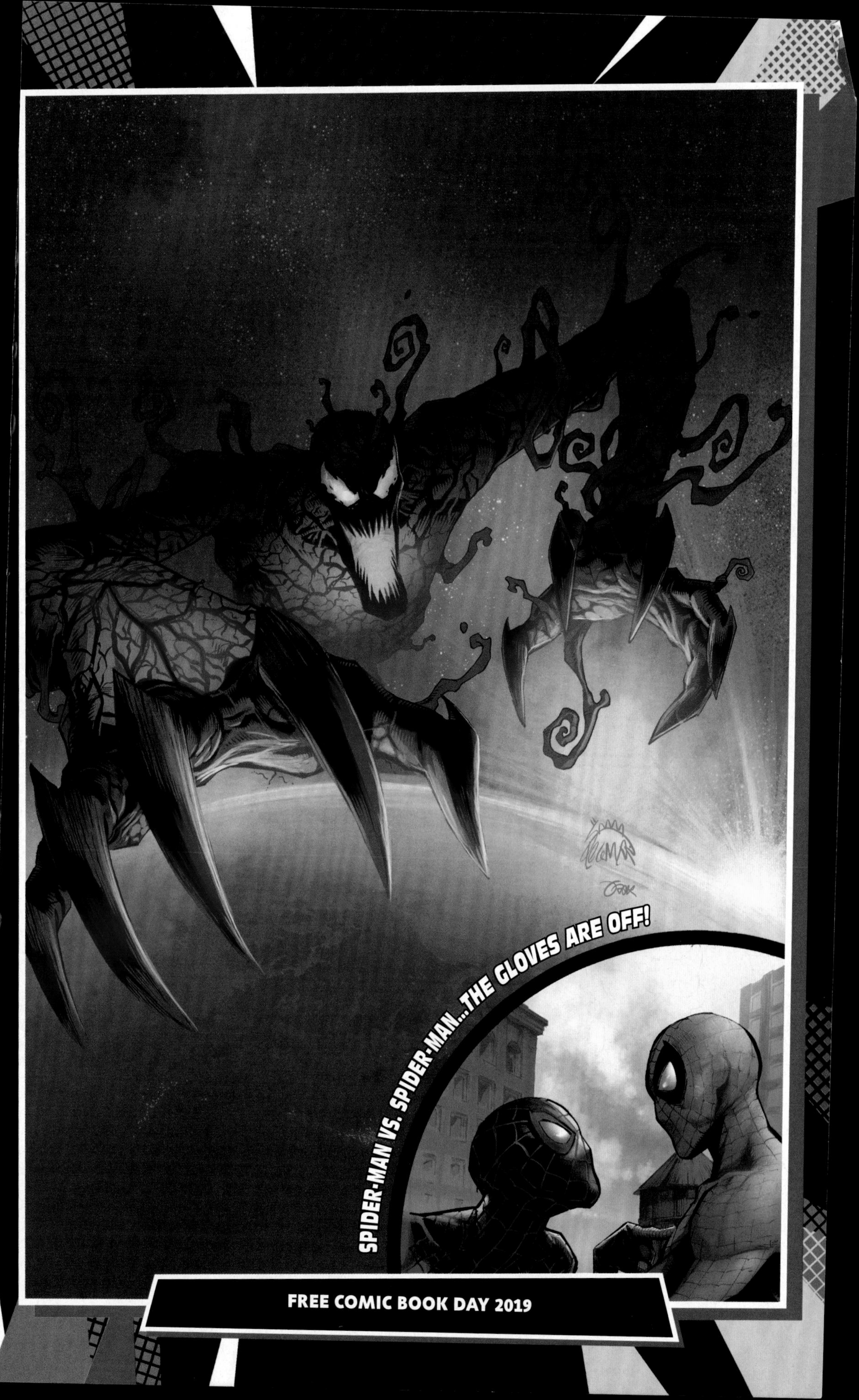
SPIDER-MAN VS. SPIDER-MAN...THE GLOVES ARE OFF!
FREE COMIC BOOK DAY 2019

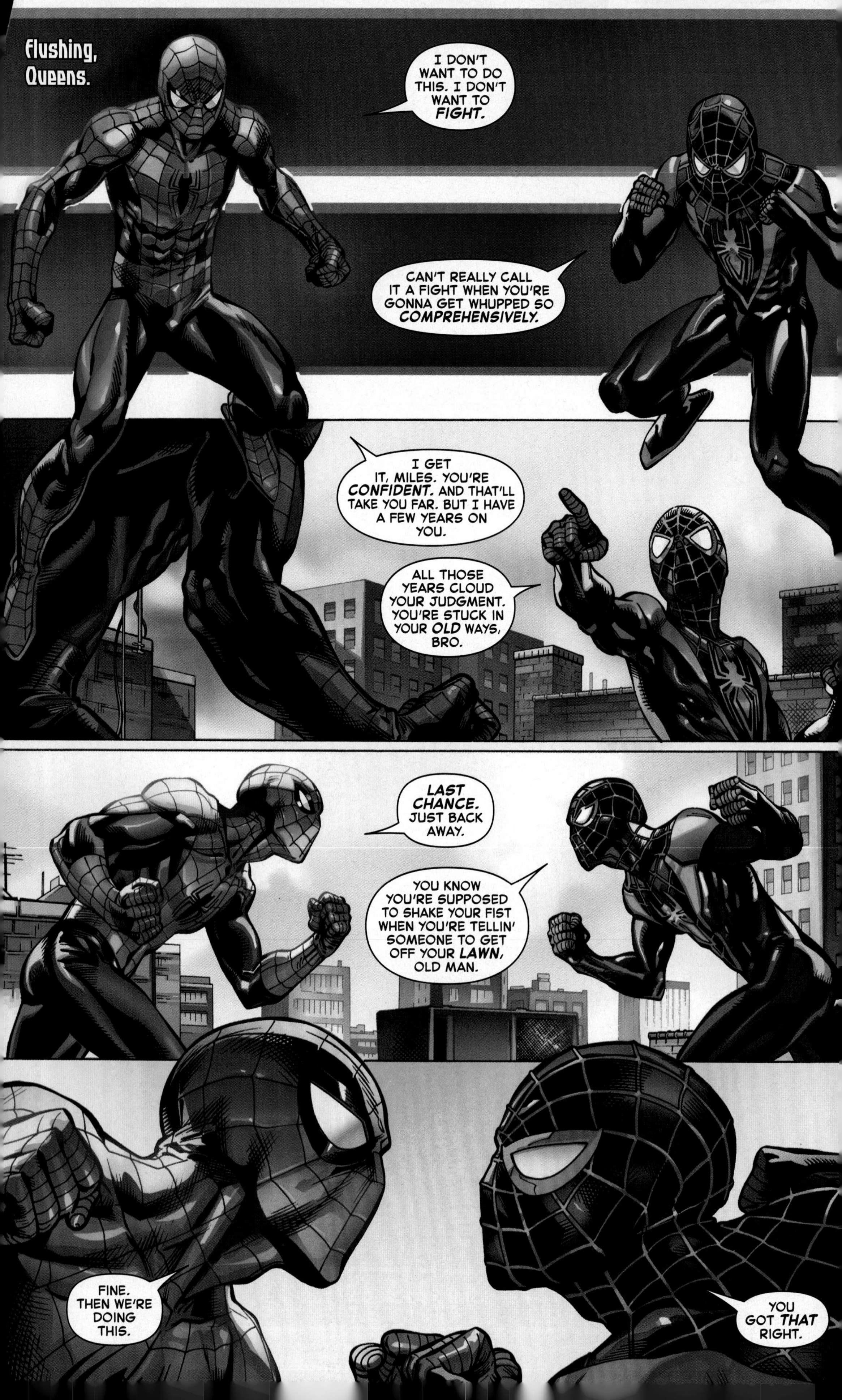
Flushing, Queens.
I DON'T WANT TO DO THIS. I DON'T WANT TO FIGHT.
CAN'T REALLY CALL IT A FIGHT WHEN YOU'RE GONNA GET WHUPPED SO COMPREHENSIVELY.
I GET IT, MILES. YOU'RE CONFIDENT. AND THAT'LL TAKE YOU FAR. BUT I HAVE A FEW YEARS ON YOU.
ALL THOSE YEARS CLOUD YOUR JUDGMENT. YOU'RE STUCK IN YOUR OLD WAYS, BRO.
LAST CHANCE. JUST BACK AWAY.
YOU KNOW YOU'RE SUPPOSED TO SHAKE YOUR FIST WHEN YOU'RE TELLIN' SOMEONE TO GET OFF YOUR LAWN, OLD MAN.
FINE. THEN WE'RE DOING THIS.
YOU GOT THAT RIGHT.

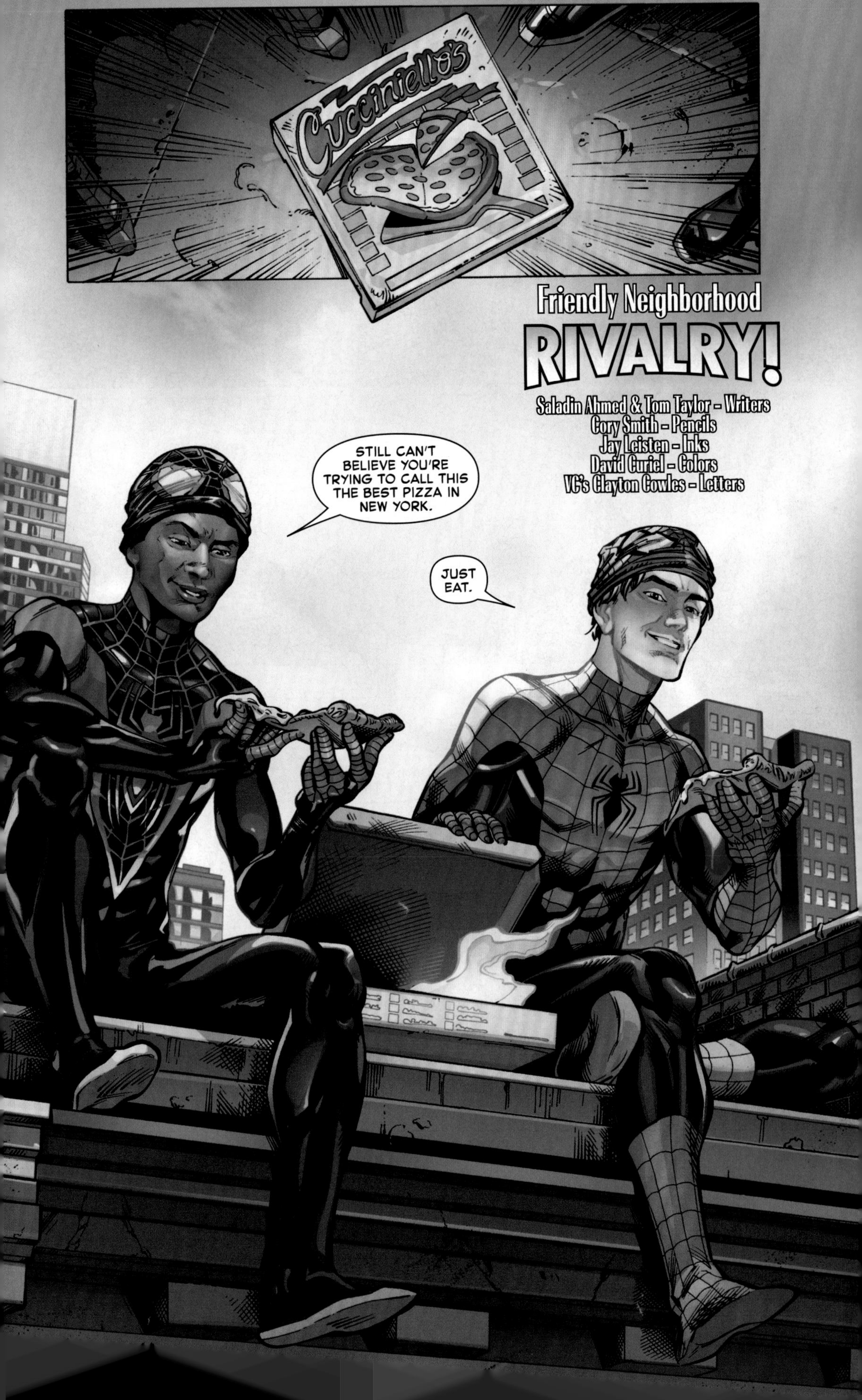
Cucciniello's
Friendly Neighborhood
RIVALRY!
Saladin Ahmed & Tom Taylor - Writers
Cory Smith - Pencils
Jay Leisten - Inks
David Curiel - Colors
VC's Clayton Cowles - Letters
STILL CAN'T BELIEVE YOU'RE TRYING TO CALL THIS THE BEST PIZZA IN NEW YORK.
JUST EAT.

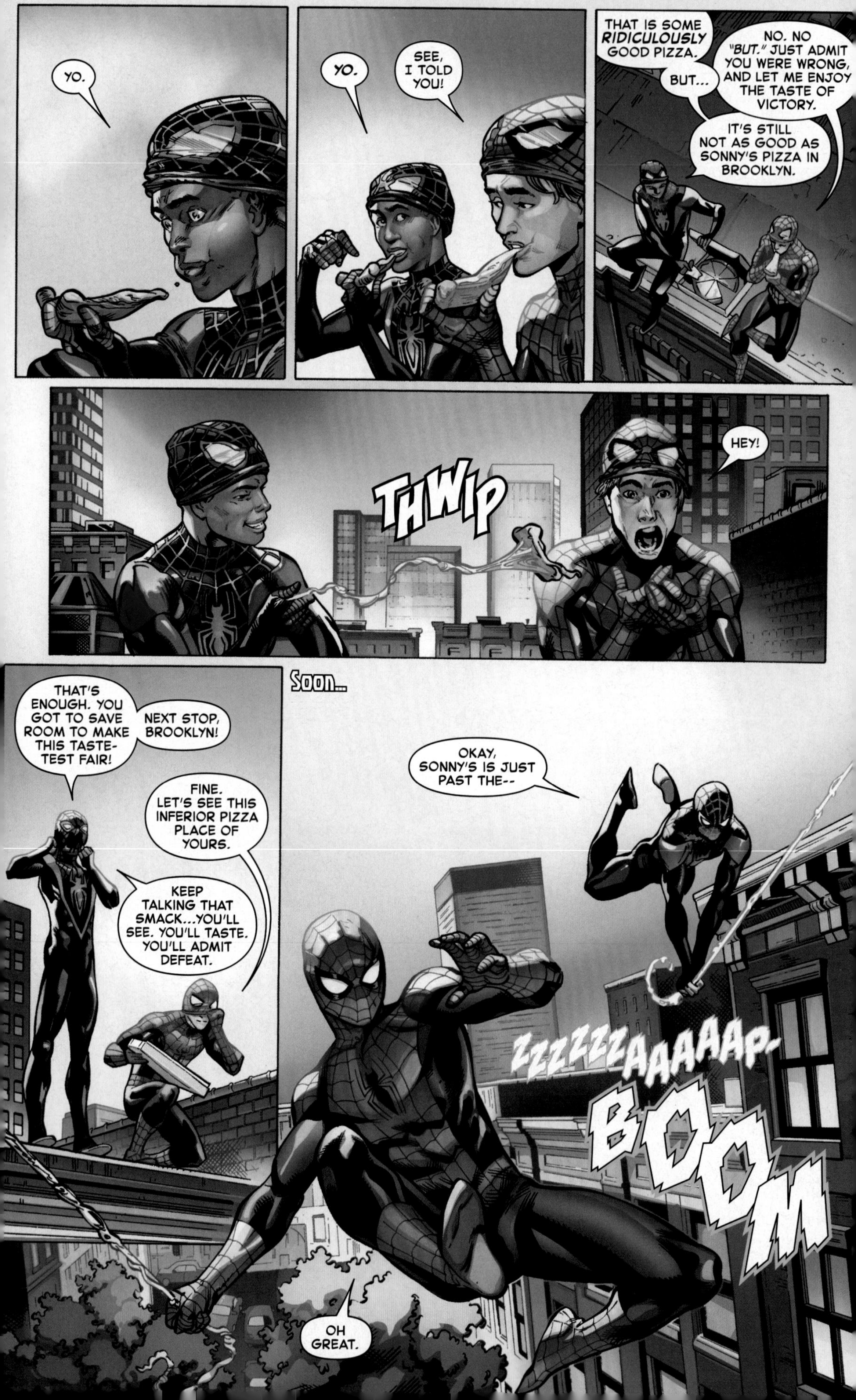
YO.
YO.
SEE, I TOLD YOU!
THAT IS SOME RIDICULOUSLY GOOD PIZZA.
BUT...
NO. NO "BUT." JUST ADMIT YOU WERE WRONG, AND LET ME ENJOY THE TASTE OF VICTORY.
IT'S STILL NOT AS GOOD AS SONNY'S PIZZA IN BROOKLYN.
THWIP
HEY!
THAT'S ENOUGH. YOU GOT TO SAVE ROOM TO MAKE THIS TASTE-TEST FAIR!
NEXT STOP, BROOKLYN!
FINE. LET'S SEE THIS INFERIOR PIZZA PLACE OF YOURS.
KEEP TALKING THAT SMACK...YOU'LL SEE. YOU'LL TASTE. YOU'LL ADMIT DEFEAT.
Soon...
OKAY, SONNY'S IS JUST PAST THE--
ZZZZZZAAAAAP-
BOOM
OH GREAT.

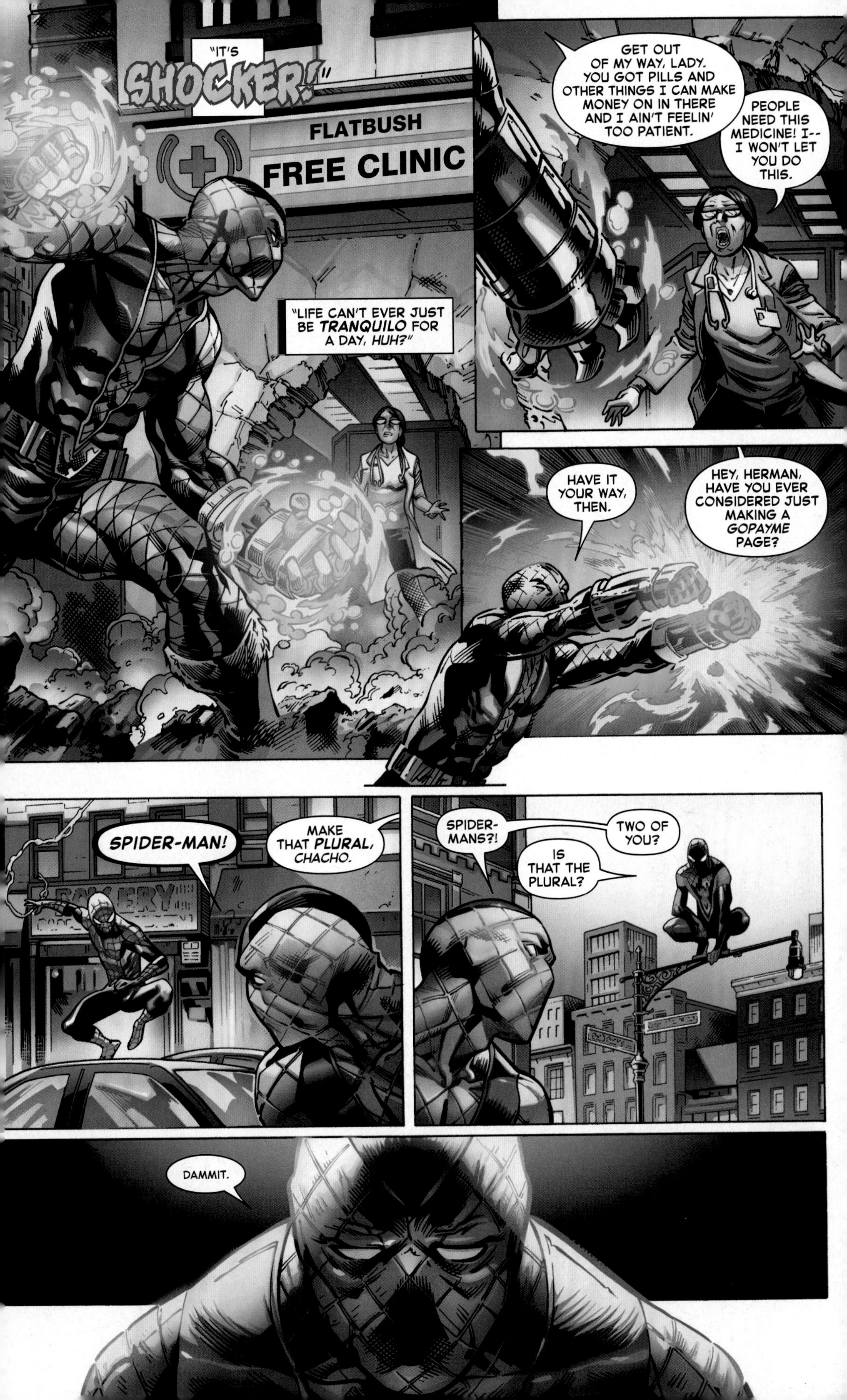
"IT'S
SHOCKER!"
FLATBUSH
FREE CLINIC
"LIFE CAN'T EVER JUST BE TRANQUILO FOR A DAY, HUH?"
GET OUT OF MY WAY, LADY. YOU GOT PILLS AND OTHER THINGS I CAN MAKE MONEY ON IN THERE AND I AIN'T FEELIN' TOO PATIENT.
PEOPLE NEED THIS MEDICINE! I-- I WON'T LET YOU DO THIS.
HAVE IT YOUR WAY, THEN.
HEY, HERMAN, HAVE YOU EVER CONSIDERED JUST MAKING A GOPAYME PAGE?
SPIDER-MAN!
MAKE THAT PLURAL, CHACHO.
SPIDER-MANS?!
TWO OF YOU?
IS THAT THE PLURAL?
DAMMIT.

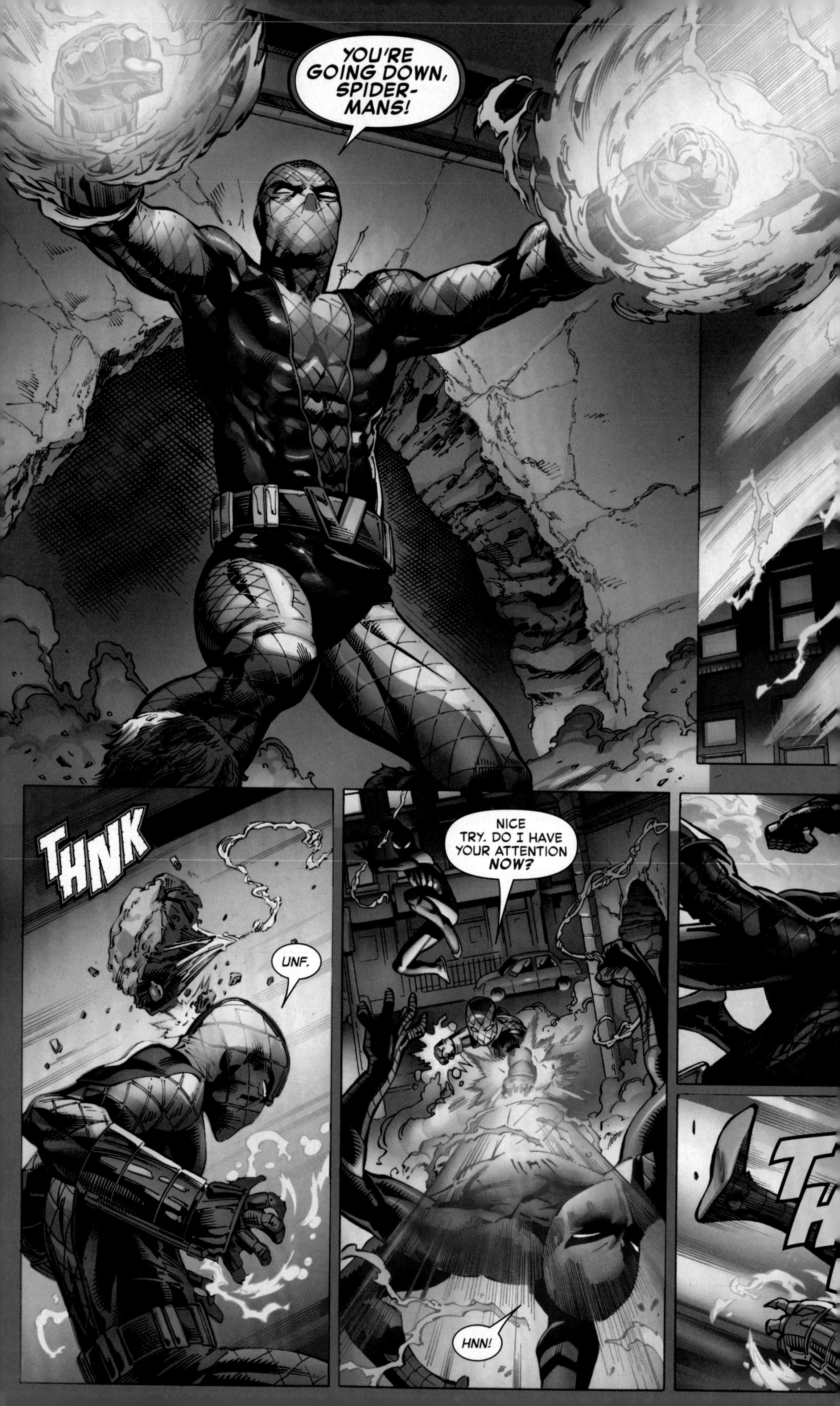
YOU'RE GOING DOWN, SPIDER-MANS!
THNK
UNF.
NICE TRY. DO I HAVE YOUR ATTENTION NOW?
HNN!

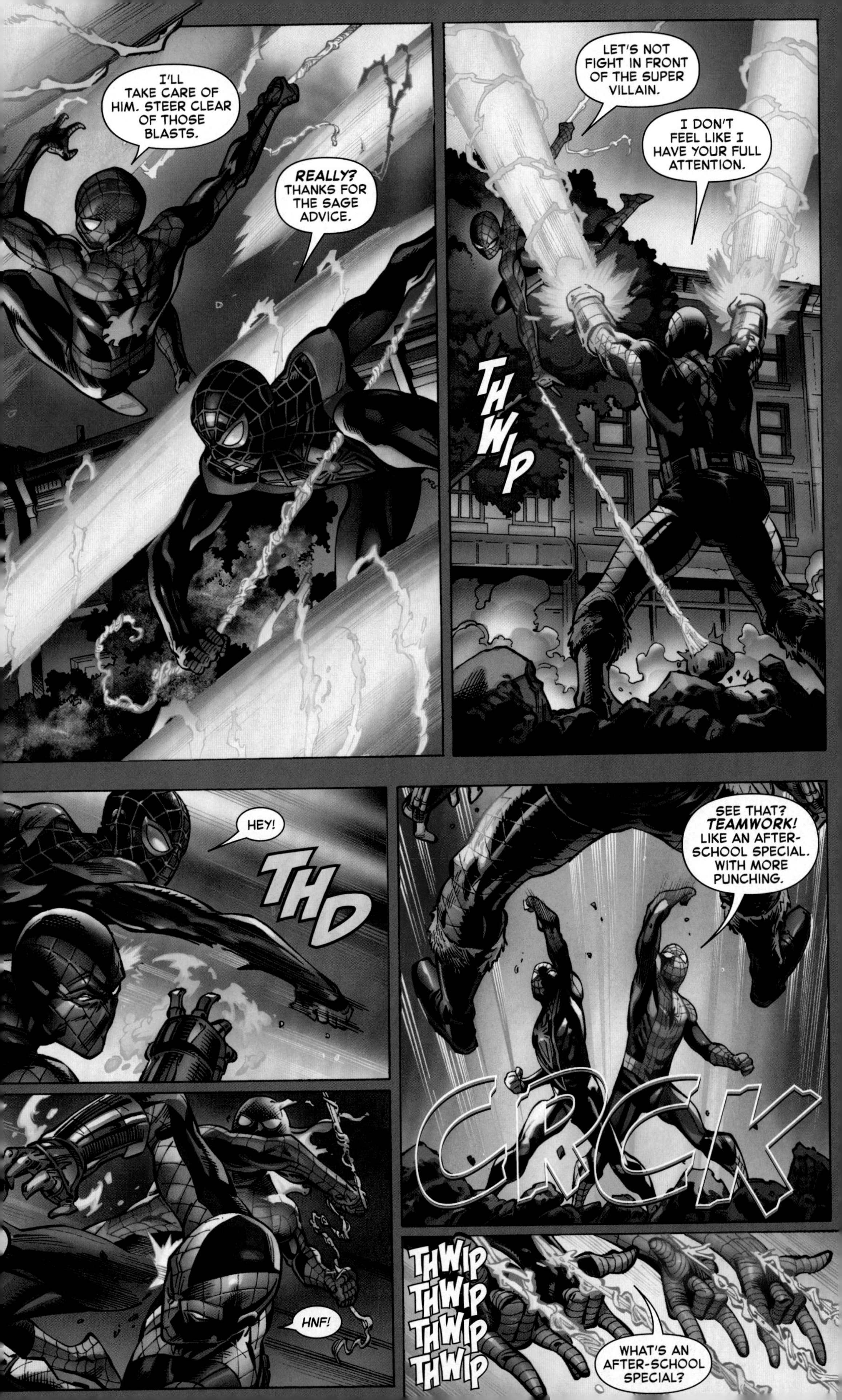

I'LL TAKE CARE OF HIM. STEER CLEAR OF THOSE BLASTS.
REALLY? THANKS FOR THE SAGE ADVICE.
LET'S NOT FIGHT IN FRONT OF THE SUPER VILLAIN.
I DON'T FEEL LIKE I HAVE YOUR FULL ATTENTION.
THWIP
HEY!
THD
HNF!
SEE THAT? TEAMWORK! LIKE AN AFTER-SCHOOL SPECIAL. WITH MORE PUNCHING.
CRCK
THWIP THWIP THWIP THWIP
WHAT'S AN AFTER-SCHOOL SPECIAL?

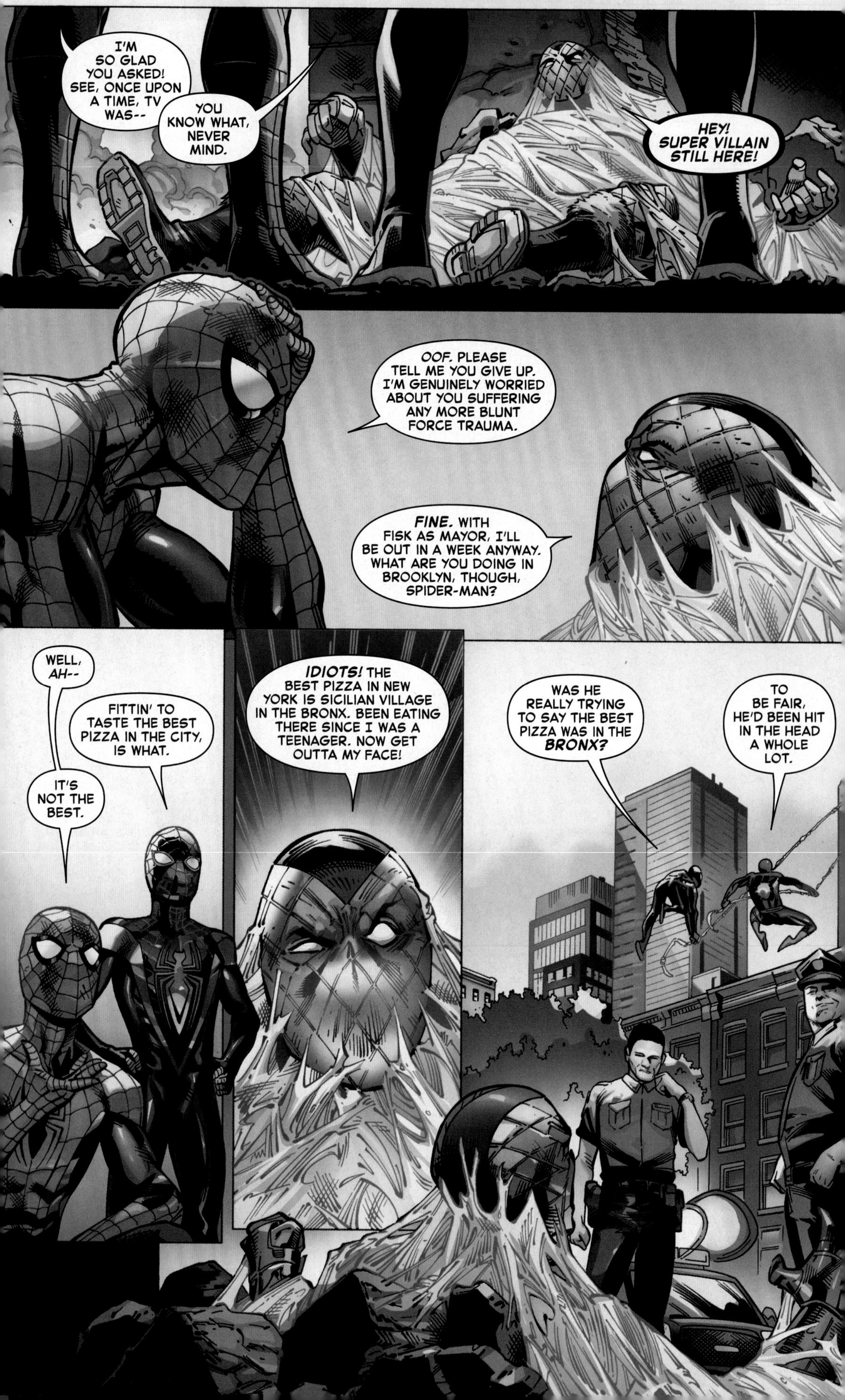

I'M SO GLAD YOU ASKED! SEE, ONCE UPON A TIME, TV WAS--
YOU KNOW WHAT, NEVER MIND.
HEY! SUPER VILLAIN STILL HERE!
OOF. PLEASE TELL ME YOU GIVE UP. I'M GENUINELY WORRIED ABOUT YOU SUFFERING ANY MORE BLUNT FORCE TRAUMA.
FINE. WITH FISK AS MAYOR, I'LL BE OUT IN A WEEK ANYWAY. WHAT ARE YOU DOING IN BROOKLYN, THOUGH, SPIDER-MAN?
WELL, AH--
FITTIN' TO TASTE THE BEST PIZZA IN THE CITY, IS WHAT.
IT'S NOT THE BEST.
IDIOTS! THE BEST PIZZA IN NEW YORK IS SICILIAN VILLAGE IN THE BRONX. BEEN EATING THERE SINCE I WAS A TEENAGER. NOW GET OUTTA MY FACE!
WAS HE REALLY TRYING TO SAY THE BEST PIZZA WAS IN THE BRONX?
TO BE FAIR, HE'D BEEN HIT IN THE HEAD A WHOLE LOT.

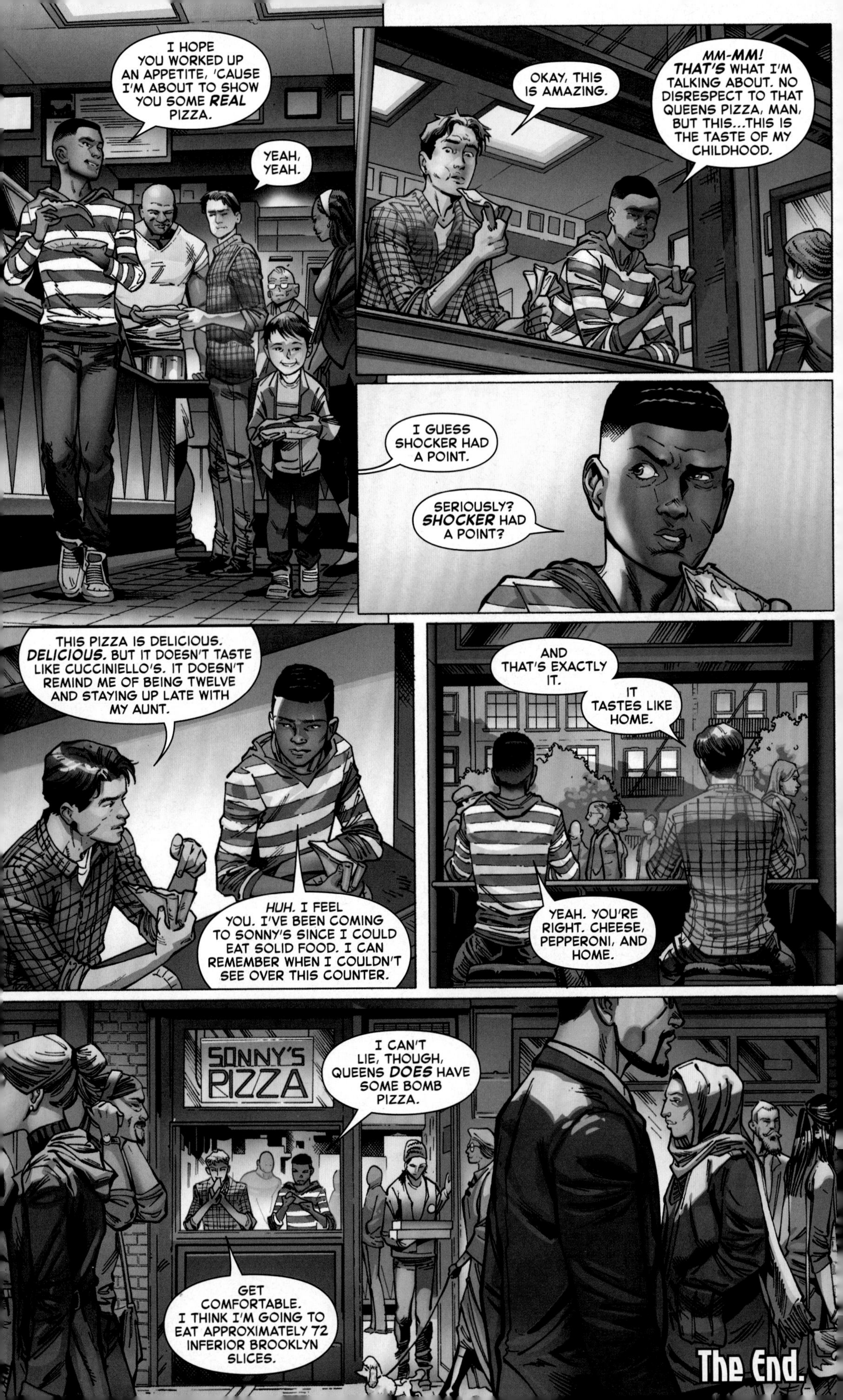
I HOPE YOU WORKED UP AN APPETITE, 'CAUSE I'M ABOUT TO SHOW YOU SOME **REAL** PIZZA.
YEAH, YEAH.
OKAY, THIS IS AMAZING.
MM-MM! THAT'S WHAT I'M TALKING ABOUT. NO DISRESPECT TO THAT QUEENS PIZZA, MAN, BUT THIS...THIS IS THE TASTE OF MY CHILDHOOD.
I GUESS SHOCKER HAD A POINT.
SERIOUSLY? **SHOCKER** HAD A POINT?
THIS PIZZA IS DELICIOUS. ***DELICIOUS.*** BUT IT DOESN'T TASTE LIKE CUCCINIELLO'S. IT DOESN'T REMIND ME OF BEING TWELVE AND STAYING UP LATE WITH MY AUNT.
HUH. I FEEL YOU. I'VE BEEN COMING TO SONNY'S SINCE I COULD EAT SOLID FOOD. I CAN REMEMBER WHEN I COULDN'T SEE OVER THIS COUNTER.
AND THAT'S EXACTLY IT.
IT TASTES LIKE HOME.
YEAH. YOU'RE RIGHT. CHEESE, PEPPERONI, AND HOME.
SONNY'S PIZZA
I CAN'T LIE, THOUGH, QUEENS ***DOES*** HAVE SOME BOMB PIZZA.
GET COMFORTABLE. I THINK I'M GOING TO EAT APPROXIMATELY 72 INFERIOR BROOKLYN SLICES.
The End.

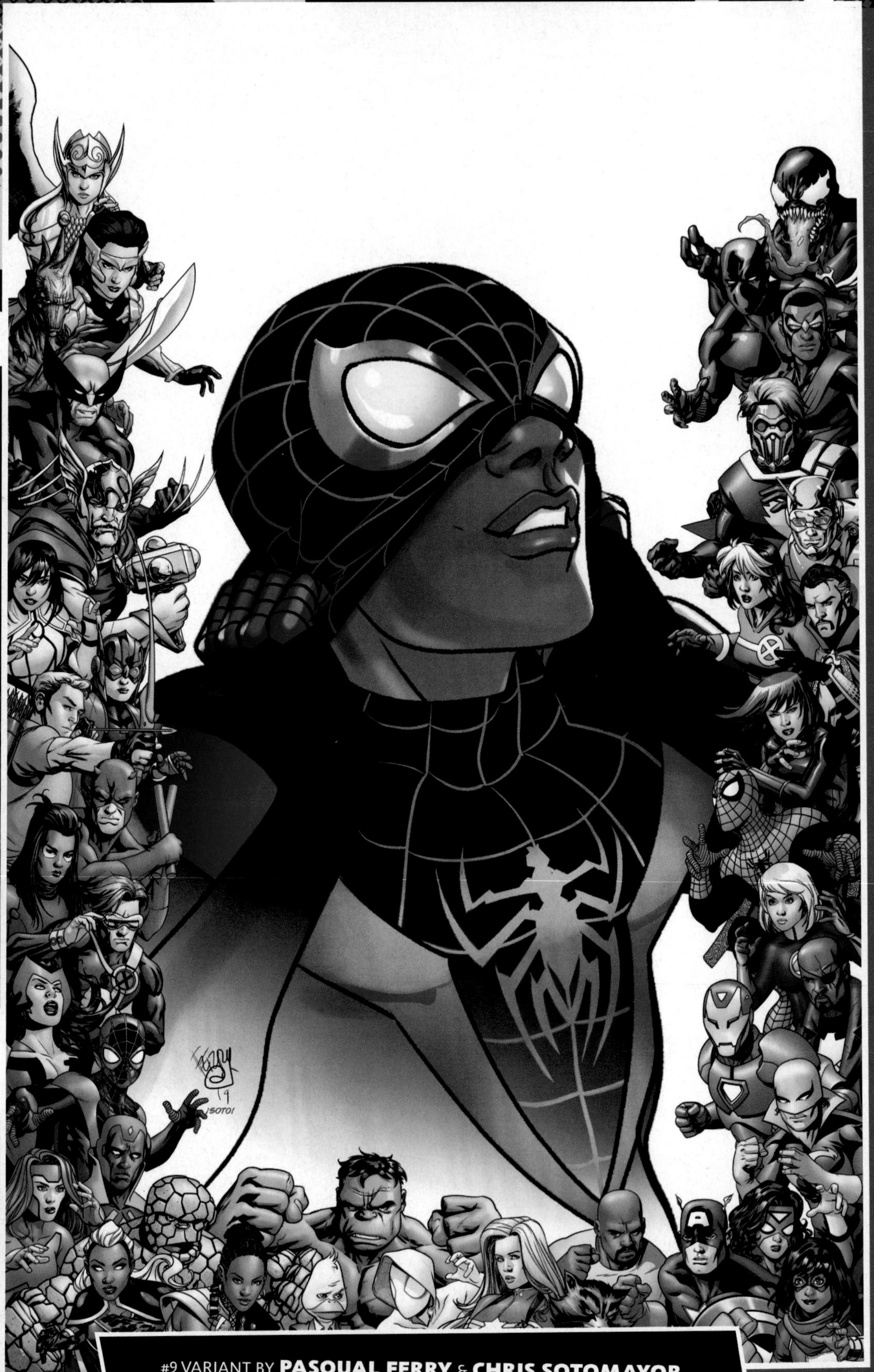

#9 VARIANT BY **PASQUAL FERRY** & **CHRIS SOTOMAYOR**

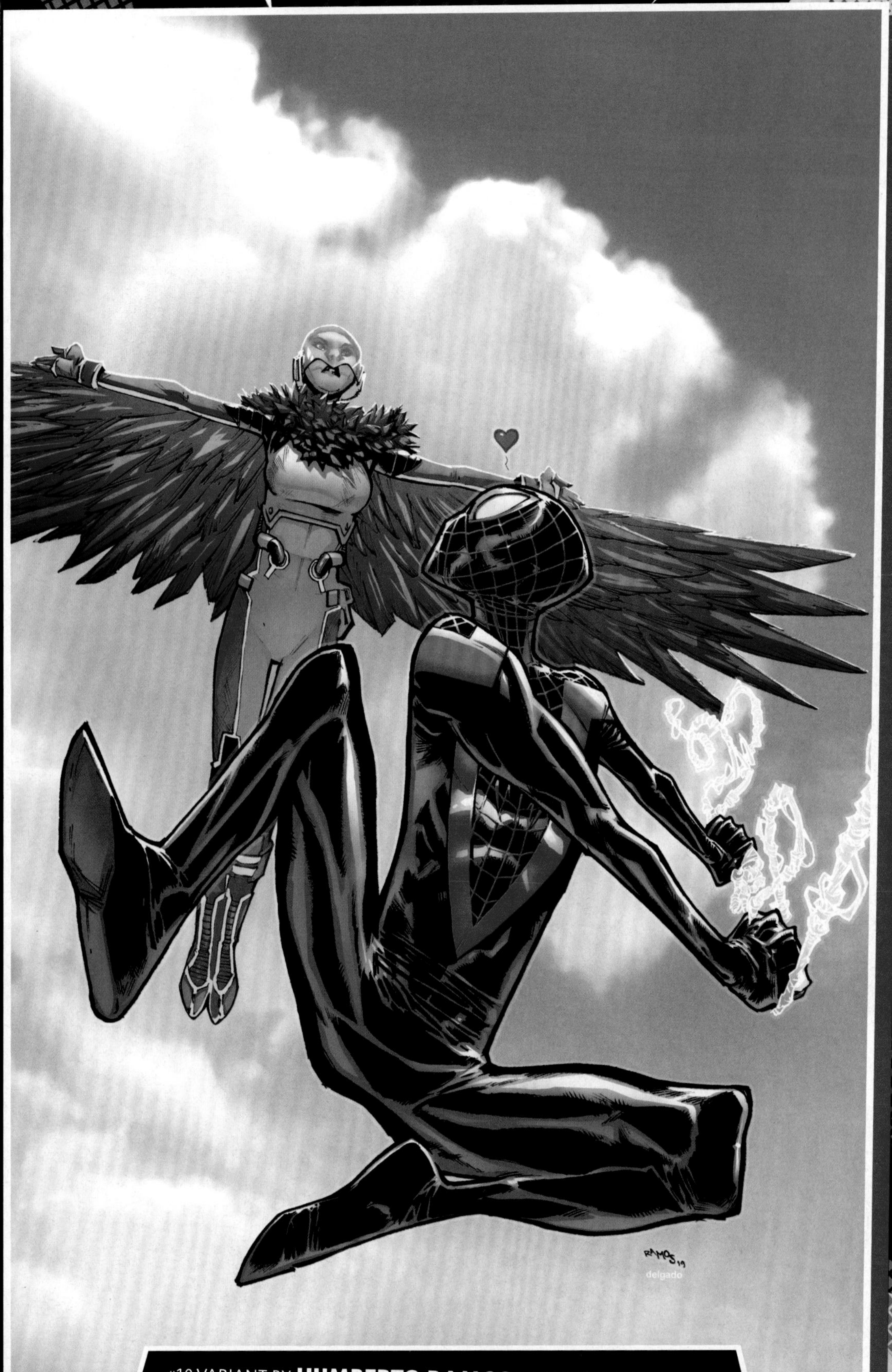
RAMOS 19
delgado

#10 VARIANT BY **HUMBERTO RAMOS** & **EDGAR DELGADO**

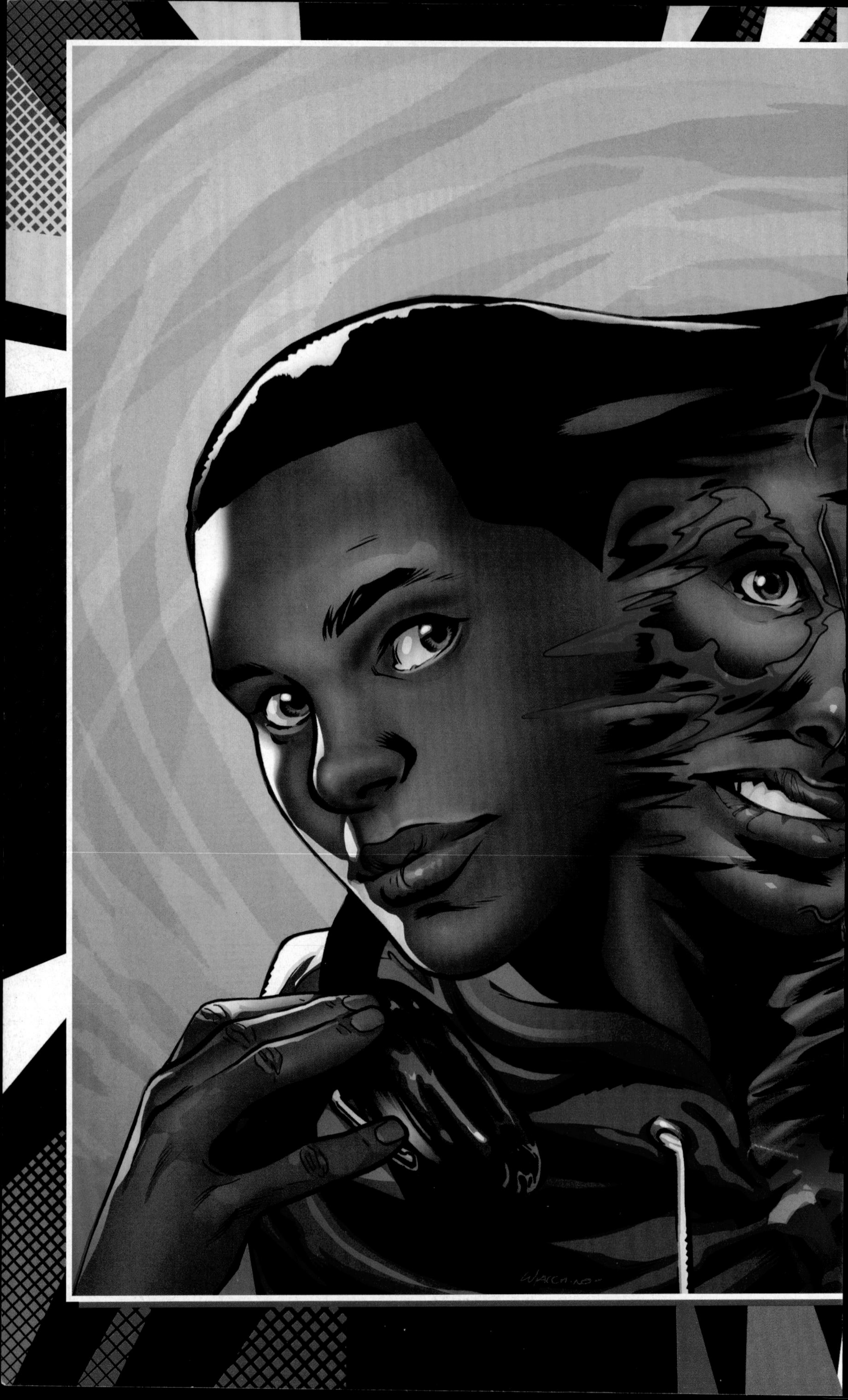

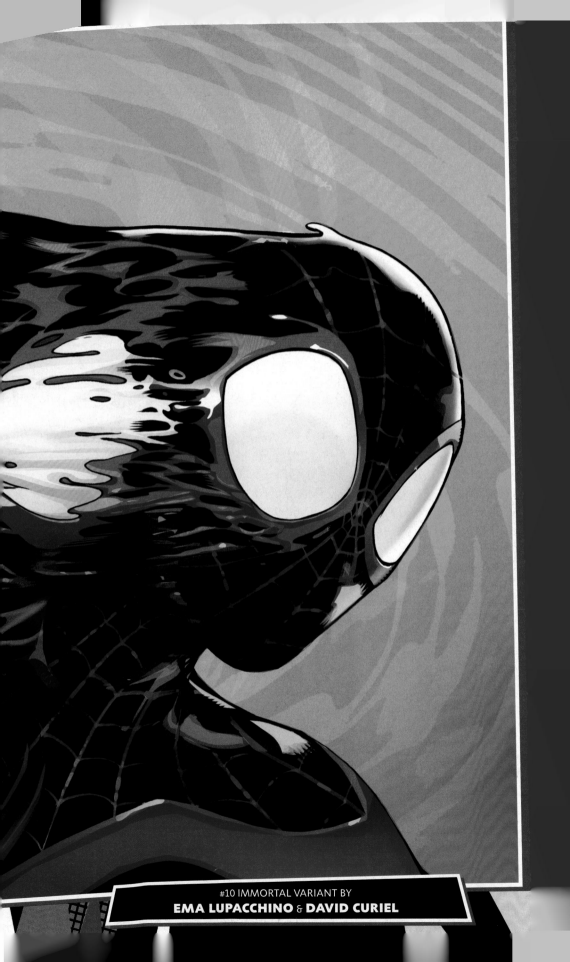

#10 IMMORTAL VARIANT BY
EMA LUPACCHINO & **DAVID CURIEL**

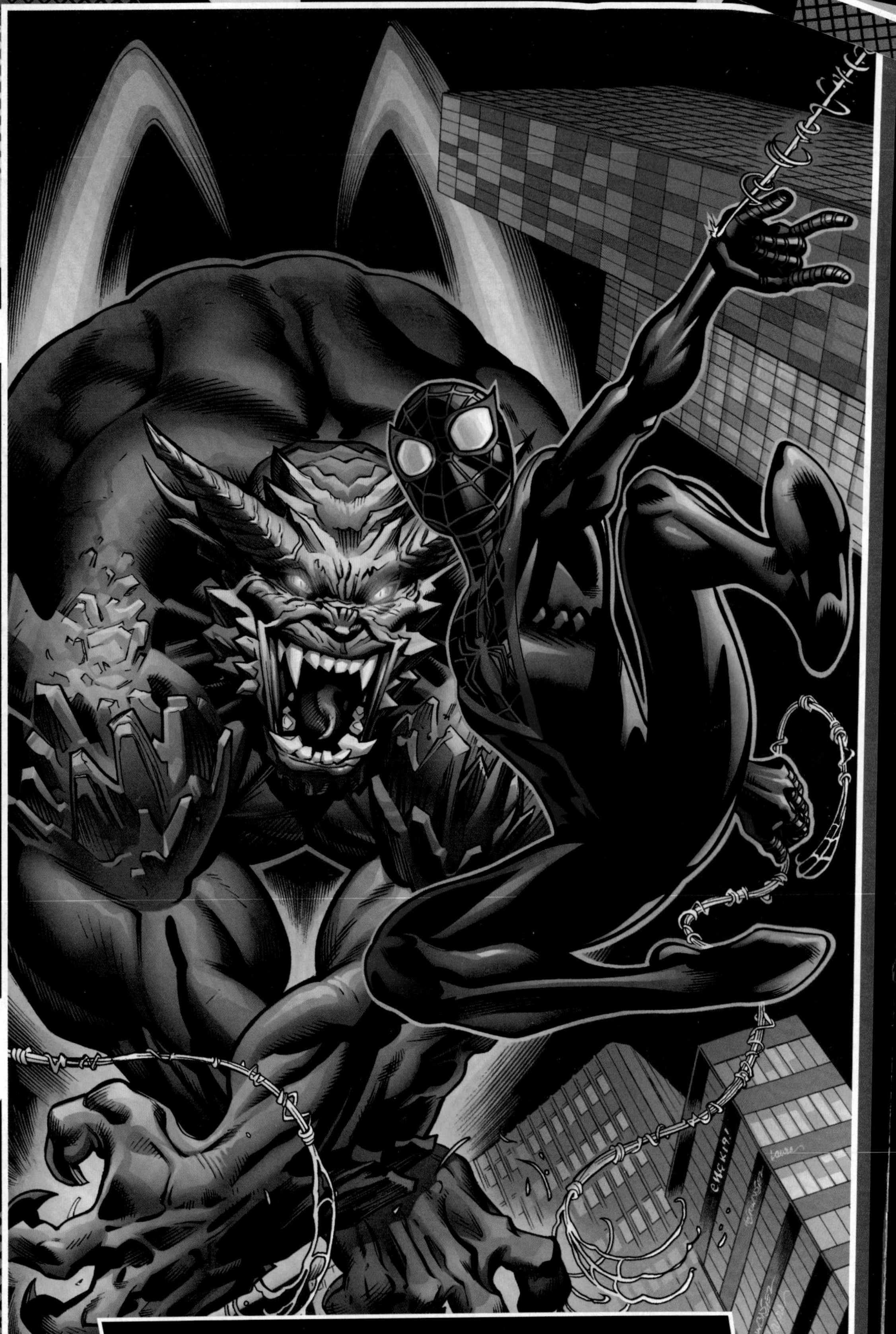

#10 VARIANT BY **ED McGUINNESS** & **LAURA MARTIN**